Information Technology and t

Information Technology and the New Accounting

Graham Jones

*Part-time Lecturer, Open University Business School and
Formerly Principal Lecturer in Accounting and Information Technology,
Polytechnic of Wales*

Terry McNamara

*Senior Lecturer in Accounting, Polytechnic of Wales and
Part-time Lecturer, Open University Business School*

McGRAW-HILL BOOK COMPANY

London · New York · St Louis · San Francisco · Auckland
Bogotá · Guatemala · Hamburg · Lisbon · Madrid · Mexico
Montreal · New Delhi · Panama · Paris · San Juan
São Paulo · Singapore · Sydney · Tokyo · Toronto

Published by
McGRAW-HILL Book Company (UK) Limited
MAIDENHEAD · BERKSHIRE · ENGLAND

British Library Cataloguing in Publication Data

Jones, Graham *1947–*
    Information technology and the new
    accounting.
    1. Accounting—Data processing
    2. Management information systems
    I. Title   II. McNamara, Terry
    657'.028'5   HF5679

    ISBN 0-07-084179-9

Library of Congress Cataloging-in-Publication Data

Jones, Graham.
    Information technology and the new accounting.
    Bibliography: p.
    Includes index.
    1. Accounting—Data processing. 2. Information
technology. I. McNamara, Terry. II. Title.
HF5679.J634   1988   657'.028'5   87–22579
ISBN 0-07-084179-9

1234 WL 898

Phototypeset by STYLESET LIMITED · Warminster · Wiltshire
and printed and bound in Great Britain by
Whitstable Litho · Whitstable · Kent

Contents

Preface

This book aims to look at the links between information technology and accountancy. Accountants have been major users of computers for many years, and the various accounting bodies have accordingly included an element of computer studies in their syllabuses to reflect this. However, for most of that time the emphasis appeared to be upon teaching the student to be a computer specialist rather than to be a user of computers. The development of better communications and new office technology, linked with better hardware and software, has changed the emphasis, and the accounting bodies are changing their syllabuses to reflect this.

The text is divided into six parts as follows.

Part 1 considers the role of the accountant, seeing him or her as a provider of information who works with modern techniques which are the results of a steady development of information handling over time.

Part 2 considers the data processing environment, looking at hardware and software and the way files are handled. We see how different types of firm will develop systems that suit their own needs.

Part 3 is devoted to a consideration of accounting and business information. It starts by considering the traditional accounting system and its weaknesses before moving on to look at the information available from current systems.

Part 4 examines the way a system is created and the steps involved in acquiring a suitable packaged system.

Part 5 looks at a subject that is of major importance to accountants, that of control. After a general introduction to the problems of privacy, security and fraud, it considers the application of internal control to computerized systems and the role of the auditor.

Part 6, on information technology and the accountant, looks at some of the developments in technology and the likely future effects on accountants.

With the speed of development, courses in accounting can no longer make only passing reference to information technology. It is becoming more generally accepted that accounting teachers should be moving towards using computerized systems as examples of the norm rather than as exceptions. The text should therefore prove useful to a variety of students. It is designed as a primer for professional accounting students, and undergraduates on business or accounting degrees, showing them the interface between their own subject and information technology. This is already affecting business from large organizations down to small local firms. The subject matter of this book is based on current practice and should therefore be reflected in a variety of other courses, e.g. certificate and diploma courses of B/TEC, accounting inputs to courses for computer specialists, etc.

Throughout the book we have tried to show the reader why, as well as how, things happen and to highlight basic trends in the development of information processing to enable him or her to see current techniques as part of an ongoing process of development. The book therefore looks at information technology and not just at computing and includes a number of small mini-cases to set certain developments in perspective.

Writing a book inevitably causes domestic disruption in the authors' families — unsociable hours, research materials that invade living space and disrupted family evenings are part of the story. On top of this, family members are frequently recruited to act as typists, proofreaders and researchers and their sole reward is a mention at the end of a preface. In the knowledge that they at least will read right through this preface, we say thanks.

Graham Jones
Terry McNamara

Part 1

The role of accounting

1

Information technology and the accountant

Introduction

Mac was worried. He was sure the guy was a villain but had to let him board the train. He went back to the office and walked in on the Superintendent, known to everyone as E. J., and sat down. 'Boss,' he said, 'I'm sure he's our man but I can't place where I came across him before.' 'Don't worry, Mac, we'll run a check through baby. She'll go back over years of work in seconds.' The computer confirmed their fears. 'We'll get Inspector Marriot to stop him at Dover before he leaves the country.' Mac warned, 'You know what it's like trying to catch him at his desk. He may not even be in his car and a radio message could be dangerous if he's working undercover.' Unworried E. J. said, 'O. K., we'll send a message on his silent communicator.'

We have all seen stories like these, and others, in countless books, in films and on television. Using smart computers which talk to the users like friends, the powers of law and order bring villains to justice, or space heros are able to conquer evil empires.

This all seems to be a million miles away from the routine life of an accountant but every month new developments are being adapted to serve the world of business, and things that were science fiction a few years ago are now being offered as business aids.

Let us go back to the opening paragraph and recast it as it might work in the accounting office.

Mrs Warman called into the office to discuss a few problems with Mac before a meeting with E. J. to review the client's accounting file. She felt sure that the client could legally make certain tax claims. Mac disagreed and further queried certain points in the accounts. They discussed the problems with E. J. who suggested they use the professional database to check on accounting standards and tax law. This type of database is due to be launched very soon and similar services already exist to check on legal cases.

They were unable to complete the review for they needed some further information from Mr Marriott. 'He's out of the office,' said Mac, 'I've tried to get him on the Cellphone but he's not in the car and hasn't transferred calls to his pager so presumably he doesn't want to be disturbed.' 'Actually he's at a site meeting at the oil refinery,' said E. J.

Firms can hire electronic pagers. The standard pager emits a bleep which could disturb a meeting, so silent pagers are available. Some pagers can also flash a simple message to the user. The fact that he is working at an oil refinery could be significant. However, pagers are available that can be used in a hazardous environment such as an oil refinery or gasworks.

We see therefore that computers and communications devices are providing new services to business users. We will look at this in more detail in Chapters 15 and 16. Throughout this text we shall consider the way that information technology is affecting the work of accountants. The work accountants perform varies greatly and the new technology will affect people in different ways. We have therefore divided the book into six sections each considering a different aspect of information technology and the way it affects accountants and business people.

The work of the accountant

Accounting can be thought of as the language of business, and the essential role of the accountant as that of communicating financial information to interested parties. It can be argued that accounting is both an art and a science. The accountant, in attempting to measure the financial results of a business organization, has to interpret the facts and figures available, which is very much an art. Also, despite the rules and regulations governing accounting measurement, the results are subject to the inherent inaccuracies of any measuring device. The science of accounting lies in the use of sophisticated techniques and logical analysis in the manipulation of accounting information for decision-making purposes.

The balance between accounting as an art and as a science has been influenced by the dramatic progress of computer technology (see Fig. 1.1).

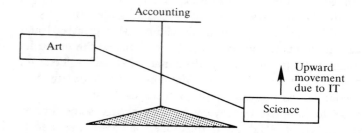

Figure 1.1 Accounting is becoming more science-orientated owing to the increasing sophistication of information technology

The use of computers in business organizations started in the large data processing areas such as payroll and sales invoicing, which involved the repetition of routine calculations and the printing of large numbers of documents. The next phase involved software programs capable of assisting managers in decision areas. For example, a program called SOLAR (Stock Ordering, Loading And Release) was developed by the Xerox Corporation at a cost of millions of dollars to handle the complex decisions involved in controlling Xerox's enormous inventory. These decisions support applications have led to another phase, which can be termed Management Information Systems (MIS). There can be integrated systems capable of, for example, enabling a bank customer to access a terminal outside selected banks to ascertain the balance on his current account, order cheque books and withdraw cash. An integrated MIS provides a database containing nearly all the information a manager may require. A manager in some organizations is able to access the database for data which can then be fed into decision models using desktop computers.

The rest of this chapter examines the work of financial and management accountants, considering their roles as involving information systems.

The work of professional accountants

In viewing accounting systems it is helpful if we label them financial accounting and management accounting. The Institute of Chartered Management Accountants (CIMA), in their publication *Terminology of Management and Financial Accounting*, defined financial accounting as ' . . . the analysis, classification and recording of financial transactions and the ascertainment of how such transactions affect the performance and financial position of a business'. Hence, financial accounting tends to have the main objective of providing information for external use; for example, periodic accounts for shareholders, banks and the Inland Revenue.

The sequence of events is shown in Fig. 1.2.

The preparation of these accounting reports may well involve the data capture of millions of transactions. Even in a very small business it is surprising how many transactions are involved in order to prepare year-end accounts.

Auditing, which is generally regarded as the province of the financial accountant, involves examining the accounting system in use to form an opinion as to whether the accounts present a 'true and fair view'.

Whereas financial accountants are primarily concerned with the collection and recording of data for the purpose of external reporting, management

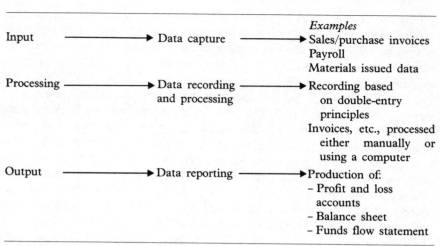

Figure 1.2 Financial system flow

accountants are concerned with internal reporting. The CIMA defined management accounting in *Terminology of Management and Financial Accounting* as 'The presentation of accountancy information in such a way as to assist management in the formulation of policies and in the planning and control of the operations of the undertaking'.

Management accounting is, however, merely an extension of financial accounting. It is concerned with processing information for managerial decision-makers. Although much of the information required for management accounting is the same as contained in the reports produced for external reporting, management accounting requires a considerable amount of additional information. Management accounting can be viewed as a system, as shown in Fig. 1.3.

In designing accounting systems for financial and management accounting the two should be integrated wherever possible rather than having two completely separate systems.

The concept of a system

A system can be thought of as a set of procedures designed to ensure that every time we come across a certain problem we deal with it in the same way, according to some prearranged set of rules. Hence, a business organization can be viewed as a set of interrelated systems, accounting being just one system designed to communicate financial information to internal and external parties.

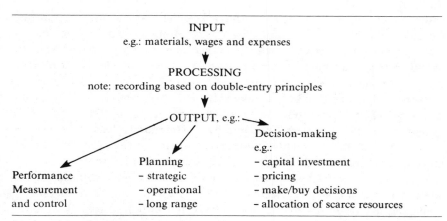

Figure 1.3 Management accounting systems

The role of designing management information systems has tended to be classified as the work of systems analysts. Although accountants are usually involved in MIS design and have traditionally been responsible for the company's information systems, this position may well be eroded unless they become more familiar with information technology.

This book is designed to provide the accountant/student with the necessary underpinning in information technology.

Trends in development
The reader will find that despite the popular conception of accountants as boring individuals, resistant to change, the accounting profession has shown great developments over the years. We shall see that the computerized systems we use today are only the current stage in a line of data processing developments that have been taking place for many years. It is no accident that accountants are to be found at the forefront of such developments. Business is about making profits and in an increasingly competitive world firms need better information to stay ahead of their competitors. The accountant's role is to provide information, and the development of better systems can increase the range of information services the accountant can offer. Managed properly, this leads to increased profits for both the accounting firm and those who employ its services.

Throughout the following chapters the reader will frequently find references to improved integration. Management tutors have for years talked of the need for team rather than just individual effort. As competition increases so the firm must reduce its costs and make increased use of the limited resources available to it. Traditionally firms were organized into functional departments, each with its own internal loyalties, and often keeping many of its own records. Certain facts were kept centrally by the accountants and used to inform management of the firm's activities. However, these facts were often less up to date than the departmental figures and were frequently couched in terms that most departments could not understand.

Faced with the need to become more efficient, managers needed better and more-up-to-date information on what was happening in their firms. The development of computers and improved communications services has allowed firms to collect details of transactions more quickly, process them in greater detail and distribute the resulting information far more quickly.

As a result, information systems are developing to serve the needs of the whole firm rather than just certain parts of it. The provision of information for managing has taken on greater importance, and improved tools have been developed to assist with management decision-making. As a result many firms are moving away from the concept of the traditional accounting system, often with a clear division between financial and management accounting and a great emphasis on historical reporting. Instead we now have the management information system, which is far wider in concept. Data is normally picked up in the departments, as close to the transactions as possible. From here it is transferred to a central computerized system where it is used to produce up-to-the-minute information for all departments. Although formal reports and summaries are still produced at regular intervals, user departments will normally be able to access the system directly and obtain answers to their questions directly from the system. The development of improved communications and better computers linked with developments in office services is what we term 'information technology'.

Firms have sought to integrate their work in this way for many years, recognizing its importance. Information technology has not made this cooperation necessary, but the new technology has made this form of reporting possible. The following mini-case study illustrates the need for integration across the firm.

Case study

Angus and Co. produce clothing that is normally sold under their own brand name. The sales manager is delighted, for he has worked for some time to obtain an order from a person he knows who is a buyer for a chain store company. The customer has asked him to consider supplying 20 000 tracksuits to be sold under the store's own brand name. If the sales are good, he stated that there might be a repeat order later in the year.

The order is large but by no means impossible for the firm to supply. The sales manager announced it at the end of the weekly management meeting; while he expected there to be some questions raised by the production people he was surprised to hear queries raised by his own staff, accounts, personnel, purchasing and the managing director. He has since received a number of memos from these sources asking him to consider certain points and provide them with more details at a special meeting. The points raised prior to the meeting include the following.

POINTS FROM THE SALES STAFF

His own staff have approached him to ask the following questions:

1. What sort of agreement did he have with the customer on deliveries? There would be a need to hire extra vehicles if there was a short delivery time. Even if there was a staggered delivery their own vehicles were committed to existing work.
2. In view of the large order that would obviously tie up a great deal of productive capacity did he want them to hold up final discussions with the firm's advertising agency on the current year's planned advertising?

POINTS FROM PURCHASING DEPARTMENT

They had a few queries for him and, in particular whether the new order would require new fabric to be ordered and the amount of time they would have to order it.

They were also concerned that if the production period was to be a short one, rather than a staggered one, they would not have sufficient space to store the goods. They were also concerned that they had agreed regular deliveries from current suppliers, and the additional deliveries coming at the same time might require extra help in the short term to clear and book in the goods.

Their final point was that they were not used to dealing with the type of fabric involved and it would take longer than usual to find the best supplier.

POINTS FROM PERSONNEL DEPARTMENT

They congratulated him on landing the order and asked if he could get some specimen garments through to the costing department as soon as possible. They pointed out that new piecework rates would need to be agreed with the unions for this type of garment and that operatives might require specialist training if there were any non-standard tasks. They would therefore like to see the estimated costs and production times as soon as possible to set up discussions.

They would also like details of whether any specialist staff would be needed or whether their existing staff would be able to deal with it.

DISCUSSION WITH THE MANAGING DIRECTOR

The sales manager, as he had expected, was asked in to see the MD and was pleased with the comments made about his department's efforts in looking for orders. They discussed the possible effects on the firm and the work that would be needed if they accepted it.

What did surprise him was that the MD said he was concerned with the long-term rather than the short-term implications. The MD pointed out that there is always the danger with such customers that they can and do increase the orders they pass to a firm such as this until they become a significant part of its business that it cannot afford to lose. At that stage they can put pressure on the firm's profit margins, in the knowledge that it may be unable to refuse for fear of losing the customer's business in total.

The MD said therefore that, in addition to looking at the figures and discussing points with other managers, he wanted to discuss implications with the board before the final decision.

QUERIES FROM THE ACCOUNTANTS

Before the sales manager popped in to discuss things with the chief accountant he commented to his deputy that the accounts department would be 'sure to want its pound of flesh'.

They asked the sort of questions that he expected concerning the selling price, costs, penalties for late delivery, etc. He knew they needed to work out the profitability or otherwise of the contract.

He had not thought of some of the other implications that the accountant raised, in particular the effects upon his side of the business. He was asked the credit terms agreed and the experience of other firms who traded with the customer. Although he was happy to assure the accountant that this customer would pay up, the accountant pointed out the extra demands on the firm's working capital that such a contract would make. There would be extra stocks of raw materials to be paid for and money had to be borrowed to finance both this and the labour involved until the customer paid. This would need negotiation of finance and there would be additional interest charges, all of which he wanted to plan and evaluate in advance. He also asked if any new machinery would be needed, as this would have an effect on the longer term financing plans of the firm.

Looking at this quickly one might form the opinion that the sales manager was the villain of the story because he had obtained a large order. It must be stressed that there is more to a successful business than just selling the goods (though this is a difficult and important part). In the firm there were many questions to be raised by all departments, and the managers concerned had to keep an open mind before the answers were obtained. Then armed with information *from all parts* of the firm they could make their decision.

2

Developments in data processing

Introduction
The accountant prepares a range of reports to assist managers at all levels. To prepare these his accounting systems must handle large volumes of data, sorting and summarizing them in different ways to meet the needs of each user. This process is generally termed 'data processing'. Accountants process accounting data to produce accounting information.

Data and information
The process starts with data, raw unsorted transactions which pass through the firm daily. These are normally large in number and must be sorted and summarized before they will give any suggestion of how the business is proceeding. They are processed through some form of accounting system to provide summarized facts, termed information, which will help managers to control the business (Fig. 2.1).

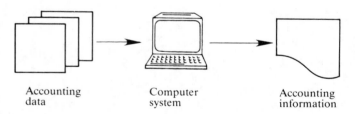

Accounting data → Computer system → Accounting information

Figure 2.1 Accounting data processing

EXAMPLE
If you think of the volume of sales data that must pass through your local electricity board, you may start to appreciate the sort of task handled by a large accounting system. Every home in their sales area is a customer and must be invoiced quarterly. Anyone trying to browse through two or three months' invoices would obtain little or no idea of the organization's progress during the

period because the sheer volume of data is too great for them to make any sense of it.

However those invoices contain a full record of the firm's sales achievements in the period and can be summarized to provide useful information covering sales to both domestic and business customers. Summaries such as these are useful in themselves, but they also provide far more useful management information when compared with planned figures for the period and the results of previous periods. In turn these results may themselves be used to prepare budgets for a future period, and so we see that information from one process may itself go on to become data for a further process.

It is not sufficient to prepare general summaries of this nature; the accounting system is also expected to deal with each customer as an individual. If any customer queries his or her account, the board's staff must be able to produce details of that particular account with the minimum delay so that the query may be cleared by a counter clerk. This sort of information requires a very different method of organizing the data. For this the system must collate and summarize all transactions relating to a particular customer.

The system here is the set of rules and methods used to process the data. Due to the volume and complexity of the business, public utilities such as this use very large computerized systems. The accounting system here is the computer programs that perform the work.

This particular example refers to a computerized system. However, accountants processed large volumes of data before computers were invented, and over the years they have developed various methods to speed up this data processing and reduce the work involved.

The effect of developments on accounting work

A government report published several years ago analysed the work of the accountant under the following categories:

1. the design and maintenance of accounting processing systems and of control systems designed to maintain the accuracy of the information produced;
2. the day-to-day running of such systems and dealing with queries that arise in the processing;
3. interpreting and advising on the information so produced.

In the past, much of an accountant's time would have been spent on the second of these, the day-to-day bookkeeping duties. This narrow aspect of the work has no doubt influenced the public's opinion of accountants. Little wonder therefore that the Monty Python sketch of the accountant trying to exchange accounting for a life of liontaming became so popular. As business has grown and become increasingly competitive, so the demands firms place on their accountants have grown. For example, we now see the post of 'systems accountant' advertised, a role that was unknown only a few years ago. These accountants work specifically on the development and maintenance of computerized information systems for their companies.

As the routine recording work has been mechanized, so ever-increasing amounts of information have become available from the same basic data. The accountant's role is changing to deal with this, and the modern accountant is required to act more as an information manager; he has to be able to help in identifying what information will be most useful and then help in interpreting and using it.

Trends in the development of data processing
As we follow the development of data processing methods through this chapter you will notice that several trends emerge.

THE NEED TO DEVELOP NEW METHODS OF CONTROL
With the development of faster, more efficient ways of processing data, accountants are no longer able to maintain their former close control of events. However, they are still responsible for the figures they produce and must work to ensure, as far as possible, that information they produce is not rendered inaccurate through fraud or error.

Early methods of control depended on the accountant's close involvement with the work and the ability to check any transaction through the system. With the development of modern processing systems, control has moved away from checking on individual transactions towards ensuring that the system itself is working and capable of preventing such errors.

INCREASED INFORMATION BUT REDUCED DATA ENTRY
In traditional manual systems transaction data has to be entered several times. For example, the details of each sales invoice are normally entered:

1. in the sales day book,
2. in the sales ledger,
3. in the customer statement.

In addition to this the sales department records the same data in their own departmental records. Much unproductive duplication therefore takes place across the business. A series of developments in the processing of accounting data has tried to reduce the amount of duplication and to bring together the various recording systems within the firm, both to provide better information and to reduce the volume of work involved.

Developments in data processing

The traditional manual system uses handwritten day books and ledgers, and this is often still taught as if it were the standard approach to the task. In practice, however, we find a wide variety of methods ranging from small firms, who adopt only a small part of the traditional manual model, through to large computerized systems which provide a far wider range of information than that traditionally provided by accounting systems.

The basic double-entry method which underpins manual systems still applies in each of the methods we consider below. What changes is the way in which the data is collected and the amount of information made available from it.

PEGBOARD SYSTEMS

These have been used by firms for many years. To see how they work we will look again at the recording of credit sales mentioned above.

Commercial stationers realized that by the use of carbon paper and carefully aligned forms one entry could be made to appear in the correct place on the day book, the ledger account and the statement. Accurate positioning of the forms was vital so they were perforated and laid on a baseboard with metal pegs that engaged the perforations, preventing movement, while the entry was made (see Fig. 2.2) on all the documents simultaneously. These were mainly used for ledger and payroll work but could also be used for job costing and other applications.

This development helped to reduce the problem of multiple entries but it did not provide additional information from the data. We can argue, however, that by reducing the system to a set of standard forms and simple operations such systems do allow a small firm to maintain a reasonable set of records without a full knowledge of bookkeeping, and therefore provide them with better information than would otherwise be available.

END-PUNCHED CARDS

This was a system designed to help produce information by faster sorting and extracting of data stored on cards. Records were stored on specially ruled cards, the centre section of which was used for the actual recording; data could be written or typed on it. Along the edges were printed a series of boxes, each with a hole at its centre (see Fig. 2.3).

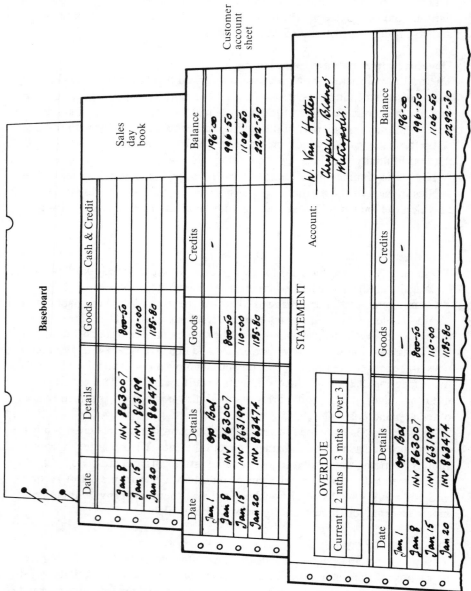

Figure 2.2 Pegboard debtors system

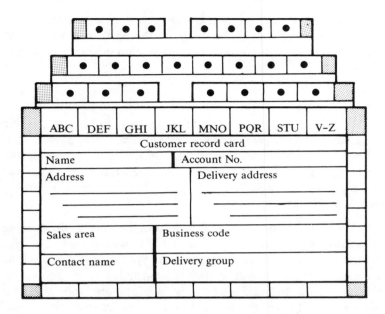

Figure 2.3 End-punched cards used to keep an index of debtors. Two cards have the JKL field punched out. Passing a metal needle through the pack on this field and lifting them by the needles causes the punched cards to fall out. Boxes on other edges could provide further analysis

A particular meaning was then allocated to each of these boxes, e.g. the boxes along one edge might represent the first letter of a customer's surname, another edge might represent sales areas, etc. On the card holding the account of a debtor named Smith the box representing the letter S would be cut out using a special paper punch.

To find all the customers in area 4 with surnames between A and D we would perform the following operation:

1. Pass a steel needle through the surname box representing A–D on all the cards.
2. Pass a second needle through the pack, this time through the holes in the box representing area 4.
3. If the cards are lifted by the needles and shaken then all the cards we seek will fall out of the pack as there is nothing to hold them on the needle.
4. Having identified the cards we seek they can now be totalled and summarized manually to provide the information.

The set of boxes around the card could be set up by the user in a number of ways to allow a variety of sorts to be made on the data. This simple but ingenious system allowed limited amounts of information to be obtained fairly quickly and easily.

BOOKKEEPING MACHINES

These were basically a typewriter and adding machine linked together for accounting purposes. They were commonly used for ledger and payroll work as these were high-volume, repetitive applications. Each account, or the payroll details of each employee, was stored on a separate card which was inserted into the machine for further transactions to be posted to it. Posting was performed as follows:

1. Once the operator had inserted the correct card, the value of the opening balance shown on the card was typed into the machine.
2. The transaction date and details were then typed in and the machine automatically placed them in the correct column and updated the balance. On a sales system it could update the account and the statement simultaneously. A copy of the transaction was also recorded on a 'proof list' kept in the machine, for control purposes, which was in effect the sales day book.

The early mechanical machines were rather ponderous and provided very little additional information. There was also the problem that, despite simple checks in the machine, operators often typed in the wrong opening balance figure. As the machines developed, many of the mechanical parts were replaced by electronics.

Ledger cards then carried magnetic stripes on their rear which enabled the machine to read information directly from the card. They still carried printed information on the front for human use, however, and later equipment was able to follow simple programs and perform simple analysis of data. As a result these came to be known as 'visual record computers'. They were very popular and allowed small to medium-sized firms to process large amounts of data quickly prior to the development of microcomputers.

These early machines set accountants a number of problems that were to become common in the computer era:

1. The volume of data being processed made it far more difficult to handle and store data documents as individual items. Accounts staff therefore had to move over to working with batches of documents rather than individual ones.

2. It was necessary to develop methods of checking the accuracy of the machine operators to ensure that they did not lose documents or insert false ones. To do this the values of documents in each batch were totalled or 'prelisted' before being sent to the machine room. After processing the totals printed on the machine's proof list were independently checked back to the prelists to ensure that they agreed. This form of control was to be developed and used in a number of ways in later computer systems.

MECHANICAL PUNCHED CARDS

In the United States, Hollerith developed the idea of using holes punched in paper cards to represent data and these were used to analyse the US census as far back as 1890. A card was used to represent each person and holes in particular positions indicated employment, age, sex, etc. They were passed through machines which could sense the information and sort and analyse it as required.

This technology was further developed and used by large organizations to process their data. By the standards of those times this equipment was very fast although cards had to be passed through the machines several times to perform very complex sorts of the data. They were very slow compared with the computers that followed them and they had no memory. Therefore operators had to intervene to reset the machine and feed the cards back in every time the data was to be used in a slightly different way.

As we shall see, computers have the advantage that they can store both data and programs, in their memories. This allows them to follow complex programs, and very detailed analysis can proceed within the machine without the need for human intervention and with the data being read in only once at high speed.

Although the development of business computers led to the phasing out of this type of equipment punched cards were to be used in business for many more years. Together with punched paper tape they came to be the main form of input to early business computing systems.

The computer

The introduction of computers made it possible to produce more information and helped reduce the amount of work involved.

Computers, being fully electronic, operated at much faster speed than had the previous electromechanical equipment. This operating speed has become almost legendary, with time to perform simple operations often measured in nanoseconds (one billionth of a second) or less. Having read this, new users are often surprised when they have to wait for information from their computer. This is due partly to the fact that they frequently fail to realize how much work the machine is being asked to perform. However the main reason is that the speeds quoted in sales literature, articles, etc., normally relate to operations taking place in the heart of the machine. Tasks that involve communicating with the outside world greatly slow things down, as we shall see in the next chapter.

Computer memory was a great development allowing both programs and data to be held inside the machine. Data now had to be read in only once. It was then stored inside the machine and could be used repeatedly to provide a wide range of information. It could also be transferred at high speed on to magnetic tapes or disks and stored until required, when it could be read back in, again at high speed.

Previous machines had required the operators to intervene and reset them each time a new task had to be performed on the data. They then had to set all the counters to zero and read in all the cards again. Computers could be programmed to perform a whole string of jobs once the data was in memory and they could carry totals forward from one job to another. They therefore allowed a far more flexible approach to work; the machine could be made to work as the business wanted and not vice versa. As a result much larger and more complex tasks could be performed and the extra cost of producing additional information was minimal. With this powerful new tool, accounting was ready for a great step forward!

Some firms took up the opportunity and developed new systems utilizing this power to provide better information. However many organizations placed the computers in the accounting department where these large, powerful machines were programmed to perform much the same sort of clerical work as had been performed manually over the years. Such users saw the advantages of computers as reducing routine work and clearing backlogs of data rather than as an opportunity to improve the firm's information system.

Batch systems

Early systems were 'batch systems' in which transactions are not processed immediately they occur, but are stored up and run sometime later as part of a batch of such items. The routine is as follows:

1. When they have a batch of documents the user department will forward them to the computer centre.
2. Here they are converted into a machine-readable form and stored until the programs they require are next run on the computer.

3.   Programs are run on the computer to a strict timetable and the required programs and files must be loaded into the machine before the data can be processed. This can result in several days' delay between the transaction and the time it is entered.
4.   As the required files will not be on the computer, staff cannot phone in to obtain information. Detailed printouts of results are therefore sent to user departments and most of their work is based on this out-of-date information.

Many of these systems were very successful despite the delays and the narrow approach involved. These expensive machines could only be bought by the largest firms who used them in high-volume areas which had always been difficult to keep up to date, and payroll and stores accounting were therefore important application areas.

Faster data processing produced information in time for it to be useful to managers. The application of computers to large stock systems reduced costs and increased efficiency. The armed forces reported great improvements in their stores accounting and no longer do we hear stories of one depot receiving a thousand pairs of left boots whilst another received a similar quantity of right boots. Computers have helped to reduce the levels of stocks held and, as the Falklands War showed, the military control of stores is now very sophisticated.

There are, however, problems with batch systems as the following true case illustrates. One of the authors visited the home of a friend one Christmas Eve. The friend returned from her job with the Electricity Board commenting on how hard the day had been. She was unhappy as two of her customers, awaiting new cookers by Christmas, had been let down at the last moment, and it had been left to her to break the bad news to them. At that time the Board operated a batch system for its stock of domestic appliances. 'A weekly printout of stocks at the warehouse is received by all branches. When a customer wants some product we check its availability with the latest printout and put through an order', she said. 'If numbers are low we ring through and ask for confirmation but they can't always give us the exact number on hand.'

In this case both customers ordered their appliances from her and she had consulted the report, finding there were plenty of units in store. However, this line proved particularly popular in the run up to Christmas and all branches had submitted orders, promising delivery on the basis of that same store's printout. As a result those orders reaching head office first were processed and others could not be completed until stocks arrived in the new year. The result was that just before the holiday customers who had been promised delivery were let down at the last moment. 'Damned computers! We would be better off without them' was her final comment. She might have added that those were two customers they were unlikely to see again.

Real-time systems

Although they helped to improve the speed of reporting, batch systems could lead to problems such as we have just seen. However the use of batch-produced information did not always prove to be a problem. Some firms with slow-moving stocks or a regular inflow of new stocks found it quite satisfactory. However, in other firms this delay rendered the information almost valueless to management. In some of these cases the computer was the victim of its own success. Information not previously available was now available in a matter of days, so managers tried to use it and found it wanting. In such cases therefore accountants were more criticized for producing information than they had been for not producing it. (Who says life has to be fair!)

What was needed was a system in which the various user departments could enter their own transaction data directly into the computer and interrogate the machine directly to obtain up-to-date information. Such a system is known as a 'real-time system'.

Once user departments could communicate directly with the computer many firms came to realize that accounting was not the only type of information that could be handled by the computer. Many now placed their computer in a management services department independent of their accountants, who themselves became one of many user departments sharing its services. Such organizations' systems were now designed to produce information for the business as a whole and the individual departmental systems were interlinked to provide better information. For example, whereas the accounting system had only recorded sales once the transaction was complete, the central system now monitored sales orders from the time they were received in the sales department through to the final sale. This benefited all departments including accounts, for the details of sales orders outstanding could help them prepare better estimates of cash likely to be received.

Real-time systems brought different hardware needs. Obviously more links were needed with user departments and as the systems had to be run in 'real time' the necessary programs and files had to be constantly available (on line) to the computer. If the necessary files are not stored on line, it is impossible for users to update or interrogate them through terminals.

One of the best known early examples of real-time systems is airline booking. Using these an agent can ascertain the current seating position on any flight and book a seat, if available. The computer file is then updated immediately to avoid overbooking of seats. These systems have run very successfully for years and provide a great deal of information to customers and to airline management. Back in 1978 one of the authors was at Heathrow in the early hours of the morning seeking a connecting flight to Berlin, during the week of a major international exhibition. Despite the unsociable hour a helpful BA booking clerk was able to search all BA flights, European and Intercontinental. No seat was available so she tapped into the Air France and Pan Am computer systems and located a single cancelled seat. This search of three systems took about 15 minutes (including general chat—well, she was attractive and they do take more care of you!)

Database systems

We have seen the development of batch and real-time systems and how data is becoming shared by departments. These methods of processing both operate by bringing similar data items together in what we call *files*. In most businesses each department keeps its own files which are seen as their own property. We have already seen how this leads to duplication of effort. It also results in certain departments obtaining information which they fail to pass on to others. As a result some departmental systems are more up to date than others in certain respects, but behind in others. We therefore have not only duplication but also contradiction in ours systems.

We saw earlier in this chapter how various developments have tried to avoid data duplication and to integrate systems. Computer scientists, in their turn, looked at these problems and found a solution that took them right back to basics.

They noted how files and the data feeding them seem to become the property of particular departments which take over responsibility for keeping them updated. This meant that very basic data such as names and addresses of customers was duplicated many times over in each department's files. The same also applied to transaction data. They suggested that all a firm's data should be held centrally with all departments able to draw on it to produce their information, with user departments no longer keeping their own files. This was the basic concept of the database.

They argued that the only way to avoid costly data redundancy was to treat all the firm's data as a common resource owned by all departments. It is, after all, the basic building blocks from which all information is produced. All data, orders, invoices, etc., are entered only once, directly into a large data file (the database). All users then work on this one set of data, so great care is needed to avoid its loss or corruption.

The system goes further than this, however, for no longer do departments have their own files. Instead they access this database and their information is built up from it directly. There is a formal program structure which defines what data each department needs to access and the way it is put together to produce information. If the database is updated, all information based on it will also be automatically updated.

With a traditional file-based system it can be very difficult to amend the system to produce different information for all the files, and related programs may require amendment. With the database system we can change the definition of any system without affecting either the database or any other system, because the programs are independent of the data they work on. The system can be visualized as shown in Fig. 2.4.

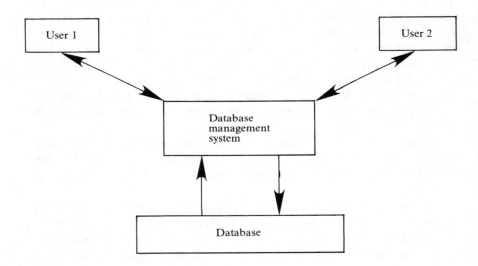

Figure 2.4   Database system

You will find that the term 'database' is often used very loosely in business. A true database is a complex thing and a vital resource, and must be properly controlled. A special set of programs called a database management system must be supplied in order to run it. These are complicated programs to control the database, and add to and remove information from it.

Summary

1. The accountant's role involves him or her with data processing systems. As computerized accounting systems have developed, the accountant has become less involved with the running of systems and more with advising on them and interpreting the information produced.
2. Data processing involves the conversion of raw unsorted facts, data, into useful information. This work is performed by the data processing system which may be manual or mechanized.
3. Accountants have worked with a number of data processing systems over the years and many of these have shown development trends which have continued into the computer age. In these developments we can identify two trends which have proved a challenge for many years:
   - a trend towards producing more information from the same data in a shorter time, and
   - a trend to cut down on the amount of data entry work involved, mainly by eliminating part of the duplication which occurs.
4. Each development in its turn has posed new problems of maintaining the necessary controls.
5. Pegboard systems were an early development and are still in use today. They used carbon paper to reduce the amount of duplication and provided small firms with a reasonable level of information.
6. End-punched cards were an attempt to provide information more quickly from data on special cards. These were of limited value and are hardly if ever used today.
7. Bookkeeping machines or visible record computers were a popular method of processing data. They allowed large volumes of data to be processed and small programs to be run. They have now been superseded by microcomputers.
8. Mechanical punched cards were the forerunners of business computers. They were electromechanical devices which could sort and resort cards, merge them and collect totals. They were not as flexible as computers and data had to be repeatedly passed through the machines. They were, however, popular with large companies and allowed large processing jobs to be performed much more quickly.
9. The computer was a great step forward, combining the advantages of memory and stored program control. This obviated the need to read data in several times and allowed far more complex tasks to be performed.

   Early computers were programmed to handle large-volume applications such as stock and payroll. The main benefits identified at the time were increased speed and the ability to perform repetitive work accurately, rather than increased information.

Batch programs served well for these sorts of applications but information produced was historical and large amounts of printed reports were necessary.

10. The development of real-time systems produced information that was completely up to date. The power to interrogate the computer and obtain current information reduced the demand for printed reports and allowed information to be used in different ways.

11. Database systems were developed to allow better access to updated information. Data is stored in a separate database and used as a common resource to update information to all departments. In such systems:
   - data and programs are independent of one another, so it is possible to change one without affecting the other;
   - the amount of data redundancy is reduced;
   - all information is produced from the same data and should be equally up to date and not contradictory.

Part 2

The data processing environment

3

Computer equipment

Introduction

Today's trainee accountants are certain to come across computers somewhere in their careers, either in their own office or at other firms. If their work takes them to a number of organizations, they may come across a variety of computers ranging from the smallest hand-held micros, rather like large calculators in appearance, through to huge so-called mainframe computer installations, which require a department of specialized staff to look after them.

Computers come in so many shapes and sizes that it is difficult at first to recognize that they are basically the same tool. In this chapter we will consider the *hardware*, the equipment itself. In Chapter 4 we shall consider the programs that make the machines perform the work we require, generally termed the *software*. In considering the hardware we shall:

1. look at some of the basic features of all computers and learn some of the terminology used to refer to them;
2. consider three case studies covering different organizations to see how the work they do affects the type of computer system that they need, from which we will see why computer equipment differs so much from one firm to another; and
3. look at how computers are being linked together through improved communication systems, and how they are leading to very different accounting systems.

Basic features of computers

Basically a computer is a piece of electronic equipment made up of a large number of very fast switching circuits, and has a wide range of uses from controlling a nuclear power station to playing a game of chess.

The accountant's interest in it stems from the following features:

1. It can handle information very quickly and with a great degree of accuracy.

2. Its power to store figures and text in an electronic memory means that these are then available to be used over and over again without human intervention. As a result it can carry out large amounts of work very quickly.
3. It can also hold a set of instructions called a program in its memory. By following through these instructions it is able to do quite complex jobs. For example, it can compare one item with another and make simple decisions based on the result of the comparison.

Figure 3.1 shows in simplified form the main parts that make up a business computer. The computing unit was traditionally referred to as the central processing unit (CPU). However, with microcomputers it is commonly referred to as the microprocessor (or just the processor). This is the heart of the system, containing the electronic circuitry which does the main work. It operates at very high speeds. In the case of the larger machines, the time taken for individual events is measured in nanoseconds or less. Printers, keyboards and many of the other devices which, as we shall see, link the processor with the outside world cannot operate at anything like these speeds.

These amazing speeds therefore relate to what can happen inside the computer if it is left to work on its own without interruption from outside. However, this is not practical for we need to enter our accounting data and programs and obtain results from it at the end.

A number of other devices known generally as *peripherals* have to be linked to the computer for it to communicate with the outside world. This term signifies that they are added on to the basic computer and, in fact, there is usually a range of them so firms can choose those that best suit their purposes.

In its everyday meaning the word 'peripheral' can indicate something of minor importance. Do not make the mistake of reading it that way in this context. Although the peripherals are added on to the central computing unit business computing could not operate without them.

The computing unit
As we have already seen, this holds the data and the program currently in use and follows the instructions in that program. For our purposes we need split it down into only two main sections: the processor and the memory.

THE PROCESSOR
This houses the main circuits that run the system. In here the main calculations are performed and the whole system is controlled. As accountants, we do not need to know how it all works.

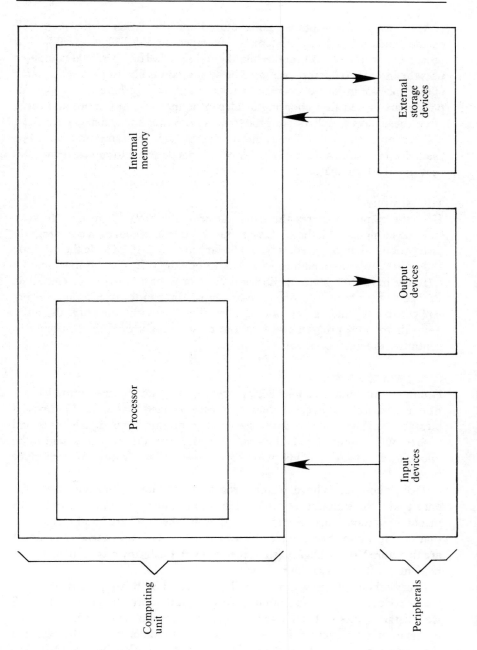

Figure 3.1 Main features of a computer

A variety of processors is manufactured and the maker of a system will decide which to use in the system; for example, the PDP 11 is a well known processor for larger machines, while the ubiquitous IBM personal computer uses the Intel 8080 microprocessor. The accountant is likely to know the name of the processor inside his machine (but not how it works); this can be important particularly when first choosing a microcomputer, because more and more often these days suppliers are producing accounting and other systems that will run on a range of different machines that have the same processor. For example, one will find a great number of systems designed to run on computers that are IBM compatible.

THE MEMORY

Here the computer stores the data and program currently in use. To keep working at high speed, the processor must be able to obtain data and program instructions when required. It would be far too slow to go outside the machine and collect this information, so it has to be stored inside the machine.

Today most computer memories consist of a large number of electronic storage devices built into silicon microchips. You can think of each as a tiny box capable of holding just one number. The larger the memory, the more room there is for programs and data to be stored, allowing the computer to continue its work uninterrupted.

HOW DATA IS STORED

Before the invention of telephones, speech could not be transmitted but a simple electrical signal could. Samuel Morse realized that he could impose a message on this signal by interrupting it to produce two signals: dots and dashes. When a message is imposed on a signal in this way it is said to be 'modulated' onto it. This was far simpler than trying to reproduce speech.

Today's computers have to store programs and data in electronic form and, once again, the simplest way to do this is to use just two symbols within the machine. Rather than dots and dashes they use the numbers 0 and 1. A system that uses just two characters in this way is called a *binary system* and 0 and 1 are therefore BInary DigiTs (shortened to *bits*). Each tiny box in memory can hold just a 0 or a 1, nothing else.

Every schoolboy knows that the distress signal SOS is represented by the morse code ... – – –... and from this we see that to represent a letter such as S we must use a group of bits. Unlike morse code, computers use a fixed number of bits to produce every character. The number used depends on the design of the processor and cannot be changed by the user. A block of bits used to hold a character is termed a *byte*. Most home micros work with an eight-bit byte while business micros such as Apricot or IBM are 16-bit machines. Larger machines use bigger bytes.

There must be some code to represent every character of the alphabet, the number set and every other character which appears on the computer keyboard. Although there is no standard code and computer manufacturers are free to use any codes they wish, most adopt the ASCII code. This is the American Standard Code for Information Interchange, originally designed to allow information to be transferred from one machine to another.

The ASCII code 00100000 represents the space bar character on an eight-bit micro. The word *micro* would take up five bytes and be represented by a string of forty 0s and 1s. The computer is able to unscramble this because it knows that every eighth bit is the start of a new character.

Advertising literature always shows the size of a computer's memory in bytes, e.g. 256K, where K refers to 1024 bytes. For practical purposes you can think of a K as 'about 1000 bytes'. Remember that one byte is used to represent each character.

Home computers tend to have from 32K to 64K of memory. Business micros based on eight-bit bytes normally have about 64K, and 16-bit machines have 256K and more. Larger machines measure their memories in Mbytes (megabytes or millions of bytes).

The size of the byte is also important when dealing with memory. If the machine wishes to transfer some character to a position in memory, the internal message to do this will need to include the number (address) of the memory box involved. To understand this let us look at how a number is expressed inside the machine.

The number 110 means one hundred and ten to most readers because they fit it into the following format:

hundreds	tens	units
1	1	0

We are counting in tens. The machine works in binary, so the column headings increase in powers of two, not ten. So 110 expressed in binary would represent:

fours	twos	units
1	1	0

This is the number 6, i.e. $4 + 2 + 0$.

In an eight-bit micro the number 6 would be represented in one byte as follows:

$$00000110$$

The largest number we can enter in one eight-bit byte is 11111111. The reader might like to check that this comes to 255. We could directly address memory boxes numbered from 0 to 255, a total of 256 bytes. This is far too small to be useful, so such machines use two bytes rather than one to hold the address number. This allows a memory of up to 65K to be addressed in this way, the limit noted above for such micros. Larger machines with more memory normally use longer bytes, allowing more memory to be addressed in this way.

We now turn our attention to the peripherals which link the computer to the outside world, transferring messages in and out. We shall consider, in turn, input devices used to collect data, output peripherals, and methods of storing data, etc., outside the machine.

Input devices

For many years the main method of inputing data to computers has involved staff typing it on to some form of input medium which could be read by the machine. In recent years a number of methods have been developed to allow the computer to sense or read in data at high speeds, saving cost and reducing errors (see Fig. 3.2).

KEYBOARD DEVICES

This is the form of input most people will first think of. Keyboards are used from home computers through to large business systems. These days they are normally linked with a display screen to form a VDU (visual display unit).

In the early days of computing punched cards and punched paper tape were the common forms of input to business computers, but these are far less common today.

Where large amounts of data such as invoices have to be typed in, *key to disk* systems are now used. A number of input terminals feed a special input device which includes a large magnetic disk. The operator types the data in and it is stored on the disk. Manual typing has always been an error-prone operation so a second operator will retype the work into the same machine. The equipment checks the two sets of data against each other, indicating any areas where they disagree. Finally it can perform a certain amount of sorting before transferring the data on to a tape for input to the main computer.

This form of input is suitable for large-volume batch systems where there is time to enter and sort data before it is processed. However, with real-time

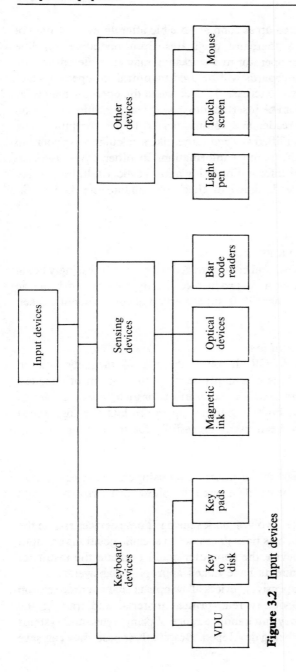

Figure 3.2 Input devices

systems, data has to be picked up as soon as possible after an event. Much of the data in such systems therefore originates from operatives in line departments, e.g. a machine operator in a workshop may enter details of jobs completed. In such cases keyboards will be used by untrained operators and unless care is taken errors will increase. In such cases the operator may wear an electronic badge which can be inserted into a *badge reader*. Information on this can be sensed by the reader and communicated to the computer. The operator may then use a simplified *key pad* rather like a calculator keyboard to enter job numbers and other simple information. In other cases users on remote terminals may input information using a full keyboard. In these cases the computer programs are designed to check or validate the data as far as possible.

SENSING AND READING DEVICES

Because keyboard input is slow and error prone, devices are increasingly being developed to capture data as a by-product of the day-to-day work of the business, e.g. data from customer tills in supermarkets is now frequently taken directly to the computer.

Magnetic ink character recognition

This method, abbreviated MICR, involves the use of magnetic ink on documents to record data. It is commonly seen on the bottom of cheques, where the dumpy characters used for the number, branch code, etc., are so encoded. They can be read both by human operators and the high-speed sorting machines, and have been used successfully for many years.

Optical input

Just as we pick up a large part of our information using the sense of sight, so optical input devices are being developed to allow fast error-free data collection.

The simpler form of device involves mark sensing. These devices enable the computer to detect marks such as ticks or crosses in specific positions on input documents. Using such a device the computer could evaluate the results of survey sheets where respondents have ticked appropriate answers.

More sophisticated (and expensive) devices allow optical character recognition (OCR). This allows the device to read printed material and transfer the content to the computer. They can handle a range of print styles, and systems for reading handwriting are being developed. Despite their cost, they can save a great deal of repetitive work. For example, some suppliers of wordprocessing equipment will use such equipment to transfer a company's existing letters on to the machine at high speed, saving hours of typing.

Bar code readers

These are used increasingly in supermarkets to capture data at the point of sale. In the past, businesses selling a large volume of low-value items could not record full sales details on the computer. However, by adding standard bar codes on grocery products and including a laser reading device in the checkout, the work of the cashier has been simplified and computer input has become a by-product of this operation.

The bar code identifies the product, producer and country of origin. It does not include price details, which are stored in the machine's memory and could actually be changed between the customer picking up the goods and paying for them.

Other devices

A great number of other devices have been developed and while these are very useful in certain applications they are not widely used in business applications. These include the following.

Light pens   These are used as a form of input to graphics and design programs. The movements of the pen can be sensed by the machine and are used to point to or redraw items on the screen.

Touch screens   These allow the user to signal certain instructions to the machine by touching a particular section of the screen. Professional journalists reviewing one business application of this technology found an unexpected problem. It worked well with only one person; when two people used it they several times, without thinking, pointed to figures on the screen. As soon as they touched the screen the computer interpreted the action as an instruction and wiped the screen.

The mouse   This is a pointing device developed to help users avoid some of the problems of using a keyboard. As it is moved around the table, a pointer on the screen (the cursor) reflects its movements. Used with special software this can be very useful. Its use is described in detail at the end of Chapter 4.

Output devices

PRINTERS

For years commentators have forecast, with the coming of the computer, the paperless office. However printers are still one of the most important devices, and a wide variety of machines exists to suit all types of business.

At the low-volume end of the range, character printers are normally used. These print one character at a time in the manner of a typewriter. Two basic types are popular.

Dot matrix printers

A print head containing a number of needles (Fig. 3.3) is fired against an inked ribbon to create each character as it is printed. Different combinations of the needles produce different characters, one row at a time. They operate at speeds of about 100–200 characters per second (cps) and the type font can be varied during printing by sending messages from the computer. Their main disadvantage is that they do not produce a high quality of print, suitable for professional purposes. Many machines today offer a second, Near Letter Quality (NLQ) mode in which characters are printed more clearly, avoiding the appearance of dots in the print, but printing is far slower. This does make the printer acceptable for a wider range of tasks, but it still does not produce high-quality print.

Daisy wheel printers

These use preformed characters which strike the print ribbon, much as happens with a typewriter (Fig. 3.4). Their name comes from the way characters are held on the end of small plastic arms on a circular plastic wheel which resembles a daisy. The wheel rotates to bring the appropriate character in line with the paper, beneath the print head. A small piston strikes it to print the character and the paper is advanced ready for the next character.

All this is far slower, about one-tenth the speed of the dot matrix machine, but the quality of print is far superior. To change the print font requires pausing the machine and changing to a different daisy wheel.

Laser printers

These are high-speed devices, first developed for high-volume applications, which operate rather like a photocopier (Fig. 3.5). Plain paper is used and a laser device transfers the computer output to the paper as a form of magnetic charge. Carbon toner is then sprinkled on to the paper and adheres to the charged areas of the paper which is then passed through a heating process which bonds it to the paper.

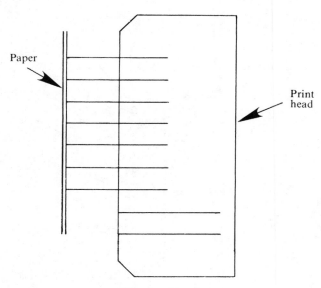

Side view of print head

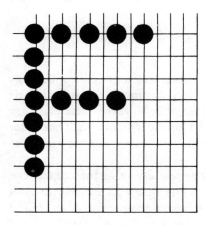

Matrix

Figure 3.3 A dot matrix printer. The print head contains nine wire pins, set vertically. Various combinations of needles are used with a matrix of five columns to represent the whole character set. In representing the upper case F the bottom two pins are unused. These are kept for underlining and to represent the tails in characters such as 'g' or 'y'. Some cheaper printers use only seven pins in the head and cannot represent true descenders.

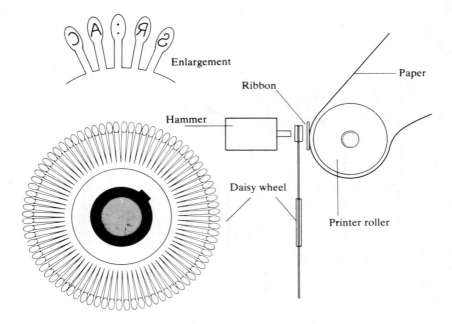

Figure 3.4 Daisy wheel printer

At first these printers were very costly and used only for larger applications such as printing electricity bills, where both document forms and their contents were printed at the same time. Recently, however, their price has fallen and smaller units have been developed for use with micros. These offer virtually printroom facilities in a small office, and their multi-copy facilities rival many photocopiers.

High-volume applications normally use line printers rather than characters. These output a whole line of characters at one time and are able to print thousands of lines per minute. A whole range of these exist, from impact printers which strike an inked ribbon through to the laser printers just mentioned which use a minimum of moving parts.

SCREEN OUTPUT
With the development of real-time systems, users are able to access the computer and interrogate it. In such cases screen output frequently suffices and there is no need for a printed report. If a hard copy is required, there are

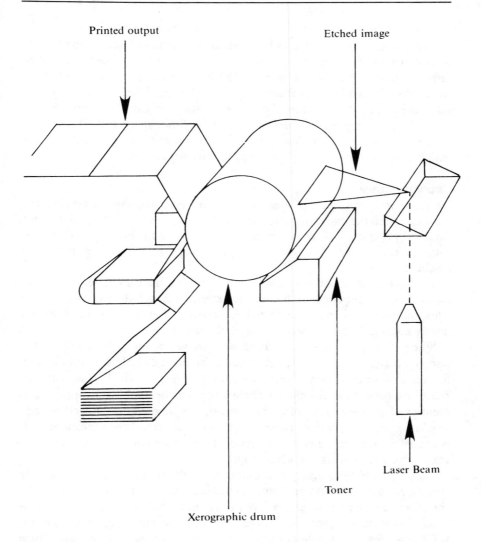

Figure 3.5 Laser printer

normally facilities to copy the screen to a printer. The design of screen reports is therefore important with such applications otherwise users will resort to slow and costly hard copies.

MICROFILM OUTPUT

With some applications such as banking, large volumes of documents have to be produced and stored in case they may be needed later. They may not be referred to very often but must be available if queried. Computer Output on Microfilm (COM) is a useful medium in such cases. A special output device takes the results straight from the computer and stores them on microfilm or microfiche. This greatly reduces the need for filing space and allows easier access to particular documents. They can be viewed on a microfilm reader which can also produce a paper copy of any document.

External storage

We have seen the need for fast internal memory capable of feeding the processor with the data it requires. However, this is used only to store current data and programs. All other programs, together with the large volumes of data produced by the various applications, are stored outside the machine.

This has to be stored in a manner which allows fast transfer back into the machine when required. A variety of external storage devices is available allowing large amounts to be stored and recovered at high speed. However, this is nothing like the speed of internal memory.

Some external devices are stored *on line*, i.e. connected directly to the computer, allowing it to access information on them directly without the need for operator intervention. Others are stored *off line*, in which case operators must load them on to the machine before they can be used. Real-time systems mentioned previously require their storage to be on line. Otherwise they would be unable to update records as events occurred. When information is retrieved from an external storage device it is read into the machine's memory from which it is available when required.

Note that anything that can be output to a printer, screen, etc., can also be transferred out to the external store to be read back in later. Such storage can therefore be viewed as an alternative form of input and output. This facility is used with accounting software where, as systems develop, progressively less is printed out, most of the details being stored in *files* on external storage. These files are updated by reading details of new transactions into memory along with items from the files, which are updated and stored outside the machine as a new version of the file. This *file handling* is an important aspect of business computing; as a result of it:

1. Most processing is done between the computer and the files, increasing speed and reducing the amount of intermediate printing required. As a result the printing done is restricted to that of summaries.

2. The lack of intermediate details can result in problems of controlling and checking the operation of the system.

The conflict between these two features has posed great problems to accounting managers. On the one side there is the need to utilize the increased speed of the computer and on the other the need to maintain overall control. Too often the traditional accountant has placed most of his emphasis on the latter while other managers have been working towards the former. What is required is a balance between the two.

External storage devices have to hold the binary data transferred to them directly from memory. They must therefore be capable of holding binary data. The main devices used today are therefore magnetic devices where a point on the surface can be either magnetically charged or not charged, representing 0 or 1. At present there are two dominant forms of storage in use, tape and disk.

MAGNETIC TAPE

This has been used for many years and is still well used, though disk has overtaken it as the most common storage medium. As the tape passes over a magnetic read/write head a series of magnetic dots can be placed into tracks that run along it, the presence or absence of such dots representing 0 and 1.

If we were able to look at the structure of the details stored on a tape file it might resemble Fig. 3.6. Of course nothing can actually be seen on the tape and the data is actually held as a series of magnetic dots.

Note the following from Fig. 3.6.

1. All the details of debtor 1 appear together in what we refer to as the debtor *record* (covered in detail in Chapter 4).
2. On this tape the debtors records are grouped together in blocks of three with a small gap between each block. This would happen because the computer program here reads three records at a time into memory and works on them. In the small amount of time while the computer actually works on the records in memory, the tape is stopped and restarted for the next one. A small gap is left as it slows down and restarts, resulting in a proportion of the tape being unused. The size of blocks and the amount of unused tape can be varied according to the machine and the programs in use.
3. The tape has special details recorded at its start and finish to help the machine control the process. These *header* and *trailer* records allow the

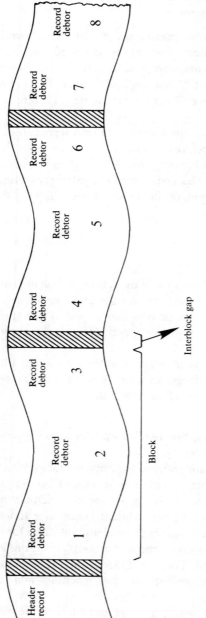

Figure 3.6 Storing records on tape

machine to recognize the tape in use, tell it where to find the records and keep a count on the number of records.

4. Magnetic tape is said to be a *serial medium*. This means that it must be worked through in order. Suppose we wished to work on the record of debtor 298. There is no alternative but to read through the whole tape, checking each record until we get to the one we require and this is time consuming.

5. As a computer tape is searched, the data on it is read into the machine's memory. If even a small part of it is altered the new data might not fit back on the same tape. It is not therefore possible to update information on an existing tape. The data must be read from the existing tape into memory, amended there and printed out on to a new tape. If the firm keeps several generations of such tape files then, in the event of problems, these can be used as safety backup versions of the file. This is a commonly used method of file security as you will see later.

The last two points put tape at a disadvantage for applications that need to search through and update only a few records on a file, so-called 'low hit rate' applications. An example of such an application might involve posting invoices to a debtors file; on any day only 10 per cent or less of them may have bought goods. On the other hand payroll is a high hit rate area as every employee has to be paid; therefore no time is wasted looking at and copying unchanged records. Such an application is well suited for tape storage.

MAGNETIC DISK

Magnetic disks have become very popular as they overcome many of the problems associated with tape. Disks are coated with a layer of metal oxide on which dots can be recorded magnetically in a series of concentric tracks. Read/write heads travel across the face of the disk to the required track to read or write data.

This is termed a *random access* device because the heads can move directly to any particular track and amend it without the need to read sequentially through all the others. A new copy of the disk does not therefore have to be produced on updating.

On large computers several disks are mounted above one another in a removable cartridge and a separate read/write head covers each face of each disk as shown in Fig. 3.7. This is a very fast form of storage able to hold large volumes of information. With removable cartridges there is no limit to the information that can be stored off line. However, if large amounts of data must be held on line, the only solution is to connect additional disk drives to the computer.

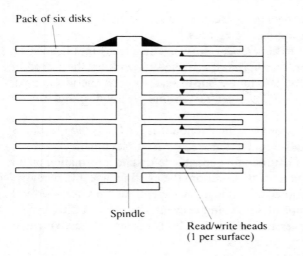

Figure 3.7   Multiple disk pack

A compact form of *floppy disk* was developed for use with micros. As they are rather vulnerable to damage these are stored inside an envelope containing slots to allow the heads to read the disk without removing it. They are not as reliable as the solid disks used on larger computers, nor do they hold such large volumes of data. To overcome some of these problems a special hard disk called a *Winchester disk* has been developed for micros that handle large volumes of data. For example with the IBM PC there is a limit of only two floppies, each holding 360K of data. However the hard disk on their XT model fits into the same space as one floppy disk drive and can hold from 5 to 40 million bytes of data.

OTHER DEVICES
Large volumes of data have to be stored and retrieved in many operations, leading to ever-increasing demands for more high-volume, high-speed storage. Various devices have been developed and others are under current development.

Bubble memories are currently in use to provide fast memory. Small magnetic bubbles on thin strips of silicone material represent the bits. This type of storage is not only fast, but is also very compact.

Optical disks have been developed to provide very high-capacity storage which is far less vulnerable to damage than most media. A laser device stores data on a disk resembling the compact disc used on home stereos. The data can be read optically and converted into signals the computer understands. The laser stores data by burning a series of small pit marks into the sensitive surface of the disk, stored underneath a protective plastic layer. This means that it is not possible to remove data or overwrite it. These are therefore sometimes called *worm* devices (Write Once, Read Many times).

Three case studies
The type of computer system a business purchases depends on the firm using it and the job it has to do. In this section we will look at three fictitious firms and see how their particular requirements lead to three quite different sets of equipment.

THE THREE FIRMS
The three firms in our case study are as follows:

1. Peterstones Ltd is a family business running a wholesale clothing warehouse which supplies drapery shops and market traders on credit.
2. Downtown Stores is a company running a number of out-of-town supermarkets around the country, selling mainly food items.
3. The County Cade Electricity Board, like other electricity boards, buys power from the Central Electricity Generating Board and sells it to industry and the public. It also sells and maintains electrical equipment.

INPUT DEVICES
We shall look first at the type of input devices each firm might consider using.

Peterstones Ltd
To date the company has computerized only its accounting function. As it develops it is likely to face the need to computerize further aspects of its business, e.g. sales orders and stock control, and its computing needs will change. Current needs are as follows. To input data the firm will have to rely on the computer's own keyboard (they are far too small to make use of any of the specialist input devices). A small firm would probably use a stand-alone micro. If it was larger, at busy times more than one person would need to be able to access the accounting information at any time. The firm would then

require two or possibly three visual display units. One of these workstations would probably be in the accountant's office, a second available in the main office to update the ledger, and the third at the reception office allowing staff to check on customers' current credit positions and deal with their queries. The latter unit would only be able to interrogate the system and would not be able to change the files.

Downtown Stores
The data they need to handle would appear to fall into two main categories:

1. Main control over the general accounting record for goods received, payments, expenses, etc., will be executed from head office with the local managers being mainly responsible for the sales side of their branches. To enable them to enter details of these transactions and to interrogate head office to find results and chase up goods they will need local terminals.

    It has been agreed that two workstations (VDU and keyboard) will be installed at each branch: one in the manager's office to obtain figures from head office along with electronic messages, the other in the general office to be used for the input of general information.

2. Details of sales transactions have to be entered into the tills but the volume of data is too large for it to be duplicated for entry into the computer. The answer is to adopt the use of POS (point-of-sale) devices to capture sales data at the checkouts. When analysed by the computer this can provide details of:

    –   which product lines are selling and the speed at which this is happening;
    –   'shrinkage' which has occurred (this is the 'nice' word for goods lost by theft and error)—by carrying out a stock count to ascertain what goods are actually on the shelves, possibly using bar codes and a portable reading device to record stock on the shelf as it is counted;
    –   the efficiency of staff, measured by the numbers of transactions they perform in a set time;
    –   the goods that need to be reordered to replace the items sold.

A number of POS devices are available but as the firm sells mainly groceries they can utilize the bar codes on products, if their turnover is sufficient. Bar code readers are included at the checkout and read the codes as the products are passed over them, reducing the volume of work and errors. The system also provides the customer with an itemized list of everything paid for. There are problems with fruit, cold meat and dairy products, which are sold by weight and are therefore not bar coded. The prices of such goods have to be entered into the tills by the checkout staff. Data collected is stored in the machine's memory for onward transmission to the firm's computer. The number of such devices varies at each store, depending on the size of the branch and the likely checkout delays.

County Cade Electricity Board

The main data processing, invoicing, etc., is carried out from the Board's head office, but customer queries, sales and receipt of cash also take place at the local sales offices. Each of these has a number of terminals linked to head office, allowing information and queries to be typed in at the branch and transmitted directly to the head-office computer.

Their largest data processing task on the input side is that of reading the meters of thousands of individual customers and billing each of them. This has traditionally been a large task and has led to a great number of errors. Although they considered using traditional key-to-disk input, the Board decided that the size of its data processing task was great enough to support the use of more advanced peripherals. What they settled for is called a 'turnaround system'. You will see that it turns the computer's own output around and uses it as input at a later stage:

1. The computer holds full details of all customers, the dates of meter readings and details of previous readings. It can also work out when a customer's meter is next due for reading.
2. Each day it prints out a list of meters to be read that day.
3. The meter reader takes this and visits the customer, filling in the current meter reading.
4. The completed form is returned to head office where it is read into the computer using an optical character recognition unit. This picks up the customer identification details and the new meter reading which are then transferred to the customer record. If no meter reading is recorded, the meter reader was unable to gain access to that address and an estimated assessment based on the past readings held on file must be computed.

Note how the task of data conversion is cleverly reduced here. The computer prints out the original document, the meter reader adds the necessary information, and the computer itself reads the information straight back in. This avoids a large number of keying errors inherent in traditional systems and speeds up the input process. However, the equipment involved is very costly and it needs a very large volume of transactions to support it.

OUTPUT DEVICES

The output devices adopted by each company are as follows.

Peterstones Ltd

The three workstations mentioned in the last section will act as output as well as input devices. On the output side these will be used to interrogate the system, and obtain management information and messages. In addition to the VDUs they will require printers to produce reports, send out debtor statements, etc. They could use dot matrix or daisy wheel printers for this work though, as noted, there will be a set-off between printing time and print quality. The choice rests with them. Due to the size of many columnar accounting reports it would be wise for them to choose a wide-column printer, as these can handle up to 130 characters in a line rather than the usual 80.

The external storage medium in this case has to be disk. The firm is working with a microcomputer system and the alternative (tape cassettes) has no practical application to business computing. The firm will need to consider the volume of its transactions and the amount of background data they need to store; only then can they decide whether floppy disks will suffice or if they require a Winchester disk.

Downtown Stores

The firm decided that they needed two VDUs at each supermarket, one for the manager and one in the office. Once again a matrix printer could be supplied with each to provide hard copies. Again the reports are for internal purposes and a high-quality print font is not required.

The type of computer to be used will be looked at later but we can consider the external storage medium at this stage. A weekly stock report must be sent to head office and stock levels will be updated every day. By its very nature this type of business holds only stocks of fast-moving goods and will therefore have a high hit rate. This would allow it to use either tape or disk. The disk can be accessed far more quickly for special reports, etc., and so would probably be the chosen medium.

County Cade Electricity Board

The main feature of the Board's business is the very high volume of customer billing work it handles. This has several consequences. On output, the sheer volume of the invoicing task is hard to imagine. To keep up with it they must use modern technology. Customer bills, final demands, etc., have to be produced at very high speed and must be of a good quality. The high level of work would justify the use of very costly, high-speed laser printers which take in plain paper and print both the form itself and the figures at very high speeds. In addition they will need a number of other printers around the building to handle other work that cannot be performed purely on the VDUs around the departments. Branch offices will also require printing facilities. The laser printer will not be used for this; it has its own specialist job on the billing side.

The large volume of customers on file means they need very large debtor files. Each of these will be billed only four times per year. This is a low hit rate application and calls for disk as a result. In a large installation like this there will probably be some tape decks and tape will probably be used at times to input data to the system, e.g. to deal with billing for purchases of customers' appliances.

THE COMPUTER UNIT
Peterstones Ltd
If the firm were computerizing only their debtors system, a single, stand-alone micro would suffice. However, they would be advised to pay attention to the future because if they were likely to computerize other areas their requirements for both size and access would change. They would have to consider whether to purchase a multi-access system or to network several micros together. If they require a multi-user system, they will need to stress this requirement early on in negotiations because there are true multi-user systems that allow several workstations to access the system and there are others that claim to be multi-access but which in fact block one user out when another is using it.

Downtown Stores
The company uses point-of-sales recording devices at each of its main supermarkets. It will therefore need the appropriate controller at each branch to work with these units. These are small computer units that read in the data from the various devices and sort and analyse it as required by the company. The summaries obtained provide details of what was sold, the amount of cash due and the goods that need to be reordered to bring the store back up to its standard stock level in each product line. The final details will be passed electronically to head office.

Although the individual stores are very large units in themselves, local management deals only with day-to-day matters. The buying is carried out centrally to obtain bulk discounts, wages are calculated at head office, and decisions on lines to be carried are made there. The group therefore has decided to install a mainframe computer at head office to deal with the group as a whole. This will be fed with summarized information from the branches through their local controllers, and head office will be able to send current prices down the line to them. As we saw earlier, the stores have access to the main computer through their terminals and can interrogate it to find the current position on deliveries, orders, etc.

County Cade Electricity Board

The main accounting and management functions are based at the Board's headquarters. Here they have a large mainframe computer which requires a fully trained staff to operate it but which can deal with a large number of jobs simultaneously. It deals with billing, other accounting functions and the management reporting work. There is no intention to replace this machine, which is working well although it is operating near to full capacity and unable to take on further work needed in connection with the current management system.

The main problem at present lies with the stock control side. The stocks of parts and domestic appliances are held at the Board's central warehouse. Each sales office throughout the region receives a weekly printout of stock balances after the week's sales have been processed. This batch system where the offices receive information that may be up to a week old has proved to be of little use to the sales offices. On many occasions they have sold appliances for immediate delivery, only to find that although the stock report shows items on hand these have already been sold by other branches.

As a result it has been decided to install a minicomputer at the warehouse with terminal links to the sales offices. This will run a real-time system, i.e. it will update the files immediately information is received from any office and will report the current balance of items on hand.

This will remove the stock work from the main computer, allowing it to take up other work required at head office. The mini will be able to communicate with the head office machine and will keep it up to date with the summarized information that management need on stocks.

We have now seen a complete overview of the three firms. Note that three very different types of system are in use. Each company chooses the computer and peripherals that will suit its particular needs. As a result a wide variety of systems is found in practice.

Linking computers and users

Today we have mainframe computers, minicomputers and microcomputers. These terms refer to sizes and classes of machine from the very largest down to the smallest. However, the development of computers is very fast and over the years manufacturers in each group have widened their product ranges. As a result distinctions are often blurred. For example, it can be quite difficult to say where the top of the minicomputer market ends and the mainframes begin. For the average accountant the distinction is an academic one anyway.

In this section therefore we shall very briefly consider the three groups of machines and look at a practical example of how some large firms are linking computers. In the light of this we will see how the connection is made and data transferred and how this can provide a wide variety of systems.

MAINFRAMES, MINICOMPUTERS AND MICROCOMPUTERS

Mainframe computers are very large, powerful units, with large amounts of memory. They are capable of multi-access working and normally support a large number of peripherals, shared among the various users. They are costly but the speed and facilities they offer are very good. They are bulky and normally have to be kept in special air-conditioned rooms and require a trained staff to deal with them. When used for multi-access (often called multiprogramming) work it appears to each user as if he is the only one on the system. However the computer works on each job for only a minute portion of time before moving off to do a little more on the next job. It is able to do this because the processor works at very high speeds, while input and output devices are relatively very slow. The processor would spend a large proportion of its time waiting for data if it worked on only one job. It therefore works on a job until it needs to move data in or out. While this is happening it moves on to the next rather than wait for the data. In this way it can support a number of users and still provide them with reasonable response times to their work.

Minicomputers were developed as smaller, less complex machines and introduced computing to medium-sized firms. Some of our minis today are quite large multiprogramming machines with far more memory than a mainframe would have had a few years ago. In fact we now hear suppliers talk of the 'supermini'.

The development of microcomputers brought machines that can be placed on a desk top. These have brought computers down to the small firm and have sold in large numbers. This has led to the development of a great deal of software designed with the ordinary user in mind, much of which has now also found its way on to the bigger machines.

As with other machines before them, the range of micros has been extended up and down. We now have a range extending from small hand-held micros, resembling large calculators, through to larger multi-user microsystems which seem very much like minis.

Organizations are not limited to using just one class of machine. Many are setting up systems that use a variety of equipment linked together. Minis and micros can be linked to one another or to a mainframe as part of a *network*. The main market (by volume) today lies with the minis and micros, as many firms are finding that a number of smaller machines at different locations can be linked together to give a better service than one large central machine. This is termed *distributed processing*.

ILLUSTRATIVE MINI CASE STUDY

Many firms are involved in the production and distribution of low-value items to retailers, e.g. cigarettes, food, snackfoods and confectionery. Some of these are developing computer networks to help process the large volumes of sales transactions and provide better information at all levels. Our case involves a fictitious company but is based on what is being done by several firms in this sector. This case will be considered again in more detail when we look at systems analysis in Chapter 10.

Albert Inder worked for Sugar Plum Confectionery for many years as a sales representative and retired five years ago. His son, John, currently has a similar post with them. Albert was very surprised recently when, with his son, he revisited the firm.

He had been one of 20 salesmen covering the country selling a product range of more than 150 lines to the shops in their area. On visiting a shop he had to fill out a standard sales order form listing each product. At the end of the day he always had at least an hour of clerical work to do, tidying up the orders and providing the summaries to be posted off to the district office. Here clerks analysed the figures and wrote up the customer documents. Fortnightly he received details of price changes and special offers and had to keep his price file up to date from these.

The firm's current system is very different. These days salesmen each carry a battery-powered portable microcomputer which is used as follows:

1. At the customer's premises, John presses a scan button on the micro which then scans through the customer records in order, showing the name on the small display screen. When it displays the one he is seeking he presses the select button and is ready to take the order.

2. In its memory the computer holds a copy of the order form (including all the prices and special offers). The salesman can scan the product lines one at a time and enter the amounts ordered. Once the order is complete he moves on to the next customer and repeats the process. He does not have to worry about updating price lists or making out order forms.

3. When he finishes the last call of the day he no longer has to spend time on clerical work. The micro is linked to a telephone line and the data it holds on each customer is transferred to the minicomputer at the district office. This done, the mini will send back details of the customers to be visited the following day plus any price or other changes. It can also send short messages to the salesman if required.

4. The district office now receives full details from all sales staff by the end of the day. Its computer can notify the warehouse of the orders and will monitor their progress, producing the necessary customer documents. It also transfers details of all sales to the accounting system and brings the debtors ledger up to date.

5. Summaries by product lines are produced and sent directly to the production-centre computers. The information is used in production planning and control. Finally, general summaries are sent to the mainframe at head office.

This brief overview of just one part of the company's system illustrates how data is captured at the earliest point and then made widely available across the business. The computer network mentioned here provides information to:

1. customers,
2. warehouse,
3. accounts,
4. production,
5. head office.

COMPUTER NETWORKS

We have seen how data is held inside computers in binary form. In this form it can be transferred to other computers or to peripherals, given the physical communications links. Computers can be networked to other computers or to peripherals. Networks may be *local area networks* (LANs), covering a small area and using private lines, or *wide area networks* where links are made over the public telecommunications system linking equipment over greater distances.

To transmit data over the public lines it must first be converted from the computer's signal into a form appropriate for the telecommunications system. This is done by a *modem*. In the past an *acoustic coupler* was used away from the office to connect computers to the public system. This fed the signal from the computer into a telephone handset but was rather inefficient. These days telephone extension plugs are more readily available and a better quality modem that bypasses the handset can normally be used.

If we are linking one computer with another, data can be transferred between them at very high speeds. However, if we are linking a computer to peripherals the rate of transfer is very much slower and the communications line is greatly underused in such a case. A piece of equipment called a *multiplexor* can be used to allow several such devices to use the same line simultaneously. It splits the messages from each device into blocks and sends a continuous stream of them along the line together with details of which device they relate to. At the other end the messages are reassembled and the user will be totally unaware of all this happening.

The demand for data transfer facilities has greatly increased in recent years and the system is being modernized to help speed up transmission. Once the signal has passed into the British Telecom system it may be transmitted in a number of ways. The traditional method has been to use existing lines for this but in many parts of the country optic fibre cables have been laid to increase the capacity. Microwave equipment and satellites are also used to transmit data. With such facilities data can be sent anywhere in the world very quickly.

This is affecting, and will increasingly affect, the way we work. For example, unlike the other commodity markets, the money market does not have its own premises in the City of London. The banks all have their own trading rooms containing highly sophisticated communications equipment able to deal with other banks anywhere in the world almost instantly. Thus there is no need for a central marketplace. The market is worldwide and consists of all the banks that take part. There is no longer a need for the trading rooms to be situated in the City. (The Chemical Bank recently moved its offices to Cardiff.) It is the communication link rather than the location that is important.

The power to network computers in this way has allowed firms to change the ways that they process their data.

The power to link computers in LANs allows better access to information and will lead to far more integration of office services in the near future. It has already allowed the development of new services such as electronic mail. The power to create wide area networks, however, can help companies make even more fundamental changes, specially in processing data. Computers can be installed at distant branches, allowing them to process their own data while head offices can still obtain all the information they need if the right form of network is used. This *distributed processing* not only changes the way the firm is managed, but can help to make it less vulnerable to computer breakdowns.

We have already seen how the demand for computer services across all departments took the machines away from the accountant's area of control. However, the establishment of a central computer, normally at head office, often proved equally restrictive even though it was no longer dominated by accounting applications. It frequently meant that branches had to submit their data to the head office to be batch-processed several times a week and wait for printed results to be returned. As well as being slow, this restricted decision-making at the local level as the information needed was normally not readily available.

Using small computers networked together branches can once again look after their own information, often in real time, with transactions entered as they take place and the files updated at that time. This provides the local users with up-to-date information useful for decision making. Several forms of network organization can be created.

Star network

With this sort of network (Fig. 3.8) a central computer, probably at head office, is in overall control of the system. All branches can communicate with this machine. They can also communicate with one another but must go through the central machine to do this. This places the central computer firmly in control, but should that malfunction the whole system ceases to operate.

Hierarchical network

Another form of network is the hierarchical type illustrated in Fig. 3.9. Local branches are equipped with smaller computers used for processing of local data. This allows them control over their own information. Above these at the next level a larger computer coordinates the work of all branches under it and produces information for the area managers. A large machine at the head office provides information for the group as a whole and is fed from the lower machines.

This tends to reflect the form of management adopted by most firms, allowing central coordination while delegating local authority. The machines are arranged in a hierarchy similar to the way in which management is organized. There is also the advantage that a breakdown of any machine in the network does not prevent the rest of the system operating.

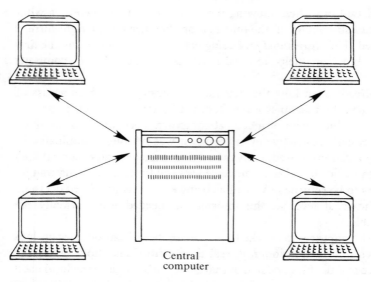

Figure 3.8 Star computer network

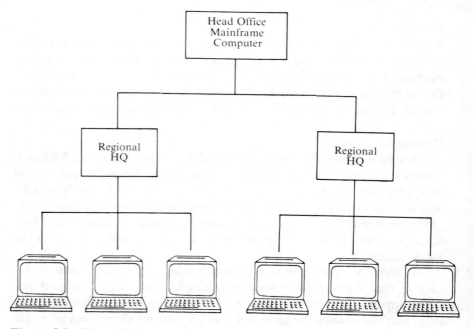

Figure 3.9 Hierarchical network

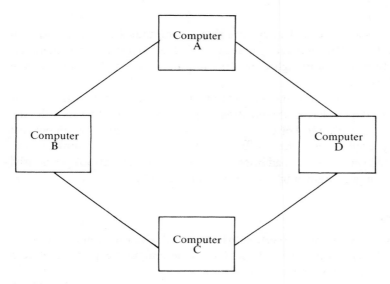

Figure 3.10   Ring network

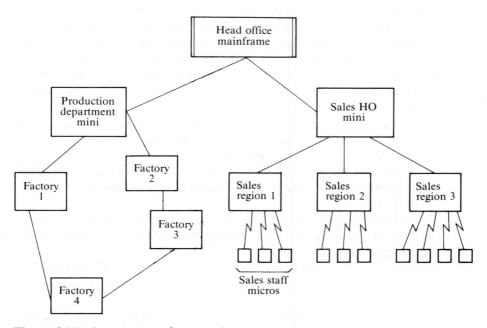

Figure 3.11   Organization of case study network

Ring network

Here all units are independent and are able to communicate with any other in the group (Fig. 3.10). Should any unit in the ring fail to operate, the others can continue to operate although their messages may have to be routed in the reverse direction.

The shape of the network depends on the organization and the way it processes its data. A larger organization may have a network that includes the above patterns within it. For example, the confectionery company in our last case study would have a head-office computer and computer links to the factories and warehouses, in addition to the sales system described previously. Its overall organization might appear as in Fig. 3.11.

Summary

1. Today's accountants are certain to be involved with the computer at some stage of their careers. They do not have to be computer experts but need a knowledge of the area for their work.
2. We have a wide range of computers from mainframes down to hand-held micros; however it is often difficult to classify machines into one of these groups as they tend to overlap.
3. The main computing unit performs its calculations at very high speeds inside the processor. The memory holds data and programs fed into the machine and supplies these to the processor to keep it running.
4. Peripherals are the units that link the computer with the outside world. There is a wide range of these designed to meet the varying demands of firms.
5. Data and programs are stored in the computer in binary form as a series of 1s and 0s called bits. The machine uses a group of such bits to form a number or letter. This group is called a byte.
6. We have a variety of input and output devices all offering different facilities. Generally, the faster the equipment can handle data, the more costly it is.
7. External storage is a means of saving the contents of memory and keeping them outside the machine. The main storage devices at present are disk and tape.
8. Data of a similar nature is stored together on one area of a disk or on the same tape for later processing. This collection of data is termed a file.

   Computerized accounting is very much based on file handling. This means that most of our processing is done at high speed by the machine, with the data and the results being transferred to and from files and only summary data printed out.

9. Files may be stored on line or off line. When a file is on line the computer can read its content with little delay. If it is stored off line, the appropriate file must be loaded on to the peripherals and read in. If many files need to be kept on line, further tape decks or disk drives can be connected to the machine.

10. Real-time systems keep the files up to date. Anyone seeking information from a file will receive up-to-the-minute details extracted from files stored on line to the system.

   The alternative is a batch system where data is stored to await processing and batches of it are processed at regular intervals. With this system the information on file will often be out of date.

11. With developments in communications, the transmission of data over large distances has become simpler and cheaper. Many firms are using distributed processing where several machines are spread around the business to deal with particular aspects of the work. These are linked so that data and results are far more widely available.

12. Computer networks allow the data processing function to be distributed around the firm, enabling local branches to process their own data and obtain information locally.

13. Local area networks link computers and peripherals over short distances and allow data and programs to be transferred.

14. Wide area networks connect computers over large areas, utilizing the public communications network. This can link computers to other areas of the firm or to an increasing number of public services, e.g. electronic mail systems.

15. Networks can be arranged in standard formats such as rings, hierarchies or stars. A large group can combine these into more complex patterns that better serve their needs.

4

Computer software

Introduction

We have seen that the term 'hardware' refers to the actual computer equipment and 'software' to the various programs and systems. Accountants use computers only because they can perform the type of work required, speedily and efficiently, and it is the software rather than the hardware that allows them to do this. Far too many people look at the make of machine they are buying rather than at the software it can run. As a result they may end up with systems that do not fully serve their purposes.

Software production is now an important industry, and a great deal of software has been developed for computers of all sizes. To simplify our study we will divide software into two main types (see Fig. 4.1):

1. *Systems software*   When we use a computer much complex work goes on, unseen, to allow the machine to run our programs. This happens under the control of a large set of programs called the *operating system* which, together with other programs, allows users to load and run their own software without having to know or understand what is happening inside the machine.

2. *Applications software*   These are the programs that make the machine perform a particular job; accounting software is an example. New applications software is continuously being developed to serve all industries, and work has been computerized which only a few years ago seemed totally impossible to place on machines. Great care is required in the choice of applications software as it can vary greatly in quality. For example, there are hundreds of different accounting programs of which only a few may exactly suit the needs of a particular firm.

Systems software

We will consider two main types of systems software:

1. the machine operating system, and
2. the language translator.

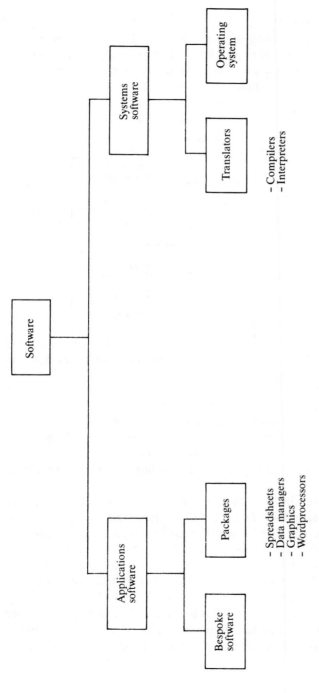

Figure 4.1 Types of software

THE MACHINE OPERATING SYSTEM

When a program is used on a computer it appears to the user that he merely has to load it and watch it run. However, behind the screen a great deal of work is performed by the operating system, which controls all aspects of running the computer. This includes the following (see Fig. 4.2):

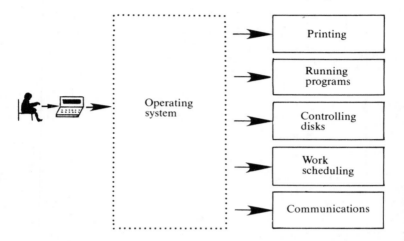

Figure 4.2 Work of the operating system. New operating systems often use diagrams and pointing devices to simplify their use.

1. The application program will have certain requirements to make on the system, e.g. allocating space in memory and on disks for both the program and its data. The operating system will check that this is possible; if so it will meet the requirements, if not it notifies the user and ceases operations.
2. Programs and data will be loaded into the machine and saved at various times during the operation. The operating system takes charge of all this, switching specific peripherals in and out of the system as required.
3. Computers are being increasingly networked in today's business world. As more communications devices are attached to a computer system so the work involved in controlling and switching them increases. In a large multitasking machine this can involve so much work that the operating system spends a large proportion of its time on it, slowing down its proper work. In such cases a smaller computer is often placed in the network purely to handle the communications and feed the main machine. This is

termed a *front end processor*. In addition to handling the communications work it may perform other tasks such as sorting data to further reduce the work on the main machine.

4. Even relatively small machines today are capable of multitasking. In such systems jobs have to share the machine's facilities and this means that the operating system has to schedule jobs and control the order in which they are processed. At the correct time a section of a program, together with its related data, has to be loaded into the CPU, be worked on and then loaded back into a particular section of memory while another task is performed.

To appreciate the complexity of the work involved we will briefly consider part of the final task above, *job scheduling*. This will inevitably remind you of certain aspects of hardware, covered in Chapter 3, which is hardly surprising as the operating system is in fact the link between the hardware and the applications software.

We saw that the machine's processor operates at such fantastic speeds that input and output devices cannot hope to keep up with it. The computer must therefore multitask if the processor is not to be kept idle for a large proportion of the time. Several people will therefore use the machine simultaneously, each job being processed for a small time slot before being placed back in memory and the next one processed in a similar fashion. This must be carefully managed so that each user obtains a fair time share and suffers no obvious delay in response time.

There are three basic types of work the machine must cope with:

1. Most business processing involves a great deal of input and output with details being moved from disk into the machine and back out to disk or printer. There are therefore natural breaks in the processing where the processor would be idle while the slow input and output devices are transferring data. These 'input/output-bound' programs are easy to multitask as the breaks release the processor for other work.

2. Mathematical programs, e.g. complex business plans, occupy far more processor time owing to the high volume of calculation. Once these 'CPU-bound' programs grab the processor they will not give it up for some time unless the operating system interrupts them.

3. In most installations some internal work, e.g. payroll, will be run in batch mode and given a lower priority than enquiries, etc., on real-time applications which must be given processor time immediately as response time is important.

The operating system deals with this work scheduling, maintaining a queue of jobs awaiting processor time, with priorities allocated to jobs according to their type. It constantly reviews these priorities to allocate the fairest possible shares consistent with efficient processor use.

With larger machines the operating system is normally supplied by the manufacturer and the buyer is locked into software provided for that machine. Microcomputers have relatively small and simple operating systems and a number of these are available.

Early eight-bit machines had their own operating systems written by the manufacturers and incompatible with other machines so that software houses had to write for particular machines only. An American company, Digital Research, wrote a standard operating system (CP/M) available to any manufacturer using the Zilog Z80 chip at the heart of their machine. This was well accepted and a huge pool of software written to work under it, making it so important that other manufacturers (e.g. Apple, Tandy) had to design special hardware to make their machines CP/M compatible.

With the arrival of 16-bit machines there was a need for a standard operating system to run the new, larger programs now possible. Digital Research entered the fray with a new version of CP/M, intent on holding their market leadership. However, the adoption by IBM of the chief competitor MS-DOS (called PC-DOS on IBMs) gave the latter a great lead. At present most machines can run both systems and a wide range of software is being written.

The next stage is the development of 32-bit machines and already the battle lines are forming. In addition to the other systems, IBM has recently offered UNIX for its AT machine. This is a popular multi-user system taken from larger machines. Although powerful it has acquired a reputation for being user-unfriendly, a criticism being overcome by the use of graphical icons to help the operator, and it is likely to become even more popular in the future.

LANGUAGE TRANSLATION

We have seen how the machine holds all data and programs as a series of 1s and 0s called machine language and that all input must end up in this form before the computer can do anything with it. At this level a program consists of very many simple operations which the computer must perform. Users could write their own programs in this way but it is very difficult because:

1. It is hard to remember binary codes for all the available operations.

2. Humans do not think this way. Even when they break a problem down into manageable portions they still approach it in a far more general way than does the machine.

To reduce errors and save time most programming is done using other languages (sets of instructions) designed to be more helpful to the staff involved. Special programs will then translate the finished work from the programming language into the binary language of the computer. A range of languages has been developed to help solve most problems. These include the following.

Low-level languages
These are close to the machine's own language and the programmer must write one instruction for every operation the computer will perform. As a result he or she knows exactly what is happening inside the machine and programs written in this form can make the best possible use of available memory.

To avoid the problem of remembering all the binary codes a programmer may use *assembly language*. Again this is very close to machine language but allows the use of simple mnemonics for the operations which are easier to remember. Numbers can also be entered in forms other than binary. The following example illustrates the difference between machine language and assembly language.

All arithmetic is performed in one area of the processor called the *accumulator*. There are several detailed instructions to transfer numbers into and out of this, and others, equally detailed, to perform the arithmetic once the transfer is complete. (It is this sequence of small, detailed steps that earns the title 'low-level' instructions.)

The instruction to transfer the number eight to the accumulator on a microcomputer would be similar to the following:

Machine language

10101001   0001   0000

The first block represents the operation code (opcode), meaning load accumulator; the other two blocks are the figure eight held in a special form. From this you can see how complicated it would be to have to remember the opcodes for all possible operations. Assembly language allows the same task to be performed more easily.

Assembly language

LDA # 8

The opcode is now replaced with a simple mnemonic (standing for LoaD Accumulator) and the number can now be entered in the normal decimal form. The # sign merely tells the computer that this figure is data and can be loaded directly into the accumulator.

A special translating program called ASSEMBLER will translate programs written in this form into machine code and check that the programmer has not broken the basic language rules (syntax) which the computer understands. Such programs have a relatively simple task to perform so they do not have to be large or slow.

High-level languages

When solving business or management problems users need to look at the overall task and not concern themselves with the breakdown into machine operations. A number of high-level languages have been developed to do this. They allow users to enter instructions in a form close to our own language where *one instruction in the program is broken down into a number of simple steps inside the machine.*

These languages are far more complex than low-level ones and the task of translation to machine language is far greater. There is therefore a limit to their size and complexity and rather than one all-embracing language, a number of specialist ones have been developed, each designed to deal with a particular area of work. They include the following:

1. COBOL (Common Business Orientated Language) This is a very powerful language for business programming. It has a good range of commands to manipulate files of data.
2. FORTRAN (FORmula TRANslation language) This was designed for mathematicians and scientists who need to use the mathematical rather than data processing powers of the computer.
3. BASIC (Beginners All-purpose Symbolic Instruction Code) This was designed primarily as a teaching language to allow students to concentrate on problem solving rather than the way the machine operates. This proved to be very popular in many areas and is the most common language on microcomputers. The Appendix to this chapter illustrates the programming of a problem in this language.
4. A number of our schools have now gone on to use a language, Pascal, which is said to improve the way students learn to program.

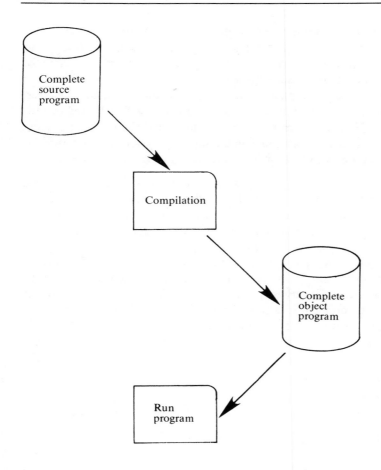

Figure 4.3 Compiled programs

The translation of high-level languages is performed by a translator program. In most cases this is done by a *compiler* which works thus (Fig. 4.3):

1. The original program (*source program*) is written in the high-level language.

2. The *compiler program* is loaded. It then reads in the source program and checks it for any errors that break the rules of the language (i.e. syntax errors). The user is notified of these and they must be corrected before the compiler will convert the program.

3. A machine language version of the program is output (called the *object program*). In the future it is this fast object file that will be loaded into the machine and run. If it proves necessary to amend the program at some later date, the changes are made to the source program and this amended copy has to be compiled again to produce a new object program.

BASIC is somewhat different because it is translated by an interpreter (Fig. 4.4). This software does not translate the whole program but only one line of it. The current line is translated and presented to the computer in machine language. It can hold only one line at a time so each must be retranslated every time it is met. The machine then moves on to the next line and repeats the process. The object program is used on the machine every time. This method of translation is very simple and takes up little room, hence its popularity on micros. This also makes it very easy to use, but it is extremely slow in operation. To overcome this problem it is possible to buy a compiler which translates BASIC programs into object files in the normal way.

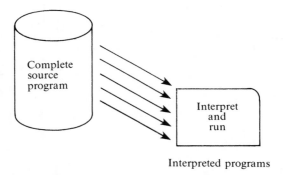

Interpreted programs

Figure 4.4 Program translation

Applications software

BESPOKE OR PACKAGE SOFTWARE

In this section we will look at how software is purchased. The detailed work involved in developing it will be considered in a later chapter.

Large companies normally have their own computer services departments with programmers and systems analysts. Many of the systems will have been specially designed for them and written and tested in house. This bespoke software is costly and time-consuming to develop, because once written it must be fully tested before it can be commissioned into use. Any errors that are missed can prove very costly in day-to-day running. The main advantage, however, is that the software is designed to perform exactly the work the company requires.

Once a system has been successfully commissioned the firm may decide to recover some of the high development costs by allowing others to purchase copies. For example, Rio Tinto Zinc has developed a large general ledger system which can now be purchased as a ready-made package system for use by other firms.

An increasing market for package systems has developed as minicomputers and microcomputers have brought computing within the reach of many more firms. Independent software houses, which for many years provided staff on contract to help develop in-house systems, have used their own expertise to prepare a range of packages for general sale. This has developed into a major industry, and new software products are regularly being developed for most sizes of computer.

In the early days of computing, packages were viewed with suspicion because they were often written specifically for the originating firm and then adapted in an attempt to make them suit other companies. As a result they were often inflexible and firms buying them had to change the way they worked to fit in with the new system. Most of today's packages are quite different, being designed to offer as much flexibility as possible. A purchaser with a particular requirement will often find that the software has a range of options built in which allow it to be tailored to his or her needs. For example, most sales accounting packages not only handle VAT-exempt, zero-rated and standard-rate goods but have room to hold up to a further five or six rates. Simple on-screen options allow these to be altered without programmer assistance. At present this facility is redundant on thousands of systems around the country, but should the government decide to levy a higher rate on luxury goods, most firms will be able to deal with it quite simply.

We frequently hear of government plans to revolutionize the tax and benefit systems when they install their own computers. Such changes can be highly disruptive and costly to the business community if their existing systems have been unable to foresee such changes and allow for them. The introduction of statutory sick pay caused many problems for firms and many had to incur great expense and effort to ensure that their payroll systems were ready in time for its introduction. One advantage of package systems is that for an additional *maintenance* fee the supplier will guarantee to maintain the software up to the requirements of current legislation. If the law changes, this saves a great deal of effort because an updated version is issued. Bespoke software, on the other hand, might well require a great deal of rewriting.

The choice between bespoke and package software is not mutually exclusive and many firms will use a mixture of the two. Computer staff in large firms normally have very little chance to develop new software, as up to 80 per cent of their time is used to maintain current systems in working order. As a result such companies now frequently have a backlog of work waiting to go on the computer and therefore help and encourage departments to process much of their own data using packages on micros.

Part of the answer to these backlogs lies in improving the speed with which such programs can be developed and improved. It would also help if we could simplify the process so that staff in user departments could develop their own work. The traditional method of creating systems involves systems analysts working with user staff to plan a system. This is then converted into detailed programs by teams of programmers, often over a long period. We now have program-generating software which allows staff to define what they want using standard systems descriptions. The computer then produces the programs necessary to perform the tasks described. These are called program generators or fourth-generation languages. The latter name helps us to place them within the knowledge already gained in this chapter; they are in effect a programming language for the general user and a natural development of computer languages:

1. First-generation languages were the binary codes needed by early programmers to talk directly to their machines, i.e. machine language programming.
2. The second generation was assembly language which helped make this low-level programming easier to understand.
3. Third-generation languages were the high-level, work-oriented languages such as COBOL and BASIC which allowed people to concentrate more on the work involved and less on what the machine was doing.
4. Fourth-generation language allows users to concentrate fully on the system and leave the machine to perform the actual coding of the programs.

The latter are still relatively new and will no doubt become far more common and more powerful as new generations of hardware are developed, providing them with the sort of computing power that they require. They have already been used by a number of firms with great success and it has been claimed that they can reduce development time by up to 90 per cent in certain cases.

It is interesting to note that we started this section by comparing bespoke and packaged software as if they were mutually exclusive. We then saw that firms today often use both types of software in their business. Finally, with fourth-generation languages, we see a bridge between the two, allowing the firm to design a system according to its needs and yet avoid many of the costs and delays needed to develop this. They may also allow staff in user departments to take a more active role in developing systems and allow them to develop simple systems to perform local tasks not supported by the firm's main system.

DEVELOPMENTS IN APPLICATIONS SOFTWARE

While mainframe machines dominated the market, software development was relatively narrow, directed mainly at systems handling large volumes of data in a specialist environment. Programs were designed to be run by trained staff with a technical background, so little importance was paid to their presentation.

The development of ever smaller machines meant that they were to be found on the desks of untrained users who had heard of the wonders computers perform and wanted their machines to do useful work for them. A consumer-led market developed, bringing great changes in the type of software produced. This new software was:

1. Better presented and easier to work with (said to be user-friendly). Users were given a series of choices through menu screens which detailed what the programs could do and asked them to choose the options they required. Help screens were developed so that a new user, unsure of what to do next, could press a help key and obtain guidance. Too many such help messages can be annoying and slow down the experienced user, so in many programs the user can now select the desired level of help each time the system runs.
2. Designed to deal with general office tasks rather than high-volume processing, e.g. to produce reports and handle general business calculations.

The development of such software led to a convergence of computing and office technology, with the numbers of machines in offices growing steadily. This allowed firms access to far more information than was previously available. However people do not work in isolation; they need to share the information they produce, so we have also seen great improvements in communication facilities at the same time.

Computers are now regularly linked together allowing high-speed data transfer regardless of the distances involved. We can now obtain far more up-to-the-minute information from all over the world which, if used properly, can yield great benefits to managers. As a result information itself is becoming an important management resource and an increasing proportion of people in our economy are employed in information-related work. We are said to be experiencing an information revolution and the term *information technology* is used to refer to developments in this area. We will now consider the sort of software which has and is being developed to meet this consumer demand and bring computers into more general use in offices.

General office software

While the amount of specialized software was and is continually increasing, software houses soon realized that a mass market existed for programs able to handle the tasks common to all offices. These involve filing and retrieving information and the production of letters and reports. This led to the development of several areas of general office software which is now found throughout business. (See Fig. 4.5.)

WORDPROCESSING

Wordprocessing, the application most people think of first, has certainly helped sell a large number of small computers into offices. There is a tendency to think of the wordprocessor as a 'smart typewriter', able to speed up the typist's work. However, it is far more than this and many accountants and managers use them to prepare draft work which is then sent to their secretaries for completion.

Text processing is possibly a more descriptive term than wordprocessing, as wordprocessors allow us to process text in a number of ways. Features include the following:

1. Having stored text we can recall it and use it for a number of other purposes. For example, complex legal agreements are often produced on wordprocessors using standard paragraphs which were stored and carefully checked for meaning and accuracy when first created. This can greatly reduce the chance of error and the time involved in checking. The term 'boilerplating' has come to be used for this process of bolting together paragraphs of prepared text to produce a final document.
2. Other documents such as price quotations, tenders, etc., can be produced simply from outlines stored in the same way. They are loaded into the

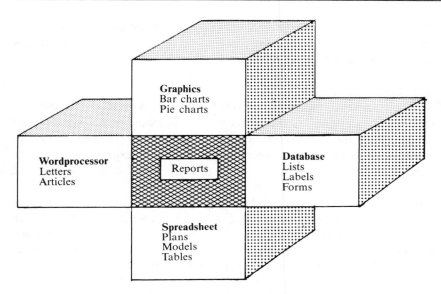

Figure 4.5 Integrated software. The development of microcomputers led to demand for general business software. At first these were developed as stand-alone packages, but they were later integrated to allow them to share the same files. Reports and other documents could now be prepared more easily.

machine and the current figures inserted. Some wordprocessors will even add up the figures and print in the totals automatically.

3. Documents prepared for one purpose can often be adapted to serve other purposes with the minimum of typing, e.g. a planned list of chapters for this book, stored on a wordprocessor, was quickly adapted to provide a progress report and a checklist for both authors.

4. The ability to cut out, insert and move blocks of text around a document can be a great help in composing reports, articles, books, etc. Many writers find that they soon compose directly on the screen which can greatly assist creativity. The writer can be further assisted by automatic word count, spell checking and even a thesaurus.

5. Firms often need to prepare a standard letter or questionnaire and circulate it to a number of people. The 'mail merge' facility on many processors allows a standard letter to be printed out repeatedly with a different name and address on each copy. The list of names and addresses is held on a separate file which is merged with the standard letter. The machine can also produce mailing labels for the letters produced.

The wordprocessor therefore becomes far more than a mere typing aid, and it is a creative tool for composing reports, etc., allowing users to experiment with ideas before finalizing documents.

DATA MANAGEMENT SYSTEMS

For many years two standard tools have been found in most offices—the card index and filing cabinet—showing that much office work involves storing and retrieving data. Both of these devices store data but offer little help when we come to analysing it. Data management systems have become very popular in recent years for their ability not only to store data but also to sort and analyse it.

Just as the amount of filing and analysis varies across firms so the range of software varies, from very simple card index-type programs, which use menu screens to guide users, to quite complex systems with their own programming languages which allow huge volumes of data to be accessed from various sources. (dBase III, for example, allows up to one billion records, and up to ten different files may be cross-referenced at a time.)

The comments above will have made it clear that these systems are helpful in handling large amounts of data but they call for a great deal of memory and disk storage and this can often be an important limitation on such applications.

These programs involve the setting up and manipulation of files. We have already mentioned the role of files and in the next chapter we shall consider in detail how they are organized. This is therefore a useful point at which to consider some of the terms used in file handling.

TECHNICAL TERMS

To help illustrate these terms, consider a simple problem, the setting up of a card index covering members of a youth club. There are four levels of data which make up the index (see Fig. 4.6):

1. *The file* This is the term given to the whole collection of cards, containing all the data. These cards are stored in the same file as they relate to the same sort of data (in our case all the members of the judo club).
2. *The record* In our case every card is a record, as it gives us all the information we have concerning one member. Items in the record each have in common the fact that they relate to the subject of the record.
3. *The field* Each card holds several pieces of information about the member, e.g. date of birth, surname, address. These are the individual facts about that member and this is the lowest level at which we may work

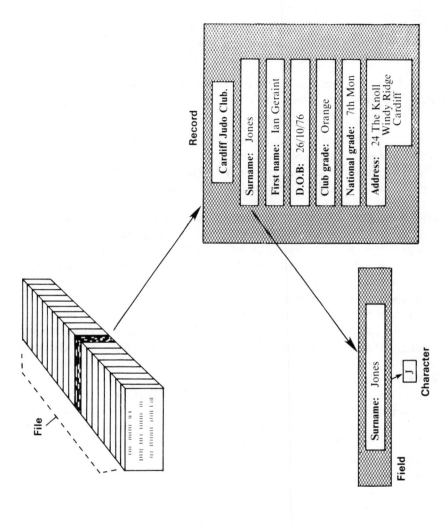

Figure 4.6 File terminology

on the cards, for example we may search for all members born after a certain date.

4. *The character* Fields are made up of letters, numbers and special items such as * , : etc. These are termed characters, and the number of characters in a field is called the *field length*.

Armed with this terminology we can look at some of the facilities normally provided by these data management systems. They vary with each package, but generally include the following:

1. All offer facilities to add, remove, view and list data on the file.
2. The power to search records for those that conform to particular characteristics in common. For example, we could search for all customers in a particular area whose turnover exceeds a given figure. All such records can then be printed out and totalled.
3. Records can be reordered within files. For example, a customer list kept in alphabetical order could be resorted into delivery-round order to provide a delivery list. Some programs actually sort the records and produce a new, sorted file while others perform a tag sort. The latter merely keep a count of the record numbers and sort these, while the original records are untouched; this is a faster method of sorting.
4. The power to sort and print can be used to produce mailing labels and various lists. Users are normally able to define their own standard report forms and the system will fill in the appropriate data after checking through the file. Circular letters can also be provided as in the 'mail merge' option with the wordprocessor.
5. Mathematical facilities in many packages allow a great deal more work to be done on the data. We may be able to make a percentage change to one field throughout the file and assess the result of the change, e.g. to assess the effects of tax changes. With such facilities the program can be a useful planning tool and comes very close to our next application area—the spreadsheet.

SPREADSHEETS

These programs have proved so popular with accountants that many people mistakenly believe them to be accounting software. This is not the case. Spreadsheets are general-purpose tools designed to allow ordinary users to harness some of the mathematical power of computers. It is possible to perform with the spreadsheet most tasks previously performed using pencil, paper and a calculator.

The screen, in effect, becomes part of a large working sheet divided up into rows and columns, giving a large number of cells or boxes. These are identified by a two-character name, e.g. cell C6 is the box where column C and row 6 intersect. Into each of these cells the user may enter only one of the following at any time:

1.   written text,
2.   a number,
3.   a formula telling the machine how to calculate the current figure that should appear in the cell.

Using the worksheet we can construct a wide variety of documents of varying complexity. Many accountants use this facility to prepare and print working papers as quickly as they were previously written out. They also have a more powerful role, however, for if we use the formulae to set up mathematical relationships between boxes on the screen we can create a business model. If we then alter certain figures all related cells will be automatically amended to reflect the effect of our changes. If the relationships we have programmed are realistic, our model can help us predict the effect of change.

The idea of a spreadsheet is difficult to grasp unless one sees it in operation and the reader is advised to take any chance available to learn the use of this flexible tool. The following illustrates the method in a highly simplified example.

A firm buys and sells goods making a profit of 20 per cent on selling price. Figure 4.7(a) illustrates the results that would appear in a model assuming they sold £1000 of goods.

Figure 4.7(b) shows the model that is entered into the computer. If the sales figures were amended to say £10 000 then the profit and expenses figures would change to the appropriate values.

Larger, complex models can be created basically by using these same simple steps. To make things faster for the user a number of further facilities are offered in most programs, including:

1.   fast methods of repeating (replicating) formulae across a number of rows or columns,
2.   mathematical functions, e.g. to find the average, maximum or minimum values of a block of cells.

GRAPHICS SOFTWARE

With these programs data entered into the machine is used to produce a range of graphs and charts. These graphical aids include bar charts, scatter graphs and pie charts.

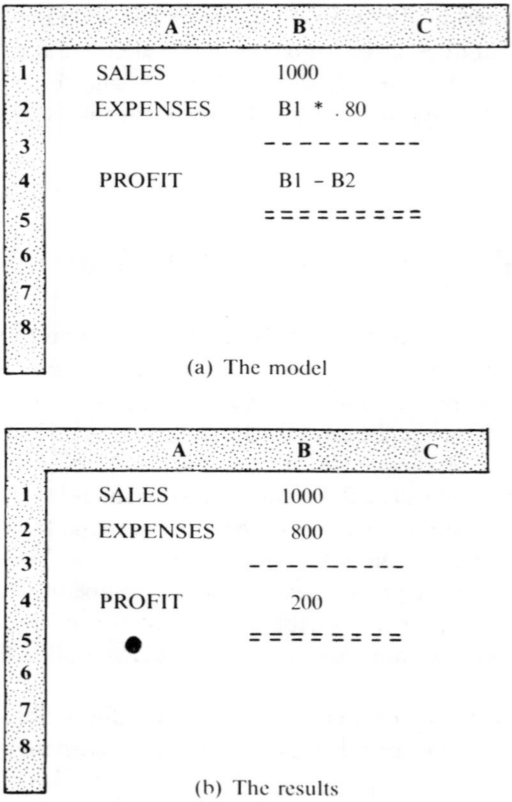

	A	B	C
1	SALES	1000	
2	EXPENSES	B1 * . 80	
3		- - - - - - - -	
4	PROFIT	B1 - B2	
5		= = = = = = = =	
6			
7			
8			

(a) The model

	A	B	C
1	SALES	1000	
2	EXPENSES	800	
3		- - - - - - - -	
4	PROFIT	200	
5	●	= = = = = = = =	
6			
7			
8			

(b) The results

Figure 4.7 The basic steps in spreadsheets. (a) The model shows the formulae and figures entered when programming. Note the asterisk used to indicate multiplication in box B2. On computers we cannot use the × as this could be ambiguous. (b) What the user sees. If the figures in B1 are changed the others will automatically change to reflect this.

The results may be printed out if the firm has the appropriate equipment. Most dot matrix printers are able to reproduce such diagrams with little trouble, but only in monochrome. To obtain colour printout the user will require a colour plotter. These can often print to paper or to an acetate sheet for use in a visual presentation. Equipment is also available from Polaroid to produce either a colour slide or acetate sheet directly from the colour screen of the computer.

It is a tedious task to have to enter large sets of figures for the preparation of such diagrams. In most cases the figures concerned will have been prepared using a spreadsheet and much effort could be saved by linking the two sets of software. As a result more and more spreadsheets, e.g. Lotus 1-2-3 and Supercalc 3, now include graphics facilities.

ACCOUNTING SOFTWARE

Accounting is a major area of computer usage and a wide range of systems are available. Unfortunately there are no minimum standards which such software must attain and the market is very much a case of 'buyer beware'. We shall look at this type of applications software in detail in a later section.

MULTI-PURPOSE PACKAGES

The above application packages have been available for many years as stand-alone units. We saw how the graphics software benefits from a link to the spreadsheet and how both wordprocessors and data management packages deal with circular letters. It was a natural development therefore when these were integrated and offered as multi-purpose packages. The manager can now draft a report on the wordprocessor, pause for a while to try out figures on the spreadsheet, and when satisfied produce both a graph and table of the results and incorporate them into the report. This is then checked for spelling and personal copies are sent to each person concerned. All this is done using various options in one set of integrated programs, which use the same working files. However, users wishing to include text, graphics and tables in the same report faced a great deal of loading and saving of the various files involved. The files produced by each were normally incompatible and a certain amount of cutting and pasting was needed to arrive at a final report. Packages are available now that integrate wordprocessing, spreadsheets, graphics and database software so that all tasks may be handled without the need to load further software, e.g. Lotus Symphony.

A major problem with any new software package is the need to learn a set of new instructions to operate it. This can be quite a task and tends to reduce the number of different packages an average user will employ. The programmers who design integrated systems do their best to standardize the menu screens and instructions across the applications in such packages.

WIMP SOFTWARE

The search to simplify packages and reduce the effort of learning several sets of instructions was assisted by the development of computer graphics. Graphical symbols (icons) have been linked with better on-screen help messsages (windows) and pointing devices to make things far simpler. This is called Window Icon Mouse Pointer (WIMP) software and is illustrated in Fig. 4.8.

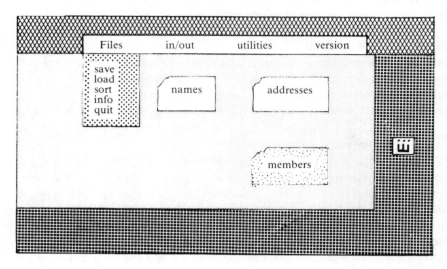

Figure 4.8 WIMP screen, designed by the authors, indicating how such software works. The user has three files on disk, and has chosen to work with the members file, which is shown shaded to indicate that it is now in use. To load this file the mouse has been used to position the cursor over the files option. On pressing the button the window of filing options has appeared on screen. The tick indicates that the user has just chosen to load this file. The window will shortly disappear off screen until called again. Note the dustbin icon on the right of the screen. To kill a file the cursor is used to drag the file icon here.

On loading the software, the user is faced with a set of icons representing the files available. To perform operations on them an arrow on the screen (the cursor) is pointed to the relevant file. For example, to delete a file the cursor is used to drag the icon across to a small icon of a dustbin. This kills the file.

Other operations that may be performed on the file, such as load, save and copy, are stored away in small windows, which can be rolled down on to the main screen as required. The user makes a choice by pointing to the required option. This done, the instruction window rolls up out of sight until needed again, leaving the whole screen to work on.

The final development was to create a device to move the cursor around the screen more easily than using the keyboard. This is the mouse, an optical and mechanical device which is moved back and forth across the workdesk. A ball bearing inside senses the movement and an optical device transmits this to the screen. The on-screen cursor will then copy the movements the mouse makes on the desk. When the cursor is pointing to the required position a button on the mouse is pressed to inform the computer. The keyboard is then used only if text or numbers are to be entered.

At the time of writing, WIMP software is still relatively new. However, further applications software is being developed and even accounting software is available in WIMP format. As noted earlier, it has also been used to help make certain applications of UNIX more user-friendly.

Appendix: Illustration of BASIC at work

This section will demonstrate the use of BASIC, a high-level language for students, to solve a small problem. It is not possible to teach the reader to program in the language within the space of a short appendix. The aim is therefore to enable him or her to understand how the problem is reduced to code and how to follow the steps in a short program.

THE TASK

Create a small program that will read in the customer name and the total amounts of four invoices (numbered 1 to 4 respectively), and print out the list together with the total and average values.

The data and the figures we seek are as follows:

Invoice number	Name	$
1	R. Smith	100.20
2	G. Brown	200.00
3	D. White	150.00
4	A. Edwards	149.80
	TOTAL	600.00
	AVERAGE	150.00

Stage 1: Break down the task

Before writing the program the task must be broken down into a series of steps which can then be entered into the machine. For a high-level language each step will consist of a small task, while with a low-level language it must be further broken down into individual steps. The general steps in this task are shown in Fig. 4.9.

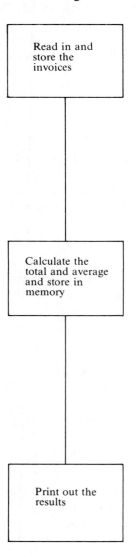

Figure 4.9 The general breakdown of tasks

(a) Firstly the program will have to read in the data it requires. This will be done when the program is run, an operator typing it in as requested by the machine. The data will be stored away in certain bytes in memory. With a low-level language the programmer would need to know the numbers of those bytes and keep referring back to them. A high-level language, however, takes care of all this. The user can give the value a name and keep referring to it that way. The machine holds a table showing against each name the number in memory and where it is stored; the programmer does not see this.

(b) Next, the program will calculate the total sales and the average. The total will be accumulated in a box that we shall designate SUM. Each time the machine reads in an invoice total it will add it to the total currently held in SUM.

(c) The final stage is to print out the report in the form shown above. The figures required are all in memory and an instruction such as PRINT SUM tells the machine to print out the value currently stored in the box called SUM.

Stage 2: Structure of the program
The program will be split into four parts as follows:

(a) The main program basically repeats the steps shown in the diagram in stage 1. The main tasks will each be performed by a small mini-program called a procedure. Each procedure is given a name and the main program will call on them by name as required.

  This form of programming is termed 'structured programming'. It is easier to develop, as the procedures can be developed separately, and easier to follow, which is why it is used here.

(b) The procedure called 'data' will read in an invoice, store the name and amount and loop back to read the next. A counter in the program will ensure that this is done exactly four times.

  Each time it reads a name or amount it will store it in a named location, the name of which is based on the current invoice number. So names are stored in

  name$(1) ... name$(4)

and amounts are stored in boxes named

  amount(1) ... amount(4)

according to the invoice to which they relate.

Note: name$ has a dollar sign at the end while amount does not. These are signs to the machine to help it check on the programmer. Any location given a name that does not end with the dollar sign can only contain a number, and this the computer can use to perform arithmetic. If the name ends with $ then it may contain letters or numbers but cannot be used in arithmetical calculations later (e.g. 2.5/R. Smith makes no sense!).

(c) The procedure 'calculate' performs the calculations; it adds the value of each invoice in turn to the running total held in SUM and finally divides this by four to obtain the average.

(d) The procedure 'printout' will do just what it says: print out the headings, messages and figures from memory.

Stage 3: The program

We will now look at the program as it would be entered into the machine. This dialect of BASIC will not work on all machines and has been amended slightly to make it more readable. Before reading the program please note:

(a) Each line of the program starts with a line number. The computer will execute the lines in number order unless the program tells it to jump elsewhere. The fact that the line numbers do not run consecutively has no ill effects; it is normal to program in this way to facilitate the addition of further lines if required later.

(b) Each line in a program must have a command word. This is a keyword which makes the computer perform some task, e.g. PRINT. These will be printed in upper case in the example to help you recognize them.

(c) The left column contains the program; the right column carries notes explaining for your benefit what is happening. The right column is not used in practice.

100 REMARK main program	The keyword REM tells the machine to ignore this line. In this way the user can put remarks and headings in a program.
110 PROC data-input	Calls up the procedure data-input to perform its work.
120 PROC calculate	Calls on the procedure calculate to perform its work.
130 PROC printout	

| 140 END | Informs the computer that the program has ended. |

....

500 DEF proc data-input	Tells the machine it is about to define or set out the procedure named.
510 FOR invoice-number = 1 to 4	This line sets the counter that will make it read in only four invoices.
520 INPUT name$(invoice-number)	This makes the machine read in the name when typed and store it in a byte named name$(1) to name$(4) according to which invoice is being entered.
530 INPUT amount(invoice-number)	This makes the machine read in the amount when typed and store it in a byte named amount(1) to amount(4) according to which invoice is being entered.
535 LET SUM = SUM +amount(invoice-number)	Adds the amount of the current invoice on to the running total held in SUM.
540 NEXT invoice-number	Makes the machine jump back to line 510 unless all four invoices have been entered. If they have, it will go on to the next line below.
550 ENDPROC	Tells the machine the procedure is complete and returns it to the next line of the main program.

....

700 DEF proc calculate	Indicates that this section defines the procedure named here.
710 LETE AVE= SUM /4	Divides the total of the invoices by 4 to provide the average, which is stored in a location to be labelled AVE.
720 ENDPROC	

....

The final procedure printout is not shown here. It uses the instruction word PRINT. For example PRINT ave would print out the figure 150 currently in this location.

The print statements are not shown here because print statements can be rather confusing to follow without some instruction in their use.

Summary

1. 'Software' is the term used to refer to programs and systems. They are equally important as the hardware and in many cases today more so.
2. For our purposes we can divide software into two main classes; systems software which runs the hardware, and applications software which performs the tasks we require.
3. The operating system is a set of programs which allows the user to run programs without difficulty. It performs a wide variety of functions from handling the peripherals through to job scheduling on multi-access machines.
4. Language translation programs convert programs from the languages in which they were written to machine language, understood by the computer. The *compiler* translates a program into an object file, stored and run in machine code. An *interpreter* translates only one line at a time, every time the program is run. This is a far slower but far simpler form of program.

5. With a low-level language one instruction must be written for every instruction performed by the machine. High-level languages free the user from the restrictions of the machine to concentrate more on the problem. As languages develop, this trend will increase, helping non-specialist users to create and amend their own systems.

6. Applications software exists for most types of organizations; some was developed specifically by the users and some was developed as packages. The increased production of good packages means that only a small proportion of medium-sized and small firms need go to the cost and problems of having software designed for them. Packages are normally a cheaper and faster way of solving a problem.

7. The market-led demand for general-purpose software, fuelled by the boom in small machine sales, has led to the development of more user-friendly packages. The standard applications for general office use these days are spreadsheets, wordprocessors, data management packages and graphics. Communication software is now becoming an important fifth area along with these. The tendency is to develop integrated versions of these, allowing users to use any tool simultaneously on the same files.

8. The development of WIMP software is aimed at simplifying the use of software and reducing the need for keyboard skills.

5

File processing

Introduction

Business computer systems often impose conflicting requirements on their designers. It is part of the role of the designer to seek solutions which provide the best compromise between these. In this chapter we will look at the role of computer files and see how such conflicts arise.

Business data processing is heavily involved with file handling, with transaction data files being regularly processed against the data currently on files. These files, which can only be read by the computer, allow us to process data at high speeds, but even at these speeds it takes some time to locate an individual item on a file. Throughout this chapter we shall see this basic conflict:

1. To minimize costs and avoid backlogs, firms wish to process as much data as possible in a given time. The fastest way to do this may involve continuous processing and the use of one type of file, which is totally incompatible with our next requirement.
2. Firms often need to obtain information quickly about a particular record, e.g. a customer or an employee, which involves searching the file for that item.

Items of a similar nature are collected together and stored as records within the files (as described in Chapter 4). Files can be classified in a number of ways according to their purpose and the information they contain. However, we need only consider two classifications.

Data files

These contain raw data awaiting processing, e.g. a file of sales invoices awaiting posting to the sales ledger (master) file. Files such as these have only a limited life and once processed against the master file, and possibly used to provide a detailed analysis, they are destroyed.

Master files

These hold standing data and information that is carried forward from period to period. These files are regularly processed to provide up-to-date information. The sales and purchase ledgers are examples of such files, with customer and supplier records being updated and carried forward from year to year.

File media

Files are stored outside the computer on magnetic media which in most cases are likely to be magnetic tapes or disks.

MAGNETIC TAPES

This is called a *serial* storage medium, because records must be stored one after another serially along the tape. As it passes at speed over read/write heads the computer records or reads a block of records at a time. Between blocks the tape has to stop and, later, restart for the next block which leaves a series of inter-block gaps along the tape. As a result, no tape is ever used to its full capacity, with the size of blocks and hence the amount of tape unused being decided by the system.

As tapes can only be read sequentially, to find a particular record the machine must search serially through the file, reading in a block at a time, until it finds the one that contains the record sought. This affects data processing in the following ways:

1. When seeking a particular record on the file a great deal of time may be lost because that record could be anywhere on file; sometimes it will be near the start and other times near the end. On average therefore the system will have to search about half the file. This is only an average, however, and a full search of the file can be quite slow.
2. If the records on the file are arranged in some order, we are said to have a *sequential file* (see Fig. 5.1). Such a file must be ordered on a specific field which is then called the *key* field, e.g. an alphabetically-arranged ledger may be stored in ascending order on the surname field, which is therefore the key field.

    If data files are sorted into the same order as the master file, prior to processing, little time is lost searching for records and the master file can be updated very quickly. (This is called *sequential processing*.) Sequential processing is the fastest method of processing large volumes of data which has been arranged sequentially. It is very slow, however, if we wish to search for a particular record.

MAGNETIC DISKS

Here the data is stored on tracks around the surface of the disk and is read by

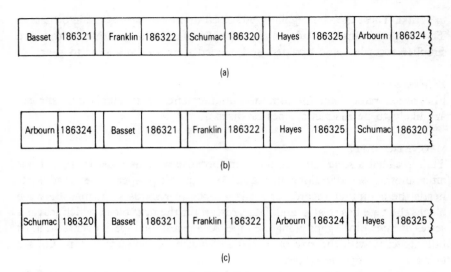

Figure 5.1 Serial and sequential files. (a) Serial file. Records appear on the file in no order. It would be very difficult to do any useful work with a file in this format. (b) Sequential file in alphabetical order. (c) Sequential file in pay-number order.

heads which pass in and out over the surfaces. As we saw in Chapter 3 mainframe computers use packs of disks with read/write heads over the faces of each disk, which can contain up to 200 tracks. With micros we may have floppy disks or a Winchester. We will consider the way the large disk packs are arranged. (The smaller single disks use similar methods, with fewer complications.)

As with tapes, the computer transfers not one but a group of records to or from the disk at any time. With tapes we called this a *block* of records but with disks we refer to a *bucket*. When we read a record into the computer the following happens:

1. The computer finds the bucket that holds the record.
2. This is transferred into memory where the machine can work on that or any other record in the same bucket.
3. Later, after processing, the whole bucket is saved back to the same disk.

With a pack of disks rather than just a single one a great deal of time can be saved by careful organization of the way data is stored. Whenever data is transferred to or from a disk there is a delay while the machine:

1. moves the heads over the correct track,
2. waits for the disk to rotate until the correct bucket is below the heads,
3. picks up the data and transfers it to memory.

This all happens at very high speeds but in large jobs it can still add up to major delays. These can be greatly reduced if the amount of head movement is cut down by storing data in cylinders.

To do this a file is started on the outside track of the first disk and data is entered there until this is full. After this, common sense would seem to dictate that we move on to the second track of that disk, but this would require a movement of the head. As all the heads move in and out together, every head will be floating over the same track on its disk surface. It is therefore faster to move on to the same track on the next disk face and so on down through the pack so that the data is in effect stored on a series of cylinders viewed through the disk pack.

Disk storage therefore has several effects on the firm's data processing system:

1. As with tape, files can be processed sequentially, if required, and the speed of data transfer is somewhat faster with disks than with tape.
2. Alternatively, the system can go directly to any bucket without the delay of working through the whole file, so if the location of a data item is known or can be calculated it can be accessed directly. This facility is termed *random access* and makes disks far superior to tape for applications that require fast search facilities.

File organization
When planning a system the designers must consider the most appropriate form of file organization and this will depend on the type of application and the information required from it.

TAPE OR DISK

Disks seem to have the advantages over tape of random access, speed of data transfer, and the fact that they do not have to be rewound each time they are used. This might prompt one to wonder why it is that tape is still a major form of storage for files. The reasons are as follows:

1. Tape is less costly than disk and therefore proves more economical in areas that do not require disks.

2. When a file is processed on tape the system cannot write the new version of the file back to the same tape, even if only one record is changed. A new tape must therefore be created on a separate drive. While this is slower it has security advantages: should something go wrong in processing the master file, the previous generation of that file can be updated and used to replace the damaged copy. Disk systems do not provide this sort of backup as data is placed back on the surface of the same disk after processing, overwriting the existing information. To obtain a copy of the disk its whole contents must be copied to another disk, using a special copying program. This means that processing of that disk must be stopped for copying to take place.

Tape is a good medium for processing high hit rate applications such as payroll where a large proportion of the records on file need to be updated. Where such an application is processed sequentially, the tape is a good medium for high-volume data transfer and there is little to compare between tape and disk.

However, where only a small proportion of records is to be amended, the application has a low hit rate and the system will spend more time seeking records than it will updating them. Such an application requires direct file access.

DIRECT-ACCESS METHODS
Direct access to records is possible with disks but the system must have some way of knowing where to find any particular record. We shall consider two methods of doing this.

Random files
With this method of file organization there is a direct link between the value of the key field and the position of the record on disk. In the simplest cases we know the maximum number of records needed and can set up an address on disk for each. A good example might be a student record file. The tutor knows the number of students in a class and that it will not change to any great extent. The student number would therefore be the key field and student 40 would be the 40th record on that file. Given any student's number, the system would know directly where to seek the appropriate record.

However, things are rarely this simple in business. When setting up a debtors ledger file the firm requires a record for each customer. But they cannot know in advance who or how many people will become credit customers, and their number will constantly change as customers come and go.

It is not practical in such a case to open a record for every person who could possibly become a customer and a direct link between the key and the record location is not therefore possible.

In such cases a formula (called a *hashing formula*) is normally applied to the key value to produce a value within the range of possible addresses on the file. A record is then stored at the location indicated by hashing its key value and access is fast and simple.

Finding a hashing formula that always creates a valid file location is complex and not a problem for an accounting student. Ideally there should be a one-to-one link, providing a unique address for every possible customer, but this is often not possible and several key values may point to the same address (called a *collision*). The system must therefore be programmed to deal with such collisions in one of several ways. The simplest method involves placing the record in the next empty location and, as this is likely to be in the same bucket, there will be no need for a further read operation and so little delay is caused.

This type of file organization is very fast in operation and is frequently used in applications such as process control. The user is totally unaware of the hashing and collision handling because the system handles all that. However, as the file is used, the number of collisions increases and so will the time taken to access records. When this reaches an unacceptable level special software is used to recreate and reorganize the file.

With files of this type, records are spread about the surface of the disk and it is not very efficient to try to process them sequentially. However, we saw above that sequential processing is the most efficient way of updating high-volume files as little time is wasted searching for records to update them. The strength of this system lies wholly in the speed of access and very little in the speed of updating. As a result it is not greatly used for business applications which frequently require both of these facilities.

Indexed sequential access method
To see how this method works consider how you might set about finding out more about the indexed sequential access method (ISAM) from your college or local library:

1. You would probably check the library for books on data processing. The subject index would save time here and guide you to the general area of the shelves.
2. The index in the book you picked out would guide you to the pages that included this topic.

3. On turning to the first of these pages you would start to skim through (sequentially) until you found a reference to the topic.

In doing this you will have performed an indexed sequential search (Fig. 5.2), and the following notes show how this would apply to a file of names. One advantage of this method to business is the relative ease with which it can handle dynamic (growing or contracting) files:

1. When the disk is created, records are stored in sequential order within various sections of the disk and a reasonable amount of space is also set aside as overflow areas for future growth. Indexes stored on the file guide users to the first and last record in each section, and room is left within each section, in addition to the general overflow areas above.

2. To retrieve a record the key value is entered, the index then directs the head to the appropriate section of the disk, and the bucket is read into memory. This contains a number of records and is searched sequentially at high speed until the appropriate record is found. We have a query on the account of a customer named Hanson and wish to examine that record. The first step is to look at the index to find the general area on the disk. Here there are two levels of index although there could be several. The subindex directs us to the bucket originally set up to hold these records. In this example the first five records were those existing when the file was created. These are in alphabetical order as a result. The rest of this bucket would have been left empty as a local overflow area. We must now search through the bucket sequentially. The record we seek is not there and at the end of the bucket we meet a pointer to a separate overflow area. We must now go back to the disk, read in the overflow area and search that sequentially. Our record is the last one in this section, which has further room for expansion. Files such as this can therefore deal with expansion but the search time increases as the file fills up. Eventually the file will have to be reorganized with existing records sorted, new indexes prepared and new overflow areas created.

3. When a new record is added the key value is used to send the head to the appropriate section of the disk and, if there is room, the record is added. If there is no room, the record is entered in one of several overflow areas created when the disk was set up. A marker or tag is placed at the end of the main section, pointing to the appropriate overflow area so that the system knows where to search for the record. This will, however, involve finding another bucket and reading it into memory so it will increase the retrieval time.

4. As the file grows, a greater proportion of records will be found in the overflow areas which will progressively fill up so that the access speed will

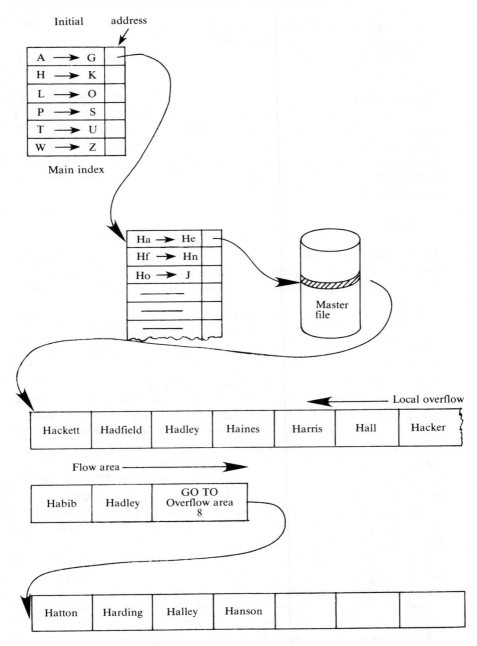

Figure 5.2 Indexed sequential access method

continually worsen unless something is done. At this stage a utility program must be used to recreate the file. It does this by bringing all existing records into the main file, creating new indexes and setting up new overflow areas.

This method is a useful compromise between the two previously studied. As the file is arranged more or less in serial order the speed of sequential processing can be utilized for updating. On the retrieval side the system allows fast access to particular records although it is not quite as fast as the last method. In applications such as ledger accounting where the system needs to be able to handle large volumes of data and yet may need to access individual accounts at short notice, this method works well.

DATABASE SYSTEMS

The development of improved storage devices and better access methods allowed data to be accessed and summarized in ways that were previously too time-consuming. Better management information was therefore possible and this in turn created more demand for information as managers realized how it could help them.

However, very large amounts of information are needed to manage the whole organization and the traditional way of dealing with this was for each department to maintain its own private system with its information stored in files which were accessible only to them. We have seen how this can lead to problems of duplication and contradiction between the various sets of data.

The development of integrated Management Information Systems seen in earlier chapters accentuated these problems. Contradiction of data was not acceptable if those figures were being used simultaneously by several departments. There was a need for data to be shared and for a wider range of managers to be able to obtain the most up-to-date information possible. The database concept was developed for just such applications. We looked at this briefly in Chapter 2 and will now look at some further aspects.

When considering the organization of a database it is important to differentiate between the *physical* and the *logical* structure of the data involved. The following example might help to differentiate these.

We all make use of a variety of information in various aspects of our lives. A family setting out on a caravan holiday might seek information from various information providers shown in Table 5.1.

Each information provider is in the business of collecting this data and classifies it according to their own system, designed to suit their purposes. The holidaymaker will have a particular itinerary in mind and is probably interested

Table 5.1

Information	Provider	Classification
Weather forecast	Met. office	Regions
Tourist information	Tourist board	Regions, towns
Traffic reports	AA/radio	Main motorways

in the attractions of a particular area to, for example, a mother, father and two small children. The information sought and the way it is used will depend on specific plans.

We can view the traveller's personal itinerary as being the logical organization of the data, as this is the way the user views it and sees it relating to his or her own personal role. This is very unlikely to be the same as the physical organization which refers to the order in which it is stored by the provider. Searching through, selecting the appropriate items and fitting them into the user's own plans can be complicated and time-consuming.

When we consider a business database those classifications are very important. Such systems contain large amounts of data, used to serve a number of specialist user departments, each with its own particular requirements as to content and presentation of information:

1. The *logical organization* is the way that each user sees the data arranged and reacting on other data to provide the information he needs. Each user will have such a picture and the systems development staff will need to bear each of these in mind when designing the various programs that access the data.
2. *Physical organization* refers to the way that the data is stored and accessed on the various storage devices. We have already seen some of the ways this can be organized. The physical organization is planned with the needs of the computer foremost in order to allow it to access the data it requires as quickly and efficiently as possible.

As with our tourist information example there is a great deal of work involved in formalizing the links between the physical system and the various logical systems involved. We saw in Chapter 2 that this task is handled by a complex set of programs, the database management system (DBMS).

With a database system:

1. data and files cease to become the property of functional departments and data becomes a shared resource with all users obtaining their information from this one common base, thus avoiding the problems mentioned earlier;
2. the data is also independent of the individual programs that access it, making it possible to create new programs or change old ones without the need to alter the way the data is stored.

A great deal of systems planning work is needed to ascertain the data needs of all the departments and the ways it must be manipulated to serve various users, and to decide who may access data and how they may be allowed to affect it.

The overall system must be capable of handling all these differing data processing requirements and so a detailed plan called the *schema* has to be prepared. This is a large plan setting out the overall links between data right across the system and showing the various programs which can access it. In addition to this a series of subschemas is also prepared, describing the way that local programs within the system relate to the data. One of these is required for every user's application area.

The DBMS controls the whole system, dealing with the way it is set up, addition and removal of data, and the links between data that provide the information.

A system of this size and complexity must obviously perform a great deal of searching and sorting of data to provide for the various applications. This would be very time-consuming and would greatly restrict the information-handling ability of the system if it required all data to be sorted every time some information were to be extracted.

Once the various uses of the data have been planned the links between data items can be identified. Then rather than place data on individual records and search right through the file for them, the system itself records many of these links between data items as they are recorded. When a sort is required it can quickly access the data items it requires and summarize them without the need to search through all the items on file.

This linking can be accomplished in several ways. We have already seen how the ISAM method of file access allows the computer to access particular data directly. In a similar way a database can be made to produce detailed indexes showing the locations of data items which conform to particular criteria. This requires the creation of large index files which are stored alongside the data, but it does allow faster access to linked items for summarizing.

Another method involves the use of pointers within data records. In this case the date is entered along with several other fields which together constitute a record. These fields point to the location of other records which are linked in some particular way with the present data item. For example, in entering sales orders which are awaiting processing, a field may link together all orders not yet filled. To produce a list of all unfilled orders the computer does not have to search all data items on file. It will find the first one and print the details, then following the pointer linking such orders it will go directly to the next order and print details of that one. In this manner it can produce the required listing very quickly. DBMS systems allow a great deal of such analysis to be performed and very complex links can be made between items with one item being linked to several others in many different ways.

The use of databases has increased in recent years but they are not the complete answer to all data processing problems. As they grow larger, the overhead involved in maintaining the various records and links increases and there is a set-off between increased maintenance and improved efficiency. However, if designed properly, they can provide great benefits and with developments in communications large databases can be accessed by users all over the world. We are seeing the development of large public databases which can search through huge volumes of data and provide up-to-date business informaton in seconds.

File processing methods
It is time to consider the way that these various types of files are processed to provide our information. To do this we will use a diagrammatic method called *flow charting*. Flow charts are used in a number of professions (including accountancy) to describe how systems operate. The sort of charts we will use are called systems flow charts. They are not very detailed, being designed to show only a general overview.

The method of processing that is carried out has much to do with the type of files that will be used. In considering file processing methods we must start, as always, by considering the information that forms the end-product of the whole operation. In cases where large amounts of data must be processed but the information is not required immediately, sequential processing is acceptable; but if users must be able to access the machine and obtain up-to-the-minute information we require real-time processing. In this section we will consider again the subjects of batch and real-time processing and see how they operate. Before that let us see how we can use a flow chart to outline our systems.

INTRODUCTION TO SYSTEMS FLOW DIAGRAMS

Flow charts help provide an overview of systems in a way not possible in narrative descriptions. The first thing to be learned is the meaning of the symbols that are used. Then we can go on to look at the general method.

To illustrate flow chart symbols, Fig. 5.3 shows a batch processing system. Do not at this stage try to understand the system—we will look at that later. At present we are interested only in the chart itself.

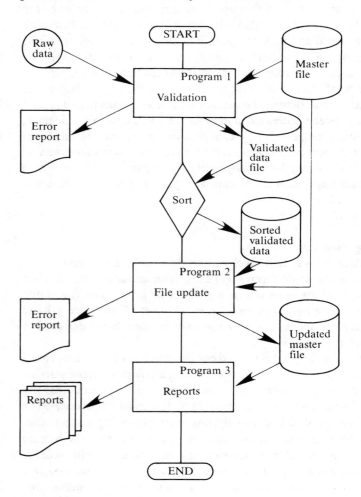

Figure 5.3 Batch processing

Symbols
The symbols used in flow charts are shown in Table 5.2.

Table 5.2

Symbol	*Meaning*
	Used to represent the start or end of the system.
	Represents a process within the system. The system will consist of a number of programs, each of which has a particular task to perform. As we are concerned only with the general overview we merely note the name of the process and what it is designed to do.
	Shows that the data from the file is sorted.
	Indicates that printout is obtained from the machine.
	Indicates input from output to a VDU terminal.
	Represents the storage of data on to tape.
	Represents the storage of data on to disk.

The method

If you refer to Fig. 5.3, you should notice the following points:

1. The chart is effectively divided into three columns:
    - The central column indicates the processes performed by the computer.
    - The left column shows inputs and outputs to and from the users.
    - The right column shows input and output to the computer's external storage devices.
2. File processing involves using the computer to update the master files from which we obtain most of our information.

Using this technique of flow charting we can now move on to consider processing methods in greater detail.

BATCH PROCESSING METHODS

Payroll, stock accounting and ledger work are examples of areas of accounting that have been computerized since the early days of computing. At first these were batch processed and many firms still run high-volume applications in batch, even though other applications may be run in real time on the same computers.

Serial files (on tape) have to be run in batch mode and, as we saw, ISAM files are often updated in this way. Figure 5.3 illustrates the general aspects of updating a master file within a batch system. We shall assume that it relates to the posting of sales invoices to the debtors ledger. However, the same basic procedure is used to deal with credit notes, cash receipts and in a whole range of other application areas.

From the diagram we can see that the routine is as follows:

1. Files relating to these applications are stored off line with each application being run according to a fixed timetable. The files are released from the library at the appropriate time and updated against all available data. As users cannot communicate directly with the machine, the input and output of such applications consist of documents.
2. User departments create the source documents, e.g. invoices, and store them up for processing. At regular intervals they will batch them and attach a batch control slip. This identifies the batch by date and number and includes several control figures that will later be compared with the figures produced by the computer, as a check on accuracy.
3. At the computer centre a control clerk records details in the batch register and arranges for it to be converted into machine-readable form, e.g. using

key-to-disk equipment. This data conversion is an error-prone task and the work has to be *verified*. One operator will key in the data, which is then stored on disk; a second operator then repeats this operation and the system verifies input by checking the two sets against one another. After verification the data is corrected if necessary and copied on to tape which is then used as input to the computer. We have now arrived at the first stage of our flow chart.

4. *Validation* should not be confused with verification mentioned above. The aim of this program is to check the data and reject those items that contain some obvious error. A variety of tests can be applied at this stage and these will be considered in more detail when we discuss controls in a later chapter. We see from Fig. 5.3 that our system uses the master file in the validation process. This indicates that it checks the customer details, names, account numbers, etc., on invoices to ensure that they agree with those shown in the ledger.

Any errors detected by the machine are listed on an error report and those items are rejected. As they will not have been included on the file they will have to be manually checked and then re-entered.

5. As this is a sequential application the validated data (invoices) must be sorted into the same order as the master file (the ledger) before updating can take place. Once this is done the updating can take place at very high speed but this is partly offset by the amount of time needed to sort all the files.

6. At this stage the various transactions, in our case the invoices, are posted to the ledger. To do this the data file and the master file are run against one another and records are matched on the key field. The actual procedure is illustrated in the following logic module. To read it follow the instructions given and when you arrive at the word RETURN go back to the line above which starts on the same indent:

READ key field on next invoice.

    READ key on next ledger record

      if invoice key > ledger

    RETURN.

      if invoice key = ledger key then

      add invoice to current record

RETURN.

This is the same approach as a human operator would adopt if posting a batch of sorted invoices. He or she would read the number of the first invoice and then repeatedly work through the records in the ledger until the corresponding account was found. The operator would then post the item, look at the number on the next invoice and repeat the procedure until they were all posted.

7. This is a very slow way to produce information; full printouts must be sent to all users as the files are off line and cannot be accessed directly. This reduction of speed and the fact that the information is not fully up to date are disadvantages inherent in this type of processing.

REAL-TIME PROCESSING

This method of processing is used with applications where up-to-the-minute information is required. Airline bookings and police checks on stolen vehicles through their national computer are two areas that would require such processing. Business firms may also use it for stock or debtors accounting where these figures are used in the day-to-day running of the business.

A real-time system is one in which the master files are updated at the time that the transaction is entered. This not only provides fully updated information but, as users can access the machine and interrogate it, reduces some of the delays involved with batch systems. Firms that use such systems normally process only part of their work in this manner because of the demands on equipment and communications. The computer involved must be capable of multitasking, unless totally dedicated to the one task, so that other, less urgent work can be run through in batch mode. The operating system will allocate such work a lower priority and will actually interrupt its processing when real-time access is required. A system such as this is different from the previous type in a number of respects:

1. Real-time users enter their own data from terminals located in their department or branch. They are not specialist data conversion staff and will therefore be slower and more likely to make mistakes; however, the fact that they are actually involved with the transactions should speed up the clearance of any queries that arise.

2. The need for direct user access to the machine means that programs and files must be stored on line to the system, resulting in a need for more fast-access disk units.

3. A large proportion of messages to the system will involve file interrogation rather than updating. Many of these can be cleared on screen, e.g. checking that a customer has not exceeded his credit limit before authorizing

a further credit sale. This will greatly reduce the amount of printing required, although the facility normally exists to print out screen details if required. The level of printing involved with batch systems would not be acceptable in this environment as it would greatly slow down response times for users.

4. As we have seen, the users may be linked to the computer in a local or a wide area network, and distance is relatively unimportant these days. For example, the British Airways booking system can be accessed from a number of countries.

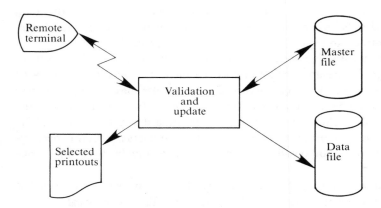

Figure 5.4 Real-time processing

In the last section we considered a real-time update of a sales ledger. We will now consider how this would operate in a real-time system (Fig. 5.4):

1. The user wishing to enter an invoice from a branch office must first gain access to the branch terminal. This may require a special key and will certainly involve logging on to the machine using a personal identification code.
2. The application to be processed will be password protected. The system will ask the user to enter the password at the appropriate time and will check that the correct one is entered. Certain staff will be allocated high-level passwords that allow them to access and change files, while passwords of less senior staff will allow access only to interrogate files but not to update them.

3. Having cleared the password protection, the system will normally provide a menu screen outlining the options available to that user. Only if he or she has authority to access files will this include the option to post invoices. The use of such menu-driven software makes the system much simpler to operate and thereby helps to reduce errors.

4. The next thing to appear will be the input screen. Increasingly these are designed to resemble, as far as possible, the actual layout of the invoice being posted. Once again this helps both to speed up input and reduce errors.

5. The program will validate data as it is entered by submitting it to a number of tests, e.g. are the values reasonable, does the input fit into the fields allocated? Failure of any of these will lead to rejection of the item, indicated by a loud beep and an appropriate error message. The system will continue to refuse the data until it is corrected.

6. Once the transaction has been accepted the system will post it directly to the ledger before any further data is accepted. In the short time interval while the user is updating the record someone else may attempt to access it. If this happened they would find that they were locked out from the record and would receive a message requesting that they try again. The record is locked during updating to ensure that users obtain the most up-to-date information possible and the short delay involved is a small price to pay for it.

7. You will see from Fig. 5.4 that although the system posts directly to the master file it still produces a data file. This file is later used to:

   - provide a detailed sales analysis for management purposes,
   - create an *audit trail* listing which is a list of all items processed by the system. This can be used by operators or auditors at a later date to check transactions through into the system.

8. This type of application is totally reliant upon fast file updating and data retrieval and therefore cannot be operated using tape as the filing media. Files using some form of direct access, e.g. ISAM, are required.

REMOTE JOB ENTRY

Some organizations use a form of processing known as remote job entry (RJE), where terminals and printers are located at outside departments or branches. They may use the terminal to input their transaction data to head office and some time later they will obtain a detailed printout of the results over their own printer.

This gives a direct link between the branch and head office but it is not real-time processing. The important factor that differentiates between the two is the way in which the files are updated. With RJE, the data from the branches is stored at head office until the applications program is next run and the files are updated at that time. This is therefore an example of batch rather than real-time processing and the branch cannot dial in and interrogate the system as required.

DISTRIBUTED PROCESSING
We have seen that it is feasible for branches to enter their own data and receive results directly. If this is the case we can go further and allow them to process their own data locally, submitting only their results to head office. This is called *distributed processing* and is currently gaining in popularity.

We have already seen (Chapter 3) the ways that networks of computers can be created to serve the particular management needs of an organization. The reader should note that both computers and peripherals can be joined together in networks, e.g. a LAN may link various items of equipment within an office. Distributed processing, however, means more than just linking terminals to a computer. In such systems part of the actual computing power, not just the peripherals, is distributed to other locations.

Summary

1. Business applications make use of the computer's ability to handle large volumes of data rather than its powers of computation. File handling is therefore an important feature of such systems.
2. When processing files firms are faced with two main requirements:
   - the need to update files by transferring large volumes of data to them,
   - the need to access individual records speedily in order to handle customer queries, produce special reports, etc.

   The type of file which is best able to handle one of these is normally inefficient in the other case. It is frequently necessary therefore to find a compromise solution.
3. Magnetic tape and disks are the most common storage media at the present time. Tape is a serial medium and cannot therefore offer random access to records. This makes it rather slow for accessing individual items. However, if the file is arranged in sequential order it is still quite fast when used for applications that have a high hit rate.
4. Disk files allow random or sequential access. They transfer data more quickly if the data is organized efficiently on the disk surfaces. For this reason large systems normally store files in the form of cylinders across a number of disk surfaces.

5. The fastest way to access files on disk is to create random files. Here a hashing formula is applied to the key field to calculate the location at which a record will be stored. Retrieval of any record is therefore very fast, given its key value.

    Although this type of file can be accessed very quickly the records are distributed across its surface in a random order. It cannot therefore be updated sequentially and updating will involve a great deal of head movement, slowing down the operation.

6. The indexed sequential access method (ISAM) is a compromise between random and sequential. When the file is created records are arranged on the surface sequentially, with plenty of room for new records. Indexes are created showing the general location of groups of records.

    This structure allows the file to be updated sequentially, gaining the benefit of fast update, and to be read using the indexes, allowing direct access. It is also able to handle files that are expanding.

7. As direct-access disk files (both random and ISAM) become full, their access times deteriorate as the system has to look for records at locations other than those first indicated. In such cases utility programs are used to reorganize the data and set up a new file.

8. With batch processing systems, files are stored off line and cannot be accessed directly by users. The files are normally organized serially and a great deal of sorting work is required to arrange all data into the same order as the master file prior to posting.

    Although validation will be carried out, this cannot be done until some time after the transaction has occurred. Delays are therefore involved while these are referred back to the originating department.

9. Real-time systems users enter their own data directly and may also interrogate the system. This requires the files to be stored permanently on line and needs direct-access files. Far more emphasis is placed on validation to detect and prevent errors and this is performed on entry. Invalid transactions should not therefore be accepted into the system.

10. Remote job entry involves entering data and receiving results through a local terminal. This is not the same as real-time processing, however, because the files are not updated at the time of data entry.

11. Distributed processing involves placing computers at various locations within the organization and linking them together. In this way data can be processed locally and summarized results or data forwarded to another part of the business.

Part 3

Accounting and business information

6

The traditional accounting system

Introduction

Manual accounting systems, in various forms, have a very long history stretching back to the early days of trade. The double-entry system, familiar to accounting students today, dates back several centuries. Computer systems are a relatively recent introduction being about 20–30 years old at the most, and micro systems have been with us only a few years. Over the history of accounting, changes have generally taken place at a steady pace until recently. Even with the advent of mainframe machines a large proportion of accounting work was relatively unaffected by the new technology. Computers were costly and were for large firms only. However in recent years, since the introduction of microcomputers, the pace of change has greatly increased and falling equipment costs have brought computers into even the smallest of firms. Since their first introduction there have been disagreements over what the effect of computerization will be.

Some authorities forecast a bleak future with mass unemployment as a result of their use, while others say that they will produce new jobs to replace many of those lost. Their introduction to accounting has therefore met with a mixed reception. Some firms and individuals were determined to master the technology while others ignored it and hoped it would go away.

Students often ask whether our existing accounting methods are out of date and whether the accountant's role is set to disappear altogether. They should remember that computers use the same basic accounting methods which have operated for years, so the accounting student approaching computerized systems for the first time will find much that is familiar. The same double-entry principles are followed but in some cases the systems designers may look at the work from a slightly different viewpoint.

On the future role of accountants there are many opinions. It has been said that developments in office systems will greatly increase the output of such workers and are likely to lead to mass unemployment. On the other hand surveys among existing accountants show them getting to grips with the new technology which is affecting the type of work they perform. It does not as yet, however, appear to have led to a reduced demand for their services. It is the view of the authors that there will continue to be a demand for good accountants but that their work will become more analytical as computers produce the required information. The advent of computers also raises challenges which accountants can benefit from; new services may be offered to clients or user departments and this will bring the accountant more into the mainstream of management. The new technology is certainly breaking down barriers between departments and providing far more information. This will possibly lead to a need for numerate managers with a wide knowledge of business. Accountants who are willing to move outside the confines of pure financial work should find an interesting role to play.

The work of the accountant can be said to cover the following three areas:

1. *Design and planning of information systems* The accounting system is designed to provide information for owners, managers, etc. A great deal of information is available from business data, given the facilities and the time needed to provide it. Using computerized systems the time involved is greatly reduced and far more can be produced. However, too much information is as bad as too little and it becomes far more important to identify what is really useful and how it should be presented.

   The accountant is the specialist in this area, being aware of the requirements of the various parties and of legal and institutional requirements such as accounting standards, company law, etc. These output requirements are important and must be identified early on as they will dictate the form of system adopted.

2. *Day-to-day running of the system* Computers are increasingly taking over more of this type of work. The demand for clerical workers appears to have fallen as their work has never been taken on to the machine. One person can, with a computerized system, provide far more information than was previously possible.

3. *Evaluation of the results* The accountant, with detailed knowledge of the system, is normally charged with interpreting the results and offering advice, and is also asked to provide specialist information to assist with particular decisions from time to time.

Computerized systems free the accountant from much of the routine day-to-day work supervising of recording and dealing with problems. This frees him or her to concentrate far more on dealing with the information produced. The result is that the accountant must become more of an information manager and adviser, providing what departments need, in a form that they can understand. Using the computer the accountant can obtain more data and create models to help evaluate the likely outcomes of various decisions; hence the comment above that accountants will need to become far more analytical.

We shall now briefly turn our attention to the traditional system of financial accounting to see how it functions and to recognize some of its disadvantages. From there we shall move on to see how computerized systems have been developed to deal with the same work.

The manual bookkeeping system

This is the system readers are likely to have met in their accounting studies. It will, however, be considered from a slightly different viewpoint from that normally taken in an accounting text, as we are only interested in the systems aspects of it.

The system is designed to handle very large volumes of data documents and, through the stages shown in Fig. 6.1, convert them into useful information in the form of reports. A reading of some accounting texts gives the impression that the annual accounts are the only reports produced by this system. That is not in fact the case; information on creditors, debtors, cash balances, etc., is being produced and used daily by staff. We will now work through the various levels shown in Fig. 6.1, taking each in turn.

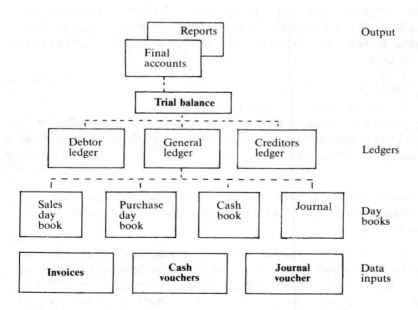

Figure 6.1 Traditional accounting system

LEVEL 1: THE DATA DOCUMENTS

These are the basic documents that provide evidence of transactions entering the system and it is a basic rule that no item should be entered into the system unless a data document exists to support it. Buying and selling transactions are supported by invoices, cash transactions by a remittance advice or a payment voucher, etc.

Even adjustments and error corrections should be authorized by a specific data document as failure to do so can make errors and fraudulent entries harder to detect. The document used to evidence this type of entry is the journal voucher. As it is used for a wide variety of items, some of them of an unusual nature, this document normally includes space for a narrative description of the transaction concerned. As a final check such vouchers must be signed by a person in authority before they are valid.

The firm's data documents hold the full story of what has happened in a period and it is by analysing the facts contained therein that firms obtain their information. However, it is too time consuming to enter full details of every transaction in a manual system and normally only total figures are entered. If additional information is later required, there is normally no alternative but to work back through these documents in detail, extracting the required information.

With a computer, as we have seen, once the data has been read in and stored on disk it can be used repeatedly. Assuming that the firm has the necessary programs, it takes very little extra time to provide additional information from the data.

LEVEL 2: THE DAY BOOKS (BOOKS OF PRIME ENTRY)

These perform a simple sort of transaction data, bringing similar items together prior to their transfer to the ledgers. For example, the sales day book performs the following tasks:

(a) It provides the first sort of data, bringing together all credit sales items and arranging them in date order. From this it also provides the daily total of credit sales.

(b) If analysis columns are included in the book, sales can be split over about six to eight classifications. This provides useful information, allowing management to monitor profitability of major groups of products. This is, however, a long way from an analysis by individual product line, a facility offered by a number of computer packages.

(c) On the control side it performs two functions:
  - The sales totals provided are also used to prepare control accounts which check the accuracy of later work in the ledger.
  - By helping to divide up the overall task of debtor accounting it helps to strengthen the control within the accounting system.

LEVEL 3: THE LEDGERS

These provide a major sort of data, bringing together items of a similar nature. The individual ledger accounts are used to collate all items which relate to a particular person or involve a particular expense, asset, etc. For example, the sales account brings together the monthly totals of credit sales (posted from the sales day book) and of cash sales (from the cash book). The combined total of them appears in the profit and loss account as the total sales for the year.

If analysis columns were used to classify sales within the day book, the ledger will contain several sales accounts, one to hold the total of each analysis column. This will enable the firm to report both total sales and sales within each analysis group.

With any information system the final output needed affects the form of system used. Thus the format of the final accounts and other reports required from the system will dictate the accounts to be found in a firm's ledger. There will have to be at least one account to feed every item that appears in the final accounts and in many cases there may be several subaccounts behind one such figure, as illustrated with sales above. Many firms use a hierarchical coding system (similar to those used in libraries) to uniquely identify each account and show how they interelate. This approach has been taken up with computerized systems and setting up the code of accounts is an important part of tailoring an accounts package to a particular user.

Early accounting systems contained only one, general, ledger that contained all the accounts needed to prepare the firm's profit and loss account and balance sheet. However, in all but the smallest firms, the number of debtors and creditors involved makes this impractical as only one person could comfortably gain access to the ledgers at any point in time. As a result most firms now maintain three separate ledgers. The debtors and creditors ledgers hold personal accounts for all customers and suppliers who deal with the firm on credit, and the general ledger holds all the accounts for income, expenses, assets and liabilities.

Despite this three-ledger system it is normal to maintain both a debtor and a creditor control (or total) account within the general ledger. They hold the totals of all items passing through the debtors and creditors ledgers respectively and serve a dual purpose:

(a) They show what the total debtors and total creditors figures should be and therefore provide an overall control over the accuracy of these two ledgers.
(b) The inclusion of these two total figures in the general ledger means that it contains all the figures needed to provide the final accounts. All necessary management figures can therefore be obtained at any time from this one ledger.

The general ledger is therefore the main one and some accountants refer to the personal ledgers as the subsidiary ledgers, existing to back up the main debtors and creditors figures in the general ledger (Fig. 6.2).

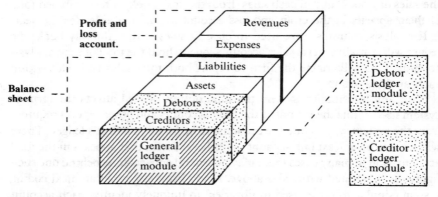

Figure 6.2   General and subsidiary ledgers

LEVEL 4: THE TRIAL BALANCE
This is a list of balances on all accounts currently in the general ledger. It is produced as a check on the arithmetical accuracy of the system and can help to detect certain types of errors.

LEVEL 5: FINAL ACCOUNTS AND OTHER REPORTS
This is the information the system is designed to provide and is therefore the starting point in designing the system. Once set up the system will treat transactions in a standard manner and provide the reports stipulated. On its own the system cannot decide what figures are needed, nor will it choose between differing accounting policies or check that accounting standards have been complied with. All this is the work of the accountant and such decisions must be taken before the system is planned and constantly reviewed thereafter.

PROBLEM AREAS

The traditional accounting system has a number of deficiencies some of which we have already identified. These include the following.

(a) *Data duplication* The same information is entered at various levels of the system. In the credit sales system we have seen the same figures entered in the day book, the ledger and customer statements.

(b) *Poor communications* The system is often criticized for being too self-contained. It is designed to collect standard data and produce predesigned reports and is often unable to deal with requests for further information. It tends to produce the figures the accountants require and pays little attention to linkages with the work of other departments. For example, accountants normally pick up details of sales when they are dispatched and leave order processing to the sales department. However, these are aspects of the same transaction and it should be possible to follow them through without having to move from one information system to another.

As a result, information presented by the accountants may lag behind that of other departments who then argue that they cannot understand the accountants' figures. Little wonder that in many firms user departments gain very little from the accounting reports they receive and consider them a necessary evil rather than a source of assistance.

(c) *Poor level of analysis* The degree of analysis in systems such as these is usually limited by the sheer volume of detailed data which has to be handled. Each sales transaction may involve several product lines and there will be thousands of such transactions in any period. Manual entry of this is very time-consuming, hence the reason that only summarized details are normally recorded, making it virtually impossible to produce further information without special work.

As a result manual systems may fail to produce sufficient information to help managers run their deparments efficiently. Although any additional information can be provided manually the cost and delay involved will greatly limit its usefulness.

(d) *Complication* The amount of work involved in a full system and the way it is split between staff make it rather complex. As a result very few of the staff working with it understand the whole system. Nor is it easy at short notice to obtain an overview of the firm's progress, as interim accounts take some time to produce from such a system.

This concludes our overview of the manual system. Having looked mainly at the problems, the reader might have the impression that it is of very limited use and that computers should be used in all firms. This is certainly *not* the case—manual systems have served a great many firms over a very long period. In a text such as this our attention is focused specifically on computerized systems and the way they deal with such problems. However, as we have seen, there are a variety of manual methods available and many firms will find that a well run manual system will serve their needs and is more responsive to changes in their business. Computers are useful in a number of cases but they are not always the best solution.

THE ROLE OF DEBITS AND CREDITS

This section has been written specifically for the accounting student who is acquainted with the terms in the heading. Such students have been taught a particular technique of recording accounting data and will therefore require answers to certain questions. Readers who are not acquainted with these terms are advised to proceed to the next section.

Most accountants have been taught to think in terms of debits and credits within an accounting system. When they come to work with computerized systems many continue to think of transactions in this way but often find that other users view the system as a set of increases or reductions to certain figures. This does not really matter for in fact these are really two ways of expressing the same thing. However, it can lead to some confusion. Even systems designers appear to be confused by the term at times, and the authors have seen two automated systems in which the term was used wrongly.

Let us look at the role of debits and credits to see why they are used. The system of double entry bookkeeping recognizes that every transaction has a dual effect on the business. This is reflected in the balance sheet which always balances, being based on the formula:

$$\text{Assets} = \text{Liabilities} + \text{Capital}$$

If the balance sheet is to remain in balance, every transaction must leave this basic formula in balance. This means that each time an alteration is made to an account a compensating alteration must be made elsewhere to maintain the formula in balance. For example, the purchase of new plant on credit terms would have the following effects:

1. The new plant will increase the total assets on the left-hand side of the equation.
2. The amount owed to the creditor will also increase total liabilities on the right-hand side of the equation.
3. The net effect has been to add the amount to both sides of the equation, leaving it in balance.

Computer systems prepare the same final accounts as do manual systems and they follow these basic double-entry principles, i.e. the need to affect both sides of the accounting equation.

The next question to ask is where the terms debit and credit fit into this system. To help reduce errors, early accountants introduced a form of cross-checking into their recording systems which works as follows:

1. All accounts contain two transaction columns. One hold all transactions that increase the account balance, the other those that reduce it.
2. They named the left-hand column the *debit* and the other the *credit* column.
3. Within the ledger there are four classes of accounts:

   assets   liabilities

   expenses   revenue

   Assets and expense accounts can be grouped together, as assets are really unexpired costs and both therefore follow the same recording rules.

   Similarly, liability and income accounts are the reverse of these and the entries in them are the reverse of those in the former types.
4. Early accountants decided that transactions which increase the balance of an asset account should be entered in the left (debit) column. An asset or an expense account will thus appear:

ASSET OR EXPENSE ACCOUNT

Date	Detail	Debit	Credit	Balance
		+	−	

Liability and revenue accounts operate in reverse. Hence a debit item reduces the balance and vice versa.

The computer does not need to use debits and credits to check on its accuracy as the instructions in the program automatically ensure that the double-entry rules are followed. However, it will print out the trial balance in that form for users. This is not a sign that the machine understands the terms; it is merely programmed to list any debit balances on asset or expense accounts in the debit column and vice versa.

It makes no difference therefore if users look at the system in terms of debits and credits or as increases and decreases. However, if user staff have a reasonable understanding of how the system operates, accountants should not try to force them to learn traditional accounting terms in order to explain it.

Brief introduction to computer accounting systems

Most computer accounting systems, particular microcomputer systems, break the accounting role down into a number of stand-alone modules. These are designed to integrate with one another to provide a range of information systems that will suit most types of business.

A firm may therefore start by computerizing only one small section of its business, e.g. the creditors or the debtors ledger. Later it may build on this towards a complete system which, as we shall see in Chapter 7, may be far wider than the traditional accounting system.

Basic financial accounting is normally divided into the following three main modules:

1. general ledger module,
2. debtors ledger module,
3. creditors ledger module.

Their roles are as follows.

PERSONAL LEDGERS

Debtor and creditor accounting are time-consuming tasks which involve very large amounts of data. They are therefore applications that firms tackle first when computerizing their systems.

Firms have to grant credit terms to customers in order to compete for their business. However, failure to control credit dealings can lead them into a financial crisis. These systems are able to provide a wide variety of reports to help managers monitor all aspects of their credit dealings.

Where these systems are operated in stand-alone form, transaction totals are printed out regularly and must be manually posted to the firm's general ledger. However, if the module is run as part of an integrated system, all these figures will be stored in memory and automatically transferred across.

THE GENERAL LEDGER

This is the key module for the preparation of reports and final accounts, containing all the asset, liability, revenue and expense accounts necessary to create them.

As we have just seen, these contain a number of sales and purchases accounts which are fed automatically from the subsidiary ledger modules in an integrated system.

The large number of accounts within the ledger are normally arranged under a detailed hierarchical coding system, the *chart of accounts*. This form of organization allows reporting at a number of levels with higher management receiving sectional totals while managers further down the organization receive details of the subsidiary accounts.

The system can be visualized as shown in Fig. 6.2, and is very similar to the traditional system illustrated above. We will consider the individual modules in detail in Chapter 7, and in Chapter 8 we will look at a number of additional modules that may be added to the basic system. At this stage we are concerned only with how far such systems can help us overcome some of the problems outlined above.

Data duplication

Computer accounting systems avoid much of the data duplication, as items are entered directly from the data documents and stored on a data file. If further analysis is required, the file can be read back into memory and analysed.

As systems are improved, data capture takes place further down the organization and it can be made available to more departments. As a result more detailed data is held on the system and more information can be obtained from it. For example, many debtors ledger packages can be linked to an invoice creation module. Sales ledger data is then captured when the invoice is prepared, earlier and in far more detail than with the traditional systems. A wide variety of reports is then available, e.g. details of sales by product, amounts to each customer, etc. (see the case study at the end of the chapter).

Communication with other systems

There are many more modules that can be added on to the system so far described. These provide figures normally outside the realm of the accounting system. For example, the addition of an invoicing module, in the last section, was basically an accounting matter. The sales orders, however, are normally received some time before this and are placed under the control of the sales department. A great deal of work may have to be done on these before the invoice is prepared and details are passed to the accounts department.

An order-processing module would pick up details of the orders as soon as they were received and follow them through to delivery. At any time up to delivery all departments would be able to check the progress of any order. On delivery the final details would be passed to the invoicing module and posted to the sales ledger. With a stock ledger module attached, the stock records would be updated and the profit on the goods involved calculated.

It can be seen, therefore, that such a system integrates the work of several departments and makes information available to a wider audience.

Level of analysis
The amount of data held on file combined with the coding system allows levels of reporting that were not possible at reasonable cost in the past. This may not be a benefit, as too much information can be as bad as too little and may hinder rather than help decision-making. Most systems therefore allow users to define the reports they require on a regular basis and will automatically produce these each period. If further special reports are required they can normally be produced as a special task, using a built-in report generator.

Complexity
With such a system, large accounts of data have to be posted between ledgers but as much of this is performed under machine control a great deal of work is saved.

The ability to call for reports at any time and the speed of their production mean that it is relatively easy to obtain an overview of the firm's progress; this is not so in manual systems.

We see therefore that the computer does go some way towards dealing with the problems identified above and offers far more information with less delay than was previously possible. There have been problems, however, and foremost among these are those of maintaining control over the system and its results. In the early days of computing, accountants often feared computers thinking that internal control would no longer be possible and that they would find themselves at the mercy of the machine. However, this did not prove to be the case and various methods of control have been developed specifically to deal with this area. This is an area to which we shall return in Chapter 12.

Mini case study: Information handling in manual and computer systems
In this case we will consider:

1. the way information on sales and debtors is obtained under a manual debtors ledger system;
2. the limitations of such a system;
3. the type of information available once the system is computerized.

We shall consider the case of C. Foster & Co., a small electrical and hardware wholesaler. Mr Foster is short of selling space and therefore wishes to measure the relative profitability of the main products that he sells. To collect this information his sales and purchases day books will contain analysis columns for each product group and as this can only provide analysis under a few classifications he has decided to split goods into the two main product groups involved, electrical and hardware.

His sales day book therefore appears as follows:

DATE	NAME	TOTAL	VAT	NET	ELECTRICAL	HARDWARE
Mar 1	H. Marvin	115.00	15.00	100.00	70.00	30.00
. .	D. Ewings	69.00	9.00	60.00	—	60.00
		184.00	24.00	160.00	70.00	90.00

Total sales from the two transactions illustrated amount to £160 before VAT, representing the total sales figure which will appear in the firm's profit and loss account.

The VAT is owed to government and posted to a VAT account in the general ledger, which records indebtedness to them.

The firm will maintain two sales accounts, one for each product group, and to these will be posted the totals of £70 and £90 respectively. Given the same analysis of purchases the firm can then calculate the profitability of both types of goods, providing information to assist in identifying those goods to be stocked.

Analysis columns such as these have been used in day books for centuries to provide greater detail. Their usefulness is very limited as they can only handle simple analysis covering about eight or nine headings maximum. Any more than this and they become unwieldly. The information provided above is hardly a great help unless the proprietor is intending to specialize in only one type of goods. In other cases he will require detailed information on particular product lines.

Consider a firm with four branches, each selling three main classes of goods. To provide a simple analysis by branch and product type would require 12 analysis columns in each of the main day books. This is a relatively simple analysis, yet if further information were requested to elaborate on it someone would have the task of reanalysing all the transactions onto working sheets, a time-consuming, costly and error-prone task.

This small example illustrates that such manual accounting systems have serious drawbacks when it comes to providing detailed analysis figures.

In a computerized system full details of every sales transaction are input to the invoicing module when the invoice is prepared. This includes details of product lines, VAT, prices, etc., and these are all stored on a data file. To prepare sales analyses the machine works back through this file and can summarize it by product group, VAT rate or any other attribute.

The general ledger will then hold a number of sales accounts to provide the level of detail required in the final accounts. For example, it may hold one for each heading in the sales analysis and, every period, the system will transfer the totals from the sales analysis directly to the appropriate sales accounts.

Some firms may require a detailed sales analysis from the machine but require less detail within the general ledger and the accounts. In such cases an overlay or additional chart is entered showing the system how to amalgamate the various figures to obtain the totals for transfer to the ledger. Thereafter the transfers can be done automatically when required.

To facilitate analysis, transactions and customer accounts may be allocated individual sorting codes which are set up by the user firm to reflect the levels of analysis they require. Even a relatively small and simple microcomputer accounting package will provide sales reports in the following detail:

> up to 99 products, by salesman, in branch order, within regional divisions.

Such analysis is totally impossible using analysed day books. To help you visualize what such a report might show, a section is outlined below:

> Sales summary   Period ....
>
> Northern Division   Branch N4
> ---------------------------------
> Sales person ..... J. Rowe
>   £
>   Printers type1   5 90
>   Printers type2   12 00
>   Disk drives   89 00
>   Monitors   19 00
>
> Sales person.........M. Smith
>   £

The coding system allows this level of reporting across the business. However, no manager could assimilate all these reports so, using the same information, the system would probably produce a series of different reports for each level of management:

1. The lower levels would outline sales of each product line for the sales person concerned.
2. At the next level the branch manager would want details of the total sales for each of his staff and for the branch overall.
3. The regional manager would only see totals for each of the branches and for the region as a whole.

As we move higher up the levels of management so the reports become less detailed but cover a wider section of the firm.

Summary

1. Double-entry bookkeeping has served the business community for centuries and continues to be used in computerized systems. In general, therefore, the accountant approaching computerized systems will find much that is familiar. However, the computer allows the processing of far more data and provides a greater degree of analysis than was previously available.
2. This has reduced the accountant's day-to-day involvement with the recording system but has placed further demands on him or her in the areas of system planning and interpretation of information.
3. The manual system worked from the data documents, through day books to the ledgers. Computer systems take far more detailed data from the original documents and store this on data file. From this they post directly to the ledger, avoiding the need for day books and providing a wider range of analyses from the data.
4. Manual systems can provide only very limited analysis owing to the time and cost involved in obtaining it.
5. Software companies use a modular approach to writing accounting systems. They supply system modules which can be linked together at various levels to provide a very wide range of systems to suit most firms. At the higher levels of integration such systems provide more than just accounting information.

7

The modular approach to accounting systems

Introduction

We have seen how computerized accounting systems are now marketed as a series of integrated modules which can be interlinked to provide a full business system. By using various combinations of these modules, together with a user's own coding system, a large variety of businesses can obtain a good system at very reasonable cost.

In this chapter we shall consider:

1. what modules would be required to meet the needs of several different forms of business, and
2. what each of the main modules does and the information it is able to provide.

Combining the modules

Management consultants, auditors, trainers and other professionals whose role involves working across a number of organizations find that, although many tasks are common to most firms, each has its own particular requirements and its own ways of tackling problems. It would not therefore be practical to design a computerized accounting system and expect to apply it to all firms. In fact there are many hundreds of accounting packages on the market, most being written for what their authors consider to be the average firm. The fact that these can greatly differ illustrates the extent to which firms can differ in their needs.

The approach taken by software houses has therefore been to design what they feel are general systems and then to modularize these, allowing the buyer to choose only those parts that are useful to him or her. In addition there are often facilities allowing alteration of the file organization, the coding system, reports, etc., when the system is first installed. In this way a very flexible approach to business systems is possible and two firms implementing the same package might end up with systems that appeared very different when in use.

To illustrate this we will consider the needs of several general types of business. The reader should bear in mind, however, that these are only general, simplified examples and that each business has its own individual requirements. At this stage we can study only the general approach; and in this area the student's practical training period has a very important part to play in preparing him or her to become expert and able to advise clients.

THE CASH TRADER

A trading firm buys and sells goods but does not manufacture them. Examples of cash traders range from small corner shops to large high street stores and mail order firms. Those at the lower end of this spectrum have not normally become involved with computers up to now but they are very much used in the larger businesses.

At their main office such a firm will need to handle the normal creditor and general ledger accounting, but as most selling is on cash terms they will not normally require a debtors ledger module. The main source of information on their sales comes through the till and there have therefore been various attempts to capture this data and feed it into the main system. The problem here is basically one of entering the large amount of data involved.

With larger, higher-value goods such as furniture or carpets, this is not too difficult as the volume is not too high for details to be recorded from cash sales slips or by linking the till into the computer system. Clothing stores have done this for years by attaching a small punched card known as a Kimball tag to each garment. When a garment was sold the sales staff removed this and sent it back to head office where it could be read in by the computer without the need for data conversion.

The major problems arise in those cases where a large number of small-value goods are sold. A good example of such a business is a supermarket. The use of bar code readers linked to tills now allows the detailed data from the tills to be fed into the computer and linked with purchasing and stock accounting modules to provide information that was very difficult to obtain previously.

Depending on the size of the firm it may or may not prepare its payroll on the computer. In fact, because of the problems involved here, many firms use a computer bureau to handle this task.

Figure 7.1 shows the sort of system that may be used by a cash trader to prepare his accounts.

THE CREDIT TRADER

This type of business is very similar in many respects to those in the previous section, but in such cases the recording and control of trade credit becomes an

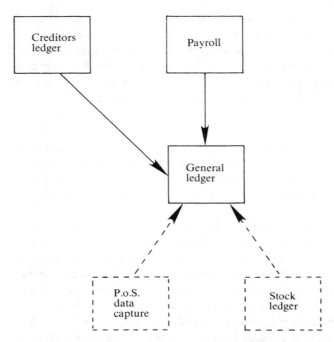

Figure 7.1 Modules for the cash trader. A cash trader has little need for a debtors ledger as he does not sell for credit. Large cash traders may run their own payroll or use a bureau. If sales data can be captured at point of sale, a stock purchase module can be useful. In other cases the work involved in entering stock movements manually rules out stock accounting.

important aspect of the work. A sales ledger package will therefore be integrated with the previous packages to feed sales totals automatically to the general ledger and to provide a detailed analysis of the selling transactions.

The handling of trade credit can pose a number of specialist accounting problems such as the need to account for hire purchase, the following up of individual debts and the provision of goods on sale or return. Finding a suitable package which can perform all the work required, in a form suitable to the firm, may therefore be far from simple.

THE MANUFACTURING BUSINESS

The manufacturing business can be far more complex to control. It may have a number of different products and need to maintain records of complex stocks of raw materials, work in progress and finished goods. If every job is different it may be necessary to measure the profit or loss on each, a job involving resorting all costs by job number. The firm also has to account for the sales of its products, whether to wholesalers or directly to the public.

Firms such as this will require all the modules above and are also likely to use:

1. a stores accounting module which not only keeps detailed records of stores balances but can also yield detailed information on the profitability of individual products;
2. a job costing module that collects details of costs and income relating to individual jobs.

Other modules

The above system will perform most of the accounting work required by such firms. However, staff outside the accounts department regularly maintain information which links with that produced by the accountants and they will also wish to use the accounting results. A good information system is therefore much more than just an accounting system. Various other modules are available to make the system perform far more than basic bookkeeping (see Fig. 7.2).

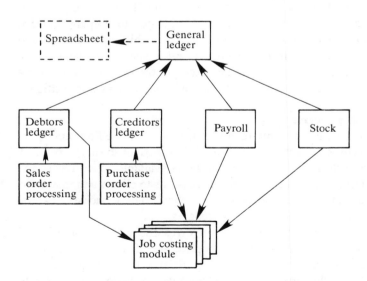

Figure 7.2 Modules for the manufacturing firm

INVOICING PACKAGES

Some debtors ledger systems are designed to prepare their own invoices while others need to be linked with a separate invoicing module. The system has to pick up certain fields from every invoice and transfer them to the sales ledger. Simpler packages are often designed to work only with a standard form of invoice so that they know just where to look for these figures. However, better packages will allow users to design invoices that suit their particular needs and will also allow them to store a number of different invoice formats to be used with particular customers.

SALES AND PURCHASE ORDER PROCESSING

The orders are originated in the appropriate departments and are the first notification the firm has of the transactions. These modules allow the user departments involved to enter details of orders and follow their progress through to delivery. They then automatically update the stocks, the debtor or creditor ledger and the general ledger. Once the original orders are entered by the originating department, all other users have access to them, saving a great deal of duplication and effort.

LINKS TO SPREADSHEET OR MODELLER

More and more systems are allowing figures from the various ledgers to be transferred into a file which can then be read into their own or another producer's spreadsheet. Here they can be manipulated to prepare budgets, reports, or to evaluate the results of possible policies. This link can be used to provide information in a form that would not otherwise be available to the firm. For example, the sales, purchases and expenses figures could be used in a cash budget to provide an updated estimate of cash inflows and outflows.

The accounting practice

Like other professionals, accountants make their living by selling their time. This requires a different form of package from that used for the above firms. A range of time recording and charging packages is available which record the time spent by staff on each client's work, charges this to clients and maintains details of actual and budgeted costs for each client. These packages can be linked to the firm's debtors and general ledgers.

The work of an accounting practice involves the preparation of final accounts for clients, often from an incomplete set of accounting records. Specialist programs are frequently used to assist staff in preparing such accounts and to simplify the handling of the many adjustments needed to finalize them.

It is stressed that there are hundreds of different accounting systems on the market for all sizes of machines. The writers of each aim their product at what they believe to be the average firm, so there can be great differences between them. It is always a problem choosing the best package for a particular client. In practice, the starting point should always be the preparation of a detailed list clearly setting out what the client requires the package to do (see Chapter 10). In the remainder of this chapter we will consider the main modules in turn. We will look at the various inputs and information associated with each.

The debtors ledger package

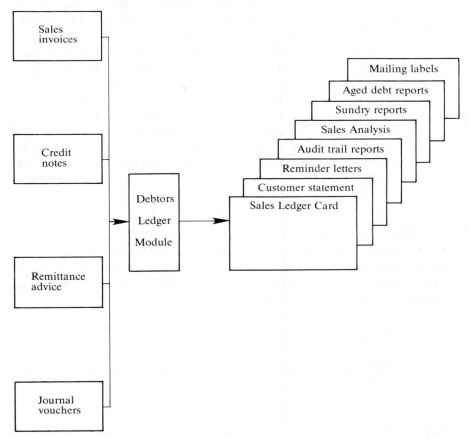

Figure 7.3 Debtors ledger module

The role of the debtors ledger (Fig. 7.3) is:

1. To maintain an individual record of every person who buys goods on credit from the firm.
2. To provide a series of reports which summarize the firm's current credit position and reduce the work involved in following up their debts.
3. To link with other ledgers it has to feed various figures to the general ledger. The following transfers (or postings) will be made automatically across the ledgers, assuming that both are installed:
    - Sales totals will be transferred to the appropriate sales accounts. With simpler systems totals are transferred directly from the sales summaries to the sales accounts. Other systems allow the user to combine several totals and transfer the combined figures to the general ledger. This means that sales analyses may be prepared in far more detail than that recorded in the ledger.
    - Details of cash from customers is regularly recorded in the personal accounts. The system will then automatically transfer the cash totals to the cash account(s) in the general ledger.
    - The general ledger will contain the debtors control account which stores the totals of all items posted to the debtors ledger. At any time, therefore, managers can obtain the total amount of debtors from this account, and the general ledger holds all the figures necessary to prepare a set of final accounts without need to refer to any of the other (subsidiary) ledgers.

RUNNING THE SYSTEM

When the module is loaded the user will be offered a menu screen outlining the various opitions available. This will vary from system to system but in its simplest form will include the choices shown in Fig. 7.4. We shall follow these through in the next few sections.

Maintenance of master file

The main task of this particular module is to keep the debtors master file fully up to date. For this to happen cash, goods, etc., must be posted daily to the appropriate accounts.

However, these transactions can be posted only if the necessary accounts exist, and in the form required by the system. The process of managing the ledger involves adding new accounts, removing old accounts and changing fields such as name or address of existing debtors. This process is termed *file maintenance* to distinguish it from the processing of normal data.

```
                    DEBTORS LEDGER SYSTEM

                            MENU


         1:  Maintenance of master file.


         2:  Data entry.


         3:  Produce reports.


         4:  Period end procedures.


         5:  Systems parameters.


                    Please enter number of choice.
```

Figure 7.4   Sales ledger main menu

These file maintenance routines are important and must be performed before posting the day's transactions. If this were not done, an invoice might be impossible to post because the account to which it related had not been created in the ledger.

The power to access the machine and make such changes needs to be carefully controlled because it can be easily abused and may lead to fraud. For this reason a number of important controls are normally built into the system. For example, a ledger account cannot normally be removed from the ledger if there is a balance on it. In such a case the balance must be written off using a journal voucher before the account can be removed.

Data entry
This option allows the user to input data to the individual accounts and access will probably be restricted by a suitable password. The user who chooses this option will be presented with a further submenu offering a choice of the type of

transaction document to be entered. This ensures that the correct entries are made in the ledger, and as a further check the input screens displayed will resemble the actual input documents involved. The main inputs in this sub-system are as follows.

1. *Sales invoices* These are used to charge customers for goods purchased on credit. These documents are generated within the firm itself. If no invoicing program is used, the invoices will have to be entered manually at this stage. However, those produced by the computer will be automatically posted to the debtors ledger accounts, avoiding work at this stage.

    The invoicing routine can also be linked directly to the stores ledger to transfer details of goods sold directly into the stores records, avoiding yet further duplication.

2. *Credit notes* These are used to reverse the work done by invoices, i.e. they reduce the customers' balances in those cases where goods are returned or not charged, e.g. due to damage.

3. *Remittance advices* These documents should accompany a customer's payment, helping identify the payer and the specific invoices paid. Many systems produce this as a tear-off portion of the statement sent monthly to customers. Unfortunately, in practice, many customers do not bother to return it and this can create problems.

4. *Journal voucher* There is a specific form of data document for each of the main transactions. These provide the authority for staff to make the necessary entry in the system. Auditors and others can later check the accuracy of transactions through the data document, a basic part of internal control.

    Many transactions such as bad debt write-offs and error corrections are far less common and do not have their own specific form of documentation. It is important, for control purposes, that they are evidenced by a document, so a general document known as a journal voucher is used. This explains the transaction, showing the accounts affected. It must be examined by a senior member of staff and signed before it is a proper authority to enter the transaction into the computer.

Period-end procedures
At the end of every month the computer must make a number of internal adjustments to tidy up the records. For example, the total of the current month's goods must be set to zero ready for the new month.

Most systems make use of this necessary break in processing to force the user to maintain adequate controls; they produce full printed listings of the month's transactions and safety copies of the files.

System parameters

This rather horrific term refers to an approach which in fact makes the system far easier to operate in practice. Many users buying a package have little idea of its full capabilities or how they may be using it after several years when it may be integrated with other modules. Many packages are therefore provided in a basic form suitable for a wide variety of users. Hidden away from the user's general view there will be facilities to change a large number of decisions or parameters. Altering these parameters makes most systems appear quite different from the standard or default way in which they were supplied. The user will start with the basic configuration and later, when more experienced, look into amending the system. The sort of parameters that can be included are too numerous to list here but a few common examples follow:

1. The system can alter the format of statements sent out to customers and if required include short advertising messages.
2. On the credit control side the system will analyse the age of a debt. On default this normally lists the portion of a debt that is one month old, two months, etc. The user can often change both the number of periods reported and the duration of these, e.g. to weeks.
3. The module can produce analyses of sales in far more detail than any one user is ever likely to require. Too much information is as bad as too little, so provisions usually exist to allow the user to define or change the way sales are analysed by the machine each month.

THE INFORMATION AVAILABLE

We now turn our attention to the end result of all this work, the information produced by the system. We must not forget that, although computerized systems can produce information that was not easily available from previous systems, this is only a benefit if it can be used properly. The modern accountant therefore needs to know what is possible and must be able to identify which information will best assist the client. In the space available we can look only at the main reports and their purposes, but the reader will find that individual packages vary in the way that this information can be presented to the user.

Individual ledger cards

The system maintains an individual record for each debtor which can be printed out to give a record of the account. However, with suitable hardware this information can be recovered quite quickly when needed, so many firms now print out far less but view accounts on screens. The full account or just summary details can be viewed, again reducing the amount of information users have to assimilate.

Manual ledger systems have always held the data needed to produce most of the information outlined below. The problem has been the time and therefore costs involved in extracting and summarizing this manually. If data has been stored on computer files then, so long as the programs exist to handle it, the cost of producing further information from that data is relatively small. As a result computerized ledgers now normally provide far more statistical information. For example, for each customer it is normal to have details of current sales, previous year's sales and the total for the year to date. Information of this type is useful for sales management purposes, not just for accounting.

Customer statements

The monthly statement of account sent to customers is an important document. It prompts them to pay and brings their attention to any items overlooked. Statements are, however, time-consuming and costly to create manually.

Computer modules offer the option to run off statements from all accounts, selected groups of accounts or only those that meet certain criteria, e.g. those that are overdue. They normally have a facility to print mailing labels using the addresses stored on file and in many cases a short message can be included on all or only selected statements. As stated previously, a remittance advice is often included with the statement.

The type of statement to be produced affects the way in which the accounts are maintained. There are two basic ways that ledgers can be maintained and the choice between them depends on the information required:

1. *Open-item method* This is used where the statement sent to a debtor needs to detail every invoice outstanding. The system keeps all such items on file even if they relate back several months. This method of maintaining accounts is the more complex of the two, as it also requires the facility to match payments against the invoices to which they relate. This can become quite involved when a customer pays a sum 'on account'. The method is useful where the firm has a large number of transactions with individual debtors.

2. *Balance forward method* This is a far simpler method of maintaining accounts, as in this case the system stores details of only those items that relate to the current month and only these appear on the current statement. All items relating to previous months are lost, being incorporated into the opening balance, and cannot be identified without going back through previous statements.

Many systems offer the user the chance to mix the two methods within a ledger, using open item for accounts that are most active and balance forward on the rest.

Credit control facilities
A number of reports can be produced to assist in this important area of management. For years accounting staff have produced aged debt listings, showing the total amounts owed and the proportion of this outstanding for one month, two months, etc.

Each debtor can be allocated an individual credit limit and thereafter the system will monitor these limits, issuing reports of debtors near to or in excess of their limits. Many systems can also produce a series of standard reminder letters and will search through the file and produce personalized copies of these for any debtor whose balance has been outstanding for a stipulated period.

Audit trail reports
These are listings of the items on the data files, produced to allow users to follow transactions through into the system. They resemble the day books in a manual system, but in a computer system they are produced purely for the user's benefit as the computer does not need to work through day books. The reports include the sales listing, credit note listing and journal.

Sales analysis
The sales transactions stored on the data file can be sorted at high speed to produce a variety of analyses. The computer's sorting power is assisted by the coding system mentioned previously. The codes may consist of letters, numbers or both and are created by the user; for example, the first two characters in a transaction code might represent the sales area, the next two the salesman involved and the next three the product. For analysis purposes these codes can be linked with a customer code, and using the two a very wide range of detailed reports can be produced. So many combinations are possible that the user normally has to define those to be produced regularly. These are then produced automatically each period. Should a different report be needed at any time, this can be produced by altering some of the system defaults.

As this was our first application we have considered it in some detail to give a general idea of how a ledger module operates. We will consider the remaining modules in less detail, with the main emphasis being on the range of information they can produce.

The creditors (or purchase) ledger

The creditors ledger (Fig. 7.5) serves a similar purpose to that of the debtors ledgers above. It maintains a personal account for every creditor and the method of organization, the available reports, etc., are very similar. There are, however, a few alternative facilities:

1. The system can search the ledger at any time and list all transactions awaiting payment. To pay these the user scrutinizes the list and keys in details of those to be processed.
2. Many systems will then process the resulting list, producing the required cheques automatically. Today these cheques are often presigned to save further processing time. However, unsigned cheques, which can be used without scrutiny and further signing, require special care to avoid their misappropriation and misuse.

    Once the program has created a cheque it will be posted automatically into the creditors and general ledgers.
3. When paying a creditor it may be necessary to indicate to the supplier the particular transactions that are being cleared. We have already seen that many firms send out a remittance advice for this purpose. However, not all firms do this. Many creditors systems therefore provide facilities allowing the firm to print out an itemized remittance advice in such cases.

LINKS TO OTHER MODULES
The main links with other modules are as follows:

1. Once again there is a general ledger link, feeding the various purchases and expense accounts, the bank account(s) and the creditors control account.
2. It can also be linked to a stores accounting module, feeding details of goods purchased directly into the appropriate stock records. In some cases a production order processing system may be integrated with these modules.
3. If a job costing module is in use, the creditors ledger will hold details of individual purchases and the jobs to which they relate. Automatic transfer

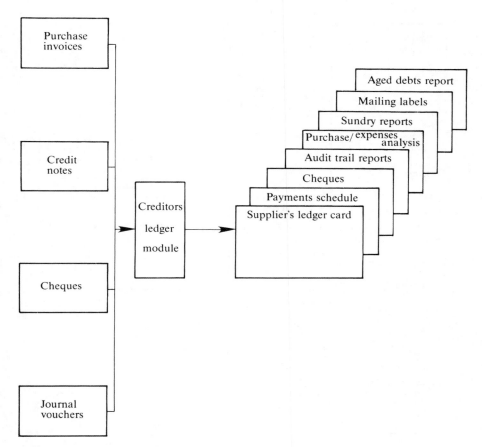

Figure 7.5 Creditors ledger module

of these figures to the job costing module saves much time and effort.

The general ledger module
We now move on to the main ledger of the system, the general ledger (Fig. 7.6). As we have seen, this contains all the records required to prepare the final accounts and other reports, i.e. records of all assets, liabilities, income and expenses.

These ledgers have been used by accountants for centuries. Their main role was to store historical figures and produce the annual accounts. However, with the speed and power of modern computers and the use of a well designed

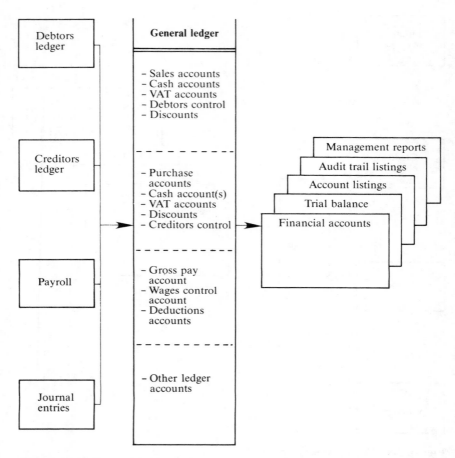

Figure 7.6   General ledger module

coding system they can be far more important than this. Properly coded and linked to budgeted figures, perhaps used with a spreadsheet to manipulate the figures, they have now become an important management tool, capable of producing a wide range of management reports which cover all parts of the business.

Once again this is a ledger updating module so many of the main options will be similar to those already mentioned. However, with an integrated system, a large proportion of the data for this module will be picked up by direct transfer from the subsidiary ledgers rather than through manual input.

Here again the journal voucher is a very important document, as a large number of transfers and adjustments takes place in this ledger, and an internally generated data document is required to support them.

THE CODE OF ACCOUNTS

The degree of analysis available from this module depends very much on the detailed breakdown of figures recorded therein. Most systems therefore contain a large number of accounts covering, in detail, every area of the business. To facilitate reporting these are normally grouped together with a hierarchical system of codes. By consolidating information at various levels of this system, reports can be produced very quickly for all levels of management.

The power to sort and report on such codes was outlined above, in the section on the debtors ledger. With the general ledger it becomes far more detailed as the coding system involved affects all departments of the business and a far wider range of reports will be required. The following example shows the sort of information that might be obtained from a six-figure accounts code, such as are used with many microcomputer systems.

A firm's ledger might contain an account numbered 062312 (see Fig. 7.7).

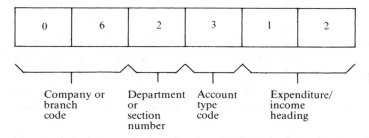

Figure 7.7 A six-figure nominal account code can be subdivided to provide several levels of analysis

Its meaning and place in the system will depend on the way the fields in the code have been defined by this particular firm. Further enquiry might show that they have chosen to set up four levels of analysis as follows:

1. Digits one and two (06): the subsidiary company or branch to which the account relates. A two-figure code such as this would allow up to 99 costing heads to be used.
2. Digit three (2): the department or section within that branch or company.

These first three digits therefore allow all transactions to be charged directly to a specific area of the business, facilitating the provision of detailed management and costing reports. There are many other ways that these three digits could be arranged to suit the needs of a variety of firms. For example, they could provide far more cost centres within one company.

3. Digit four (3): the type of account (income, expense, asset or liability).
4. Digits five and six (12): a subcode further classifying the income, expense, etc., item involved.

This particular account code therefore holds a great deal of information about the account and its place within the organization, if the computer can only unlock it. The account code used above might for example represent the rental cost of the sales office in the Bristol branch. Using this six-digit code the computer can select accounts which are related in some way, e.g. all accounts for the Bristol branch. It can then report these individually or summarize them to provide a large number of reports ranging from very general figures for higher management to very specific figures on some specific aspect of the business. For example at either end of this spectrum this might involve the following:

1. Searching and accumulating totals on the first field to produce a general report on a specific branch would assist regional managers to compare the general results of their branches. For example, a profit and loss account for branch 1 would involve summarizing all accounts with 01 in the first field and the general code for income or expense accounts in field three.
2. Providing a detailed expenses report for the manager of department 9 at branch 6 would require a further sort and printout of the individual accounts involved. The report would list each one, itemizing the expenses for the current month and the year to date. If the accounts also held budgeted figures, the report would list these and calculate the variances from budget in each case. The result is a very detailed report that assists local managers but is far too detailed for head office purposes.

The amount of detail involved makes this sound rather complicated, and to design and install a full coding system in a large organization involves a great deal of work. However, in practice, once the system is installed and the report formats have been specified the work becomes automatic and the system will produce the required reports with very little user involvement.

Our example gives an idea of the amount of detail available from a six-digit code. A larger code allows far more detailed reporting. A number of smaller packages are limited to six-digit codes, but others allow about a dozen characters. One IBM package allows the user to set up a 15-character unstructured code plus a further 40 characters for analysis purposes!

This form of coding allows the preparation of budgetary reports on a departmental basis. The next stage a company may require is the ability to accumulate and compare costs job by job. As we will see later, this is the role of a further module.

The task of creating the coding system is a vital one. It will affect all departments of the firm, and staff will have to live with it for some time. It is important, therefore, to plan it carefully and allow a degree of flexibility to deal with future development. For example, a group which already has nine subsidiaries would be very unwise to allow only one digit to represent the company concerned as a further acquisition would render their coding system obsolete.

The coding system must reflect the information needs of the firm and is designed to allow the system to accumulate and provide that information. It is therefore false economy to purchase a system with a restricted chart structure and try to squeeze the company's system into that.

OUTPUTS FROM THE SYSTEM

The volume of detailed information available from this module means that it can produce a huge variety of reports. Its usefulness lies in the fact that many of these will be designed by the firm's own managers to suit their particular purposes. In looking at the outputs we cannot therefore hope to illustrate the entire range of reports that are available, and must concentrate on the general types that are offered.

THE FINAL ACCOUNTS

These are the reports that most people will first associate with this ledger. Most systems offer a wide degree of flexibility in designing the layout of the profit statement and the balance sheet.

These reports can normally include comparative figures for one or more previous periods plus budgeted figures for the current one, in addition to the current figures. It may also be possible to regroup the expenses together under other headings and provide reports for specific managers.

The effect is that reports can be far more useful to the firm's staff and may be laid out in the best format available to help them understand the results of their actions. Once managers have learned to use this updated information there will often be a demand for more useful information from the system and far less reliance on purely financial accounting reports. This means that when evaluating possible systems senior management must be flexible and allow for future growth. Given a successful system, the demand for information will greatly increase as managers come to rely increasingly on the system. With experience of the sort of information available they should also become more adept at specifying their own information needs.

TECHNICAL REPORTS
These are reports printed by the system to allow users to check the way it has operated. It may be necessary to do this before an error can be corrected or to provide more detailed information on a particular area of the work. The main reports of this sort include the following.

The trial balance
In traditional accounting systems this was a list of balances on all the accounts in the ledger. It was produced to ensure that the sums of the debit and credit items in the ledger were equal. In a computerized system this control task is performed far earlier in the system. Every time data is entered in one of the ledgers the total amounts processed are agreed with manual totals of the input data, and totals are checked across the ledgers before the system can continue.

The trial balance report is still produced and used by accountants to check on balances in various accounts before they incorporate their period-end adjustments into the ledger. The above checks ensure that this report is automatically in balance. However, in the past this task involved a great deal of work as staff had to check back through the ledgers searching for errors and amending them.

Audit trail reports
When data items are entered into the system they are stored on a data file. From here they are used to provide information summaries and possibly to update other files. The audit trail report is a listing of data items that have been posted. It will contain sufficient information to allow the items to be traced back to the original input document. With some larger systems every page of an audit trail report is numbered as a security measure to prevent information being added or removed.

It is normally possible to call for a selective list of transactions. For example, the user may ask for a list of all transactions posted to a group of accounts or all items over £50. This can prove helpful in clearing certain queries which arise from time to time.

Individual account listing
This will provide a full printout of any ledger account that the user wishes to review. It shows the opening balance, the transactions in the period and the closing balance.

MANAGEMENT REPORTS
These are the reports mentioned above, which make the system a useful tool rather than purely an accounting record. The wide range of reports available gives management the power, if used properly, to find out far more of what is happening in their companies. Armed with this knowledge they can take corrective action where things have gone wrong.

However, the power to provide such information depends on the efficiency of the coding system used. This has to be set up when the system is installed and can be difficult to change thereafter. We have noted how a successful system is subject to heavier demands as managers learn what is possible and become more adept at specifying their information needs. However, at the time the system is installed they may have little idea of what can be done and what will be required. The accountant therefore has an important role to play in helping to install any system and should try to help other users at this important stage.

Most systems allow budgeted figures to be prepared for all accounts in the ledger. This is an important function which will almost certainly be needed by most users when the system is running. The degree of sophistication offered varies greatly, however, from one package to another. Normally the user estimates the total annual figure for each account and the system will break this down into period details. The simplest systems may merely divide the total figure by 12 to give a monthly figure, based on the assumptions that the firm accounts on a calendar month basis and business is spread evenly across the year. Better systems allow far more sophisticated cost breakdowns to be performed and, once again, this is an area the accountant needs to look into carefully before a system is set up.

This module therefore facilitates the provision of departmental reports and possibly the use of cost centres. If the firm wishes to go a stage further and bring together costs and income relating to individual jobs, it will need to integrate a job costing module into the system.

Summary
1. Software firms normally produce a range of standard accounting modules which can be bolted together into full systems. This method is very flexible and allows systems to be created for a wide range of firms. The

ability to alter system parameters provides further flexibility and allows the system to grow with the user to some extent.

2. The basic financial accounting system consists of three ledger accounting modules:
    - general ledger module,
    - sales (debtors) ledger module,
    - purchase (creditors) ledger.

3. Some firms will add further packages to this to give them a full financial accounting system. These are:
    - stock ledger module,
    - payroll module.

4. These systems can be further expanded to provide management information which assists other departments of the firm. Modules that may be added on include an invoicing module, order processing and job costing.

5. The chapter outlines the inputs and outputs of the three main financial ledgers.

8

Additional modules

In this chapter we shall consider the role of the additional modules mentioned in the previous chapter.

Stores (or stock) accounting

Accounting for stocks can involve a great deal of time and effort, especially where there are several types of stock located at various places within the firm. The volume of transactions to be recorded in such cases can be very large. The use of a stock ledger package can greatly reduce the amount of data entry, as it will pick up most of its data from the sales and purchase subsystems. Many firms find that although a stores accounting package can yield great time savings it can still pay to leave certain lines off the computer and control them manually. The control of 80 per cent or more of the stores items will normally fit into a standard package. However, the remaining minority of items may pose special problems, e.g. unusual units or splitting bulk, which could increase systems costs and complications to an unacceptable extent.

Stocks provide the link between the buying and selling sides of the business, acting as a buffer which allows the firm to balance the differences between them. Control and storage of goods can be a costly function for the following reasons:

1. The firm must purchase or hire suitable storage space, heat it and make it secure.
2. The wages of stores staff are a direct stock-holding cost.
3. There is always the risk of damage, loss or obsolescence of the items stored.
4. In addition the firm must borrow money to finance the stocks held and this, too, costs money.

THE STORES ACCOUNTING TASK

Storekeepers are charged with physical control of goods and the maintenance of accurate stores records. This has traditionally involved:

1. receiving goods into stores and checking them against the delivery notes from the suppliers;
2. recording the receipt of goods on stores cards or bin cards maintained for each store item;
3. ensuring physical security of goods during their period in the stores and issuing them in rotation to avoid wastage;
4. notifying purchasing staff of those items running low which may need to be reordered;
5. issuing goods from the stores against properly authorized issue notes from the various user departments;
6. recording the allocation of materials against particular orders to ensure that the records do not show more items available than are actually free.

The storeman's job therefore involves a mixture of physical and clerical control over stocks, which can lead to problems. Many staff may be very good at handling the goods but poor at clerical work and vice versa. No firm relies totally on the computer system to control the stocks. They supplement this with regular stock counts to verify the recorded balances. Where these indicate material differences between book stocks and actual figures, a formal investigation into the cause takes place before the differences are written off.

Links with other parts of the accounting system

LINKS WITH THE SALES SIDE

The stock package can hold details of the selling price of every stock line. Indeed many packages are able to hold several such prices for each line. They may hold a normal price for general customers, a trade price for trade customers and perhaps a special group price to be offered to fellow members of their own group.

When a sale is made to a customer the appropriate price code must normally be entered into the invoicing package. With some packaged systems a customer can be allocated a special code to show what pricing group the firm belongs to. In such cases the system will automatically produce an invoice at the appropriate price unless the operator overrides this function.

Any selling transaction will reduce the amount of stock held. This could affect a number of stock lines and involve a great deal of clerical work. Many manual systems do not keep full stock records because of this volume of work. All this detail will, however, have been entered into the invoicing module and with the computer it can be transferred across the modules.

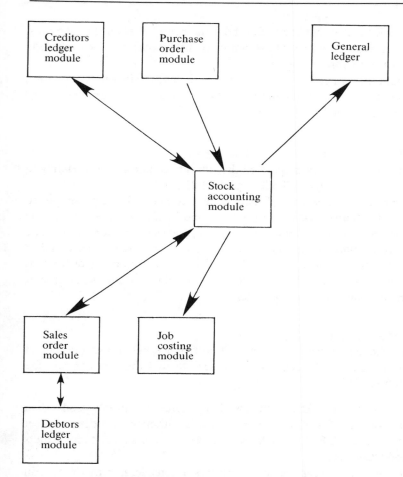

Figure 8.1 Links with other modules

If the system includes a sales order routine, this will follow the progress of a transaction through from first order to final dispatch. At the time the order is received this will allocate stocks to it in the stock records. The physical stock balance will not be reduced but the balance of free goods will be. This helps staff to monitor the current stock position and reduce the danger of stockouts.

LINKS WITH THE PURCHASING SIDE
In addition to the selling prices, the stock records also hold the purchase price

of every stock line. In fact they often hold the prices of several of the most recent deliveries for each line. These figures are useful both for stock valuation and to assist with forecasting.

Once again the figures may be entered directly into the ledger system but if there is a purchase order module the details will be picked up sooner and transferred across modules.

LINKS WITH THE JOB COSTING SYSTEM

Where a job costing system is operated the aim is to collate all costs relating to each job and measure its individual profitability.

Direct material is one cost element which is normally quite simple to allocate to jobs. Some goods are purchased specifically for one job and the entry of a job number in the purchasing system allows such information to be gathered. Other materials are issued from stores to be used on jobs, and in such cases the stores issues notes will identify the code numbers of the jobs involved. There is a great deal of data to sort and collate but this is not a major task given the power of the computer.

COST VERSUS SERVICE

Stores management involves seeking a fine balance between a number of conflicting objectives. Management must seek to find the best compromise between these:

1. *Avoiding stockouts* The main task of any stores is to supply goods when they are needed. They must, therefore, hold sufficient quantities to meet expected demand. Failure to do so could lead to a loss of customers, halts in production, etc.
2. *Minimizing investment* Stock represents a considerable investment in the goods themselves, and also labour and premises to store them. Management will wish to reduce the investment in this area to the minimum value consistent with service.
3. *Efficient purchasing* The firm's buyers will seek the best prices they can for goods. Most suppliers will offer larger discounts for buying in larger quantities. The benefits to be gained here must be weighed against the costs of holding larger stocks.

Mathematical models have been developed to help managers calculate the optimum balance between these and find the optimum purchasing policy for each line. Computers can help managers find the best buying policies and will calculate economic order quantities.

They can also provide a level of day-to-day monitoring which would be difficult to achieve using manual methods. For each stock line on file they will regularly monitor:

1. the minimum stock balance,
2. the maximum stock balance,
3. the reorder level.

Most systems will automatically report details of any lines where the stock balance is approaching any of these monitoring levels, as this helps avoid over- or understocking. Some will also, if required, initiate an order using the standard reorder quantity stored on the file.

BATCH VERSUS REAL-TIME STOCK CONTROL
We have already discussed the difference between such systems (Chapter 2). The method used will depend upon the type of business and the sort of information required.

In certain large out-of-town retailers selling high-value goods such as furniture, the stock accounting system is a key part of the system. A real-time multi-user computer system allows customers and sales staff to find the stock position on any line immediately. The customer's payment is recorded through an electronic till which simultaneously updates the stock system and instructs the stores to prepare the order ready for collection. Such firms place great reliance on their stock systems and must seek a fine balance between stock costs and stockouts. A real-time system is vital to such firms because stock control is at the centre of their operations.

At the other extreme many firms still prepare their stock records on a batch system with regular printouts being sent to user departments. Many businesses find that the information provided is satisfactory for their needs and that the additional cost of a real-time system would not be justified in their work.

ALLOCATION OF COSTS
One feature of today's business world is the regular changes that occur in the prices of raw materials. These are so important to business that they are regularly monitored by government as well as industry. Firms, particularly those competing in international markets, need to be aware of the effects such changes have on their costs.

All amounts paid for goods must be recovered by being charged against the jobs that use them. We have seen that the stock records are able to hold several different delivery prices for the goods held in store. The problem therefore arises of what price to use when charging goods to a particular job. This problem is not new and accountants have identified several methods of dealing with it. Each of these has advantages and disadvantages in practice and it is part of the accountant's role to advise on such problems. The methods adopted include the following:

1. *First in first out method*   This assumes that the earliest goods are issued first and allocates costs in that order, leaving the stock valued at the later prices.
2. *Last in first out*   This is the reverse of the above, assuming that the most recently purchased goods are issued first and that stock is valued at old prices.
3. *Average cost*   This is a compromise between the above methods and issues goods to production at a weighted average of the costs to date.

Each method requires a great deal of detailed work but once the user has chosen a method, using the system parameters, its operation will be automatic.

IDENTIFYING SLOW-MOVING STOCKS
It is important to identify slow-moving and obsolete stocks, because unless they are written down the value of stocks in the firm's balance sheet may be overstated. While stores staff may be aware that certain stocks are obsolete, they are unlikely to be able to identify all slow-moving items. These can be identified by scrutinizing the stock records and identifying the pattern of issues. This can be very time-consuming, but luckily computers can be made to log the date of the last issue for each stock item and the number of issues each period. A report can then be produced on all items which have not been issued since a certain date or where the number of issues in the period is small. A review of the records involved can help management decide whether or not their value needs to be written down.

ASSEMBLIES
Many firms produce goods made up from a large number of subcomponents; such products are termed *assemblies*. In many stores no great harm may result if they temporarily run out of one product line; however, where subassemblies are involved failure to supply one item may halt production even though there are ample supplies of the others. It is useful therefore to group these items together in reports so that they may be monitored as a group.

Most stock control systems will allow such components to be identified as belonging to a particular assembly. Reports can then be produced relating to individual components or to the assembly in which they are used.

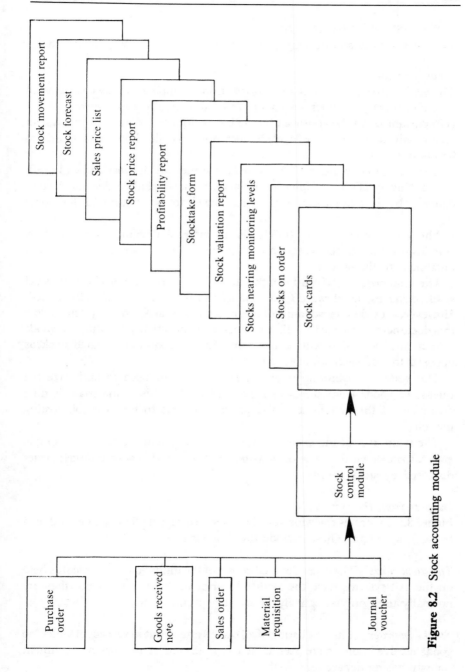

Figure 8.2 Stock accounting module

INPUTS AND OUTPUTS TO THE SYSTEM

The main inputs and outputs to the system are summarized in Fig. 8.2.

Input documents

The *purchase order* is used to order goods from a supplier. It may be generated automatically by the stock system or prepared manually. In the former case it is important that it be approved by the buyer prior to its issue: as the system reacts only to the reorder level, it does not normally know if a line is to be discontinued.

In simple cases an order will be issued for immediate delivery and will result in one delivery of goods. However, in larger firms one bulk order may lead to delivery by instalments and this may need to be monitored for some time.

The *goods received note* (GRN) is an internal document produced by storekeepers when the goods are delivered. This is an important input document to the system.

The *sales orders* received from the firm's customers do not affect physical stock balances, as these do not change until goods are actually issued. However, they do give advance notice of a stock issue so most systems allow this document to be used to allocate stock to a particular job. Until the goods are actually issued they will be shown on all stock reports as allocated stock, as opposed to free stock which may be issued.

The *material requisition* is an internal document used to authorize the release of goods from stores to a particular job. This is the main issuing document of the system, and also provides details to feed the job costing module.

The main uses of the *journal voucher* in this system are to amend simple errors, write down the value of slow-moving stocks and deal with discrepancies disclosed by stock counts.

Outputs from the system

Figure 8.2 illustrates the wide variety of detailed reports that can be produced by such a system. These include the following:

The stock cards   These are detailed copies of the individual stock records held on file. All systems have the facility to print out such reports but they are normally used only selectively to answer specific queries.

Stocks on order   This is a listing of all orders issued but in respect of which no goods received notes have been issued. It is an important working document for purchasing department staff.

The stock movement report and the stock price changes reports These summarize the data handled in the current period and provide useful information for managers about what is currently taking place.

Stock valuation and profitability These reports are very important as they help to measure the firm's profitability. However, in manual systems the amount of work involved severely restricts the information available in these areas.

The stock report will value stock on hand using the costing methods adopted by the firm, e.g. average cost. Slow-moving stocks, etc., will have been written down in value using journal vouchers.

The power of the system can be seen from the profitability report. The stock records hold details of items sold, cost price and selling price for every stock line. From this data the profitability of each product or group of products can be prepared.

A simple listing of all items, with the current balances omitted, provides a stocktake form for use by staff performing a physical stock count.

Stocks nearing monitoring levels Items that have reached their particular monitoring levels will be included in a series of reports so that necessary action can be taken. Such reports will cover:

1. stocks above the maximum level,
2. stocks below the minimum level,
3. stocks below the reorder level,
4. stocks with no balance unallocated,
5. slow-moving stocks.

Sales price lists A listing of items and the selling prices recorded against them can be used to produce regularly updated sales price lists. For internal use these may list all the recorded prices, but if the lists are to be issued to customers a separate trade and general price list can be prepared.

Payroll accounting
Payroll is one subsystem that has an effect on every employee of the organization. It can involve a large volume of data and poses a number of problems, including the following:

1. The fact that it affects everyone in the firm means that it is a highly sensitive area. Each employee expects his or her salary to be paid on time and delays of even one day can lead to major problems. Accuracy is also

important, as a clerical error can result in a family trying to live for a week on a reduced income until things are corrected. Such errors may not only affect the employee concerned but may also have serious effects on industrial relations because they reduce confidence in the employer.

2. If bonuses and overtime work are to encourage employees to put in additional time and effort, there must be the minimum of delay between the time they are earned and their appearance in the wage packet. Given an unreasonable delay, staff will fail to link the effort with the reward and this can be a great disincentive.

3. Privacy is another important matter. Staff do not want colleagues to have access to personal details of their earnings, tax position, etc. Breaches of security here can have very serious consequences and lead to a number of personnel problems.

4. The payroll task is large, complex and repetitive and must be completed to a strict deadline. The combination of these factors increases the likelihood of processing errors in a manual system.

5. Payroll can be one the most complex accounting systems operated by a firm. There are many different methods of calculating pay, and a whole range of deductions to be made, and there are several systems of making the final payment to the employee. In large firms the payroll system may have to be very flexible to handle a wide range of staff from many operational areas, employed under various contractual agreements.

6. Over the years government has become increasingly involved in this area as more detailed rules have been developed, covering income tax, national insurance and more recently sick pay.

An organization must therefore have complete trust in its payroll system. If it fails, they face major problems. A computer malfunction with no backup facilities will involve drafting in large numbers of staff to perform the work on time. If the tax or social security systems change or if new forms of payment are introduced, months of programming work may be required to update the systems and test these updates.

Faced with all these problems it is hardly surprising that a large proportion of firms decide not to tie up internal data processing resources in this application area. They frequently subcontract it to a computer bureau which makes its money by processing other people's data for them. It normally services a wide variety of clients who prepare their own input documents and send them in. The bureau processes these, using its own programs and machines, and sends the results back to the firm. Despite the spread of computing among firms and the growth in the use of microcomputers, these bureaux are increasingly picking up new payroll clients. Indeed, as legislation becomes more complex, they foresee further increases in this aspect of their work. We have been promised a complete overhaul of the social security and taxation systems at the end of the decade. This will involve major changes with benefits being paid by employers through a negative income tax. Although firms are aware that this is promised, there are no details available and they cannot therefore start to prepare new systems. Such changes are likely to require major rewriting of many existing systems and this will take a great deal of time. The reason for the delay in implementing this scheme is that the government service itself cannot operate it until they install new computer systems. The fact they they will have to develop and test their own side of such systems may, hopefully, result in a better awareness of the problems faced by employers and, possibly, more realistic implementation deadlines.

There are several advantages in employing the services of a bureau in this area. They include the following:

1. The bureau, as a specialist user, can gain economies from large-scale processing. It operates large, sophisticated machines, and its wide client base makes it economic to purchase larger payroll systems which offer a host of advanced features and can deal with most problems a firm is likely to face. Such software would normally be far too costly for all but the largest firm.

    As the bureau earns its fees from a limited number of such systems it will employ systems development staff specifically to maintain these. The client firm therefore receives the benefit of such software and has no problems of software maintenance.
2. The cost to the client firm is normally very competitive considering the complexity of such systems and the fact that its own data processing resources are left free to concentrate on the more basic day-to-day problems.
3. There are also security benefits with this type of processing. The fact that employee files and data are stored on the bureau computer, away from the employer's premises, increases confidentiality. In the event of a computer breakdown the bureau normally has standby facilities and will still be able to process the payroll.

LINKS WITH OTHER MODULES

Just like other packages, payroll may be treated as a separate module or integrated into an overall system. The links with other sections of the accounting system are shown in Fig. 8.3.

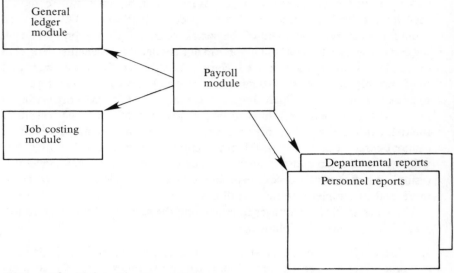

Figure 8.3 Links with other systems

LINKS WITH THE GENERAL LEDGER
Totals from the payroll will be transferred automatically to the general ledger
to feed the following accounts:

1. The total salaries and wages figures appear as an expense in the profit and
    loss account and must therefore be accumulated in the general ledger. If
    the firm produces departmental reports, these departmental subtotals will
    be calculated by the payroll module and used to feed the departmental
    wages accounts in the general ledger.
2. Items such as tax, national insurance, superannuation, union dues, etc.,
    will have been deducted from employees' wages and must be handed to
    the bodies involved, e.g. Inland Revenue. A set of deductions control
    accounts in the general ledger record the firm's indebtedness to these
    bodies and, once again, the figures for these are transferred over from the
    payroll module.

LINKS WITH THE COSTING SYSTEM
Once again the computer's sorting powers can be used to present wages figures
under a number of different headings to assist the firm's managers. We saw
above that departmental wages totals can be accumulated, which allows

reports by department or cost centre. If the system includes a job costing module, employees will have charged their time to particular jobs and full details of these will be held on file. The system will resort wage payments by job number and transfer the figures across to the job costing module.

LINKS WITH THE PERSONNEL SYSTEM

The personnel department is charged with the overall management of the staff function, including control of the number and grades of staff employed. They must attempt to match staff to the available jobs according to age, training, etc., and will have collected a great deal of information on staff from the time they were hired and throughout the years of their employment. This information covers training, work experience, health, etc., and can provide useful information for management. Once again many firms have the data they need but, because of the work involved, many have been unable to pull the facts together to provide the necessary information. Much of this data is of a personal nature and the firm has a duty to look after it and not divulge it except for the purposes for which it was collected.

If this data has been entered into the computer for payroll purposes then, given suitable software, it can be sorted and summarized to provide a wide range of personnel reports. As a result, firms are once again finding that an integrated system provides far more than just accounting information. If such data is used purely to prepare a payroll, it could escape the provisions of the Data Protection Act. However, if it is used to provide general personnel reports, as outlined here, the firm will have to register and will be legally bound to protect the data involved.

An obvious further step is to use the available payroll data with a spreadsheet or planning software to create a model of the firm's pay structure. This might be useful in planning personnel strategy, the design of bonus schemes, etc. In this way the firm's current accounting data can assist management to plan future strategy and no longer serves merely a passive, historical role.

INPUTS TO THE SYSTEM

Before a person can be paid a wage or salary there must be a personal record on file. The first input form in the system (Fig. 8.4) must therefore deal with master file maintenance. A *starters* or *leavers* form is created by the personnel department and is their authority to the payroll staff to add or remove a record on the master file. This involvement of the two departments strengthens overall control and the two sets of independent records will be regularly reconciled as a check on total numbers employed.

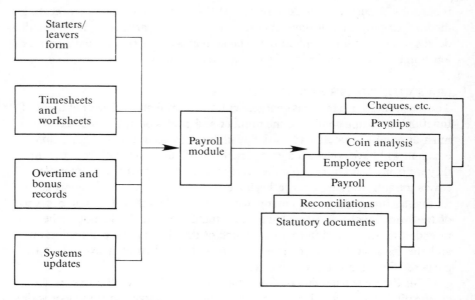

Figure 8.4 Payroll module

The first stage in the payroll run involves calculating the gross pay of each employee before any deductions are made. Students frequently think of this as a simple task, merely involving multiplying the hours worked by the pay rate. However, as we have already noted, payroll is frequently far more complex than this:

1. While office staff are frequently paid on an hourly basis, others may be employed on piecework terms where their earnings are related to the amount of goods they produce. The firm's payroll system may therefore have to handle several different methods of calculation. The input forms used in such cases will include both *timesheets* and *worksheets*.
2. Many firms run a bonus scheme which allows employees to increase their earnings if they complete more than a standard amount of work in a given time. There are many such schemes and they can be quite complex, some measured on individual output and others on group output. Bonus earnings may be calculated and entered manually or may be covered by the programs.
3. Employees may be entitled to additional payments over and above their basic pay. These can include overtime payments (which may be

calculated in a number of ways), and special payments for additional skills and responsibility or as recompense for undertaking unclean or dangerous work. Any such payments must be independently authorized by the personnel department.

These and other regular payments are authorized on a *personnel changes form*, which is also used to authorize changes in pay rates, promotions, etc. Overtime and non-recurring payments will be authorized through the timesheets.

4. Many employers use the payroll system to repay travelling expenses, etc., incurred by staff in the performance of their duties. These are not normally taxable and most packages can be set up to handle a number of such items. In most cases staff submit expenses claims to the accounts department and these are checked by clerks. If the claims are approved, the details are entered manually and the system will do the rest.

As a result the input side of the system can be very complex with a wide variety of inputs. Although systems are very flexible these days there are particular problems with some firms that may lead them to calculate certain employees' gross wages manually and then enter these into the system to be processed alongside those calculated by the system. This may surprise the reader but, as we saw with stocks, a standard package might be able to handle all but a few employees, and to design programs to handle the few exceptional, items might be totally uneconomic compared with the small amount of manual work involved.

Next the system will go on to calculate the deductions for tax, national insurance, superannuation, sick pay, etc. These will be calculated automatically and the net pay computed. To do this, the system must store details of tax rates, superannuation rates, etc. From time to time these rates and even the methods of computation have to be changed. To deal with this the software suppliers or the firm's own computer staff will issue *systems updates* to amend the system. Such changes to the system must be subject to careful controls, as unauthorized changes would leave the system open to fraud.

OUTPUTS FROM THE SYSTEM
The reports available from the module are also shown in Fig. 8.4. In addition to the written reports, a great many queries will be cleared on screen.

Payslips
Every employee will receive a payslip detailing gross pay, any expenses reimbursed and all amounts deducted. The net pay shown thereon will be the

amount payable. For most employees this was traditionally paid in cash either weekly or monthly, while office staff were commonly paid monthly by cheque. This is now changing and an ever-increasing proportion of employees have their earnings paid directly into a bank account. Many employers and, apparently, the government would like to see this proportion increase as it reduces the costs of handling such amounts. However, there is reluctance on the part of many employees to move away from cash payment and as the law stands employees cannot be forced to accept this type of payment. There have been discussions about changing this aspect of the law, but this has proved to be a highly emotive issue as it may involve repealing the 'trucking acts' which were originally created to protect workers from abuses in the days of the industrial revolution. However, it seems likely that over the next few years we will see increasing numbers of people paid through the bank, allowing the transfer of monies to their accounts using computers.

Coin analysis

Where wages are paid in cash the pay section has to collect money from the bank and make it up into pay packets. The firm draws from the bank the exact amount of money required to cover the payroll, so that if no errors are made there will be no surplus or shortage at the end of the task. To facilitate this task the computer provides a coin analysis which tells staff exactly how many notes and coins of each denomination are required to make up the packets.

This is quite easy to program: with each employee's net pay, the computer first divides it by the highest denomination of note, and the answer is the number of such notes required. The remainder is divided by the value of the next smallest note, showing the number of those required. This process is continued down to the lowest denomination of coin or until the full amount is covered. The machine maintains a running total for each note and coin and prints this out at the end.

In some firms pay is rounded to the nearest pound or 50p to avoid the problems of handling lower denomination coins. This saves time but is sometimes unpopular with staff who can be very conservative where their earnings are concerned.

Cheques and other forms of payment

Where some staff are paid by cheque, the system may be able to print out the cheques automatically, using presigned cheque forms. With a large payroll it can take a great deal of time to print out cheques and distribute them among staff who will then have to take these to their bank and possibly wait for them to be cleared. In recent years the banks have developed a number of systems to make such payments easier.

In most cases firms can avoid preparing and signing large numbers of cheques by using a bank giro which lists the employees, details of their bank accounts and the net payment due to each. The firm then draws one cheque on its own account to cover the total amount and sends this with the list to the bank. The latter will then make all the necessary transfers on the firm's behalf.

Although this saves both time and costs it is still time-consuming to print out the list of payment details from the computer and then send them to the bank where they will all be retyped into another computer. Firms with computerized systems can make use of the BACS (Bankers Automated Clearing System) system which prints the pay details out on to a computer tape that is sent to the bank and read in at high speed by their machines. This tape obviously has to be produced to a standard format which can be read by the bank's machine. Further information on the BACS system and other methods of transferring funds are given in Chapter 15.

Employee report

All the details on file relating to a particular employee can normally be printed out in the form of an employee report. There are also facilities to print out selected information covering a range of staff. This could include a great deal of information including personal data, details of pay and deductions to date, and costing details such as departmental codes, etc. Much of this information is likely to be used from the screen rather than printed out.

Payroll

The payroll provides a summary of all payments and deductions relating to a particular pay period. In addition to providing summary details of pay it is used to check output totals with manually produced control figures.

Where departmental accounting is operated, the payroll is normally produced under departmental headings and shows the totals charged to each department or cost centre. These totals will be used to feed the general ledger accounts if the two modules are integrated.

Deduction summaries and reconciliations

Large sums of money are deducted from employees' earnings every year, and the company deducts these in trust for the final recipient, e.g. the Inland Revenue or a superannuation scheme. At the year end they must therefore account to the employee and these other bodies for their stewardship. In addition, certain statutory reports must be made by all the employers.

For taxation purposes an employer must provide each employee with a summary of tax and pay for the fiscal year, summarized on a form P60; a computer-produced form is now acceptable for this purpose. An employee who leaves must be provided with a P45 form that will allow a new employer to deduct tax properly. There are also other forms and summaries required for National Insurance, superannuations, etc. The system can save a great deal of detailed work by producing and printing these.

Further steps in integration

We have seen how computerized systems have moved away from the narrow confines of accounting systems and have become far more general information systems, serving most departments of the organization. The developments described in the last two chapters show the more common integration of modules. This trend towards integration is continuing and manufacturing firms in particular are creating ever-wider links between the various systems they operate. For example, in addition to the more common modules mentioned above, the following are now available:

1. Cost estimating packages allow the firm to use accounting and production figures to estimate the likely cost of jobs. In arriving at such figures the module will need to link with the accounting and production control systems, as the computer may need to work out if and how such an order can be fitted into the firm's production schedules.

2. Within the production departments the computer can help with the complex task of controlling work in progress. Through the use of input devices such as simple keypads, the progress of any job can be monitored and controlled by the computer. Information on such jobs allows production controllers to monitor the progress of jobs and take action to reduce delays. The same information can be used by a costing module to calculate and monitor the costs of individual jobs.

3. Industrial firms are increasingly using computer aided design and manufacture of their products; this development is termed CAD/CAM. In such applications design packages are used to plan the product. Once this is complete the detailed data from the design can be transferred to computer-controlled machines which will then manufacture the product to the exact specification. The system can estimate machining times, and the data provided can be linked with a costing module to prepare budgets and measure production efficiency.

The result is that in certain areas the computer is helping to change the way organizations are managed and is providing more and better information which is available across departments and reflects the current state of the business. When dealing with such systems we must cease to refer to them as accounting systems—we are now dealing with management information systems and must take a systems rather than a functional view of the business.

Summary
1. This chapter looks mainly at the role of the stores and payroll modules.
2. A stores accounting module provides a great deal of information, not only on stocks but on the profitability of different product lines.
3. Stock was one of the earliest and most successful application areas for computers. Stock management involves finding a balance between stock holding costs incurred by the firm and service to the user. Computers help monitor stock levels and reduce stocks to the minimum investment consistent with the required level of service.
4. The payroll accounting module not only prepares the pay for employees, but can be linked into the system to provide figures for the final accounts and for management reports.
5. Payroll is a complex area of work and may involve a number of payment methods, bonus schemes and various other payments. Add to this the fact that legislation, tax rates, etc., are constantly changing, and it is not surprising to find that many firms subcontract this application to a computer bureau.
6. The computer can handle the process up to the stage where money has to be withdrawn and made into pay packets. Where payment is made by cheque, the transfers to the bank and through into employees' accounts can all take place on computers. There is increasing pressure on employees, therefore, to accept payment through a bank account. The proportion of our workforce paid this way is increasing, although the UK lags behind many other countries.
7. The payroll module can link with other accounting modules to exchange information. It can also provide invaluable information for the personnel department. While firms have always recognized the confidential nature of such information, they now have a statutory responsibility for its protection.

9

Software for accountants

Introduction
In Chapters 7 and 8 we have seen the types of software developed to handle the accounting function within a wide range of firms from traders to manufacturers. The accounting practice is an example of a different type of organization, the professional firm, which exists to sell its own services rather than a product. In this area, too, software has been developed to help manage and account for the business. You will note that many of the services provided, such as debtor accounting, are common to all types of concern, while others such as incomplete records systems are specific to this type of firm.

Incomplete record systems
Incomplete records is a term to strike fear into the hearts of many accountants, especially those trained in small practising offices where this constitutes a large proportion of the work. It has been common practice for many years for a market trader or smallholder to breeze into the office carrying several shoeboxes or carrier bags full of papers. A brisk and businesslike 'I have brought my accounts in for audit, let's see if your people can get the job done without bothering me this year' sent partners running for cover. Office juniors and admin. staff suddenly remembered visits that they had to make, and invariably the slowest (or newest) typist was left to hold the fort.

Incomplete records is the term reserved for those clients who do not run a full accounting system. These can range from the extreme case, where no books are kept and invoices, receipts, etc., are stored on a metal spike, through to almost complete systems, e.g. where only the sales ledger is omitted.

The general method of tackling such jobs involves analysing bank statements, invoices, etc., and reconstructing sufficient of the transactions to produce a general ledger, from which a trial balance and final accounts can be prepared. This involves several stages:

1. The transactions identified have to be summarized to produce totals for the general ledger.
2. Any bank or cash records have to be analysed in detail and again summarized for posting.

3. The ledger postings completed, a trial balance is normally produced to prove the arithmetical accuracy of the work.
4. A review of the figures and comparison with previous years will normally show up a large number of queries which have to be taken up directly with the client in order to reconstruct much of what has been omitted from the records. Hence the client's comments above about disturbing him.

Once suitable explanations have been obtained the accountant will incorporate these into the books and ensure that full double-entry rules are followed in order to avoid errors.

This done, the final accounts can be constructed and any final adjustments incorporated before the notes to the accounts are drafted and the accounts finalized.

All this involves a great deal of routine work, much of it summarizing and analysing data. Such work is suitable for computerization, and incomplete-records software packages were developed and have now been in use for a number of years.

The computerized system consists basically of a set of data recording procedures able to handle all types of transactions from VAT to cash items. This module feeds a general ledger system, often with very sophisticated report-generating facilities.

The accounting clerk running a job feeds in details of the transactions together with their appropriate general ledger codes. The machine then processes these and transfers them to the ledger. As with most information handling systems it is the efficiency and detail of the coding system that dictates the level of analysis possible.

Once the transactions are posted a whole range of reports becomes available similar to those we saw when studying general ledger systems. These may include budget statements, management reports, etc.

Modern incomplete-record systems may include any of the following functions:

1. They are normally able to hold several live jobs on the system at any one time. This is useful, allowing staff to proceed with one job while waiting to interview a client on another. When the accounts are finalized a client's information is normally dumped to a client diskette which can be used in future years and may be stored along with the client's papers. This disk will be used the following year to pick up the opening balances and comparative figures for the final accounts.
2. As with many general ledger systems the data can often be converted into a format consistent with a spreadsheet package. This allows the figures to

be transferred across and used to prepare models and analyse results.

3. The output from such systems is a set of final accounts suitable for the client and the system must therefore hold formats for sole traders, partnerships, companies, etc. Some accountants would argue that the notes to the accounts are often more problem than the accounts themselves. Modern systems are therefore able to provide standard notes, which may be tailored by the accountant to suit a particular client. These have to be cross-referenced back to the final accounts and here again the computer can help.

4. Some systems allow a variety of data sources to be used for input. In many cases this is done from original transaction documents, leaving the computer to perform the detailed summarizing. In other cases some of the data may be entered in ready analysed form, e.g. from a client's day book. Some systems even allow a staff member to visit the client's premises with a portable microcomputer and enter data directly into this, coding it under the appropriate headings. On site the operator can produce certain simple reports, and the data can be downloaded to the office computer later, for processing through the incomplete records system in the normal way.

5. Such systems are particularly helpful when discussing queries with clients because adjustments can be entered easily and a trial balance or draft set of accounts produced very quickly. With manual systems this was a time-consuming and error-prone task. In addition to this, many routine tasks such as entering depreciation or handling provisions can now be performed automatically by the system, given the necessary values.

Although basically designed for use with small business concerns with incomplete systems, such software is now in use in a wide range of accounting offices from the very small through to major international firms. Some of the latter also use them on large audits, finding them invaluable for preparing working schedules, handling adjustments and preparing the accounts and accompanying notes. The use in larger offices of networked systems allows a range of staff, including partners, technical staff and secretaries, to access the same data and programs and work on them.

Time charging and billing systems

'Time is money' is a statement that is particularly true in a practising accounting firm. They make their profit by charging clients for work performed on their behalf. In many cases the fee agreed will depend wholly upon the work involved, while in others there will be an agreed fee which cannot be changed without mutual agreement.

To help firms control their time and charge it to clients, many software houses market time charging systems. These keep a full record of time worked across the office and the way it is spent.

The next stage is to charge this time to the appropriate clients and store details in the client's account in a debtors ledger. For this reason a combined time charging, billing and fees ledger system is normally marketed. Figure 9.1 illustrates the inputs and outputs to such a system.

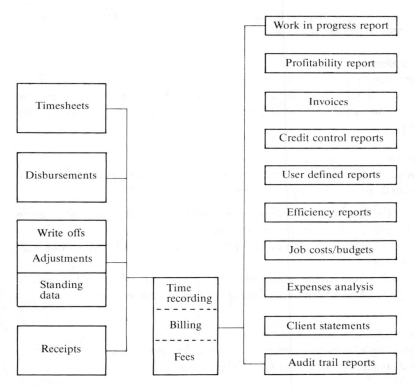

Figure 9.1 Inputs/outputs of a time charging system

INPUTS

Timesheets

The basic method of charging time to individual jobs is through the use of timesheets, and every employee from the senior partner down to a junior clerk has to produce one at regular periods, e.g. weekly. These forms will normally allocate times in either half-hour or quarter-hour minimum blocks.

It is unlikely that everyone in the office will be able to charge each quarter-hour of the week to a chargeable job and so the timesheets are designed to highlight this 'non-chargeable time' and analyse it under a number of headings. The proportion of such time must be carefully monitored and controlled, and although the firm will seek to minimize such time it is not all wasted. Some staff may be involved in public relations work which cannot be charged to any client but may later generate additional client work. Others may, with the approval of the firm, spend part of their time on work for their professional body which although non-fee-earning may help improve the professional standing of the firm.

Disbursements

The firm may need to pay out sums such as travelling expenses on behalf of a client and this will have to be charged directly to them. Details are entered on to coded disbursement forms and will be charged to the appropriate accounts.

Adjustments, write offs, etc.

A number of other details will have to be stored in the system and will need to be updated from time to time. These include:

1. standing details such as information on staff members, their hourly cost to the firm and their charging out rates;
2. personal details of clients and details of any agreed fees or charging methods;
3. bad debts (as with any other debtors ledger system) which will have to be written off and various adjustments made across accounts.

Receipts

Cash paid by clients must be posted to the fees ledger and will have to be matched against the invoices to which it relates.

THE SYSTEM

Once again the system stores large volumes of coded transaction data. It then uses the sorting powers of the machine to sort and collate such details and produce various management reports. The system performs three main kinds of work.

Time recording and control

This involves the routine work of collecting and analysing timesheets, ensuring that all are received and that each covers all working hours in a week. This is not difficult but is very time-consuming when performed manually.

From these details a range of reports can be produced allowing managers to monitor staff time. These are outlined below.

Billing

Using the time records mentioned above, the staff rates and the billing details held on the system invoices can be produced in the format required by the firm. Once the invoice has been produced the details will be automatically posted to the client's personal account in the fees ledger.

The fees ledger

This is the firm's debtors ledger and will provide the normal range of reports described in the previous chapter. The credit control function is vital in a professional office. Unless debts are followed up regularly, clients frequently feel that there is less pressure to pay such bills compared with those for suppliers of goods, which they normally process regularly.

OUTPUT

Like many other computer systems these often include a report generator which allows users to design a set of reports to serve their own particular needs. In addition to this they also normally provide the reports shown in Fig. 9.1. Many of these were described in the previous chapter, so only the new ones will be mentioned here.

Work in progress reports

The partners will need to know the amount of work that has been performed but cannot yet be billed. If, for example, some jobs are left incomplete, this may adversely affect client relations. It will also affect the firm's liquidity because while the firm is paying the salaries involved these are not being converted into cash flow from clients.

The report may list work in progress by individual client, under the partner or manager responsible for the job. A further analysis of this data can produce a detailed summary of work performed in a given time period by the whole firm or by a particular partner/manager group.

Profitability reports

If both the internal salary rate and the charging out rate of each member of staff is held on file, the machine can produce a simple measure of profitability.

Again this can summarize the profitability by client, manager or partner involved.

The reports can list all cases where the job costs have exceeded the agreed fee and the firm has had to accept a loss. However, it would be poor management if such losses were recognized only at the time of final accounting. Most firms therefore budget the hours and costs they expect to be incurred on each job. Regular reports are produced comparing the budget and actual hours to date on jobs and it is part of the work of managers to review these and report back to the partner involved.

Staff productivity reports
The timesheet details hold a great deal of data on the work patterns of individual staff and can be used to provide an analysis of how the firm is operating. We have already mentioned that the office manager will need to control the level of non-chargeable time. Reports can be produced showing the productivity of individuals or groups of staff over a period.

In previous chapters we have seen accounting software used to control and monitor the work of trading and manufacturing organizations. Here we see that the professional office itself can benefit from the same sort of services that it advises its clients to implement. This type of package is useful not only to accountants but also to other professional firms such as architects and solicitors. In the case of solicitors a special cash control package is normally added because the Law Society imposes strict financial controls upon them, designed to ensure a complete separation of client monies from solicitors' own business funds.

Decision support software
Accountants are often criticized for working in the past, labouring endlessly to find missing pennies in order to produce figures which are out of date and therefore of very limited use. While this may to some extent apply to financial accounting it is certainly not true of much management accounting work where figures are produced at short notice to aid decision-making. At this level useful accounting reports have been said to contain much 'guesswork which needs to be revised very quickly as new information comes to light'. To assist with this type of work, decision support software was developed.

Such tools are used in a number of areas to help managers react to facts and information which are frequently changing. For example, a decision whether to invest in a project, and if so how to finance it, would be sensitive to interest rates and tax rates, and would probably involve comparing a number of competing schemes, each of which might be beneficial in certain circumstances. Using such software the financial adviser is able to prepare a model of the situation and then try it out in a number of situations, e.g. at different tax and interest rates.

Financial planning and control involves the setting of targets and preparation of budgets. Actual results are then compared with the plans and corrective action taken. This is certainly a fast-moving area of work where information needs constant updating as further facts come to light:

1. At the budget-setting stage the firm will seek the best general plan to follow in order to reach its objectives. This could involve several competing policies in a situation where costs, markets and prices are changing. The preparation of a business model, against which various policies can be tested, is a fast-growing application area.
2. In day-to-day running, such software is often used to highlight the areas where targets have not been met. Managers must then decide on any corrective action that needs to be taken, and here again they will find it useful to test their plans against their business model.

One area where this software proves particularly useful is in the control of cash funds. It is vital that the business has sufficient liquid funds to operate; however, they do not wish to have excessive amounts of cash or near cash assets which are not earning any return. They must therefore pursue a careful balance between these two extremes and once again the variables involved are constantly changing. Interest rates may change at any time, the timing of receipts from debtors is always unsure, and unexpected payments can cause serious problems. The use of decision support software allows financial managers to prepare a model of the situation and test this to find the critical factors. The example later in this chapter shows how they might prepare a simple model to estimate the likely receipts from debtors over a period.

SPREADSHEETS AND MODELLING SOFTWARE

We have already mentioned the first type of decision support software, the spreadsheet, in Chapter 4. This is a very popular tool with accountants as it allows them to create simple models very quickly and the technique is very easy to learn. A model can be set up, and by altering certain figures the effect on other items such as profit can be viewed. Not surprisingly this has come to be called 'what if' analysis because the accountant is in effect asking 'what will happen if I change this particular variable?' Using modern spreadsheet packages large and quite involved models can be developed. These often start out as fairly simple models which are then refined as the firm uses them in practice and sees how they can be improved.

To evaluate the effects of changes the user must alter certain figures on the spreadsheet and when this is done the original result is overwritten. This can be quite restrictive when large volumes of data are involved and many items have to be changed. For use in more complex systems such as these, modelling packages (modellers) have been developed.

A modeller is more complex than a spreadsheet and it normally requires the use of a number of separate files:

1. First, the detailed model has to be written. This is created in a special high-level language developed for the package. This model is the list of instructions that the computer must follow to reach the results. Like any other program written in a high-level language this must then be compiled and the machine code version is stored on a model file.
2. The instructions to extract the results and print them out as final reports are normally stored on a special report file.
3. Finally the data to be run against the model has to be input, again on to a separate data file.

When all this has been done the data file is run against the other files to produce the required reports. This takes longer but it allows far more data to be handled; the modeller therefore comes into its own in those areas where the spreadsheet is almost at its limit. As it is more complex to operate it is not so useful for simple one-off cases, but it is useful for those areas where the model will be used repeatedly. A complex model of a highly dynamic situation can be prepared and then tested under a wide range of different situations. (This would give it particular application to areas of economic modelling, etc.)

EXAMPLE: MODELLING CASH RECEIVABLE FROM DEBTORS
The cash budget is used to forecast the firm's cash position. To do this estimates of receipts and payments must be made and these are brought together in the cash budget. In this section we shall look at a part of the work involved in creating the cash budget. We will look at a budget designed to take the estimated half-year annual sales and break these down into receipts for each month.

The final report is shown in Fig. 9.2. We shall now consider particular aspects of it.

Inputs
The firm will have prepared a sales budget for the period. The total sales will

VAT rate 15%
Est. sales (6 mnths)   500 000

Expected recpts (%)

Cash sale	10
1 month	60
2 months	30
	100

Month	%	Net	VAT	Gross	January	February	March	April	May	June	Debtors
Op Drs.				20 000	12 000	8 000					
Jan	15	75 000	11 250	86 250	8 625	51 750	25 875				
Feb	12	60 000	9 000	69 000		6 900	41 400	20 700			
Mar	17	85 000	12 750	97 750			9 775	58 650	29 325		
Apr	15	75 000	11 250	86 250				8 625	51 750	25 875	
May	20	100 000	15 000	115 000					11 500	69 000	34 500
June	21	105 000	15 750	120 750						12 075	72 450
											36 225
	100	500 000	75 000	595 000	20 625	66 650	77 050	87 975	92 575	106 950	143 175

595 000

Figure 9.2 Cash budget

either be entered manually here or, with many packages, it can be 'imported' directly from the file containing the sales budget.

The VAT rate is held in the model but can be changed by the user if required.

The user must next make some estimate of the expected receipts and enter the percentage figures.

The split of the total sales between months (in the bottom section) could be entered manually or it could be imported from a sales model file again.

The input complete, the model will take care of the mathematics and produce the report shown.

Using the model

Assume that when the full cash budget was put together the firm found that it would exceed its borrowing powers in the first two months and after looking at other receipts and payments it was obvious that the flow of funds from debtors was vital. What was the firm to do?

The model can now be used to help analyse the problem by asking a series of 'what if' questions. One possible action might be to influence the credit terms. A large proportion of cash sales would help. This leads to a number of questions that need to be tried on the model:

1. Assuming that they feel this can be done, what difference will it make?
2. If cash sales could be increased to 15 per cent of sales, what difference would it make if these affected:
   - people who would have taken one month's credit?
   - people who would have taken two months' credit?
   - a mixture of both?

   The results of any combination could be tested very quickly and from an analysis of the results the managers could evaluate how sensitive the results were to these particular variables.
3. What would be the effect of altering the pattern of sales over the months?
4. What would be the effect of combining the above policies?

All the above could be done manually but each change would involve a great deal of recalculation and take some time. With the model, changes can be made very quickly and more complex situations can be tested. For example, in this case any alteration in the credit control policy might be expected to affect the volume of sales. This in turn would affect profits, cash, purchases, etc. To

	A		B	C	D	E	F	G
:	VAT rate		15					
:	Estd sales		500000					
:			========					
:	Expected recpts							
:	Cash sale		10					
:	1 month		60					
:	2 months		30					
:			--------					
:			(1)					
:			========					
:	Month	%	Net	VAT	Gross	January	February	March
:	Op. Drs				12 000	8000		
:	Jan	15	(2)	(3)	(4)	(5)	(6)	(7)
:	Feb	12					(8)	(9)
:	Mar	17						(10)
:								
			(11)	(12)	(13)	(14)	(15)	(16)

1.	SUM(B5.B7)	This adds contents of boxes B5, B6 and B7 together.
2.	B2 * A14/100	Changes A14 to a percentage then takes that proportion of total sales.
3.	B1/100 * B14	Changes VAT rate to a percentage and calculates VAT on the month's sales.
4.	B14 + C14	Adds sales and VAT for the month.
5.	B5/100 * D14	Calculates cash portion of January sales.
6.	B6/100 * D14	Calculates those taking one month's credit on January sales.
7.	B7/100 * D14	Calculates those taking two months' credit on January sales.
8.	B5/100 * D15	Calculates the cash portion of February sales.
9.	B6/100 * D15	Calculates those taking one month's credit on February sales.
10.	B5/100 * D16	Calculates cash portion of March sales.
11.	SUM(B13.B16)	Sums the receipts for the current column.
12.	SUM(C13.C16)	Sums the receipts for the current column.
13.	SUM(D13.D16)	Sums the receipts for the current column.
14.	SUM(E13.E16)	Sums the receipts for the current column.
15.	SUM(F13.F16)	Sums the receipts for the current column.
16.	SUM(G13.G16)	Sums the receipts for the current column.

Figure 9.3 Spreadsheet model

evaluate all such changes manually would be very tedious and the work would probably not be done. However, once a model has been created it can be done quite simply and quickly.

WRITING THE MODEL

In this section we shall look at how a model such as this would be written, using a spreadsheet. The actual instructions and formulae used might vary from one package to another but the method would be the same. Figure 9.3 shows the basic instructions which go to make up the model. In Chapter 4 we mentioned that any cell of a spreadsheet could contain:

1. a label (a word or phrase),
2. a variable (a number the user may alter),
3. a formula (which allows the package to calculate the current value of the cell).

In Figure 9.3 any text would be entered as a label and any numbers would be entered as variables. It is the formulae that make the model work; these are indicated by a number in brackets, which refers to the following note carrying the same number. The notes give the formulae that would be contained in that cell of the model together with a brief explanation. For simplicity and brevity we will look only at the first three months of the model.

Part 4

Setting up the system

10

Setting up the system

Introduction
All computer users face one common problem, that of finding suitable applications software to make the machine perform the work they require. For small and medium-sized firms the answer normally lies in finding a suitable, ready written, software package which operates in the manner they require. They do not have the time or the funds required to develop their own bespoke systems. Today, even large firms are increasingly turning to packaged systems, because, as such systems have become more sophisticated, they allow users to tailor them to their own needs and can save a great deal of money.

However, many larger organizations still have to develop their own systems. In this chapter we consider the way such systems are developed, and in Chapter 11 we will consider the work involved in acquiring a ready-made packaged system.

Data processing staff
Systems analysts are the data processing specialists normally charged with developing new systems and with overall management of a project. Reports from accountants in industry and commerce indicate that they are frequently called upon to make a major contribution towards systems development, but in larger companies this will probably mean working with the systems development staff as the representative of a major user department. Accountants in smaller organizations often find that in their role as information provider they may be called upon to play a leading role in the acquisition of software.

We shall start our consideration of the systems development process by looking at the role of the main groups of staff within the data processing department. Such a department might be organized along the lines shown in Fig. 10.1.

THE DATA PROCESSING MANAGER
The DP manager heads the data processing department, with overall responsibility for its running and for ensuring that it operates in line with general

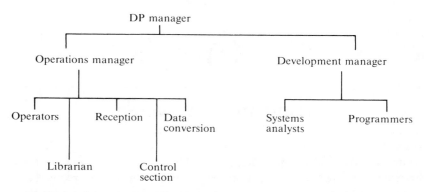

Figure 10.1 Staff of a computing department

company policy concerning computing. This manager has the overall responsibility for controlling the data processing activities of the business and his or her staff will advise and help user departments on all aspects of computers and related problems.

Below the DP manager are two specialist managers, one in charge of the day-to-day machine operations and the other in charge of the development of new systems. We will see later that this basic division can help us to strengthen control.

COMPUTER OPERATORS

The operators deal with the day-to-day running of the machines. Although the machines can process programs without human intervention, operators are needed to load and unload disks, load paper into printers, distribute printed copy and deal with running problems.

DATA PREPARATION STAFF

Data has to be converted into a machine-readable form before it can be read into the computer. Data preparation staff perform this function. For many years this normally involved card punching, but in recent years it has moved over to visual display units with key-to-disk systems.

This has always been a relatively error-prone area of work and new methods of data capture are being developed, wherever possible, that pick up data at the point of sale, etc., reducing the incidence of data conversion errors. With real-time systems many users now input their own data directly from terminals, again reducing the need for specialist conversion staff in the computer centre.

LIBRARIAN

A specialist librarian is often employed to take physical control of files when they are not being processed. This helps prevent illegal access to files either to copy or to alter them, and also prevents the loss or accidental erasure of live files.

CONTROL STAFF

These are employed to reduce the risk of errors in processing data. With batch systems they prepare control totals of all data going on to the computer and later check these against totals generated by it.

DEVELOPMENT STAFF

The systems development task is shared between both analysts and programmers. In some organizations the two grades are quite separate with the analysts designing the system and monitoring its progress while the programmers write and test the programs that make up the system. In other organizations the work is shared by a team, some of whom will be classed as analyst/programmers.

A good system cannot be developed by systems staff in isolation; they must work with staff from user departments who can offer their own specialist experience to help ascertain:

1. the work performed by the current system and the way it tackles this;
2. any problems and delays being experienced with the current system;
3. what information is required at present and likely to be needed in the future, and how it can best be produced.

Good analysts require a mixture of skills and experience which takes many years to acquire. They need a good knowledge of business systems, skill in dealing with people and a wide knowledge of business. The normal career path is through the data processing department, working up through the various grades. It is sometimes argued that this background does not necessarily give them the breadth of business knowledge they require. However, the fact that the systems development team includes staff from the various user departments concerned helps to bring a wider view and different experience to the project.

Computer steering committee

In many larger organizations the overall policy on computer developments is placed under this committee which will consist of:

1. senior management staff from the organization,
2. the DP manager and senior systems analyst,
3. representatives from other user departments.

This type of committee emphasizes the fact that data processing is a common service and not under the control of any one user department. The fact that senior management sit on the committee adds authority and ensures that all developments approved comply with the firm's computing policies.

The steering committee will:

1. receive proposals for new schemes and, if they accept them, set up a development team and then monitor its progress;
2. ensure that the firm's adopted procedures on hardware, software, etc., are compatible across the organization, to prevent individual departments from purchasing their own equipment which might be incompatible with that used in other departments;
3. order a feasibility study for any proposal that it feels should be considered and receive the results of such studies;
4. (in many organizations) audit the new system to ensure that it achieves its original objectives.

Stages in project design

We can identify a number of distinct stages which occur in the design and implementation of a new system. These are set out in Fig. 10.2 and will be considered in turn in this chapter.

STAGE 1: THE FEASIBILITY STUDY

A study of this kind is normally carried out before a new computer is purchased and before any new system is designed. As we will see later, a full systems investigation is costly and time-consuming and management will want basic guidance as to whether a project seems likely to succeed before they invest in a full development project. They therefore order a feasibility study to be carried out as the first stage of evaluation.

As its name implies, this is a basic study to assess whether or not a scheme is likely to prove feasible and is therefore worthy of detailed consideration. This is an important stage, as it can save a great deal of cost later and can give some idea of the best way to approach the project. The study should be performed by experienced staff, who will be able to make reasonable estimates of the likely costs and benefits of various alternatives. Their objective will be to reach a tentative opinion on the scheme without incurring the costs and delays of a full investigation.

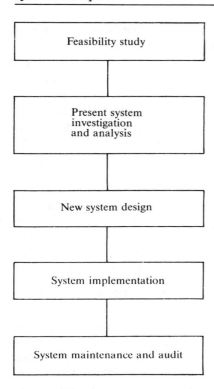

Figure 10.2   Stages in a systems project

Original proposals for a project are addressed to the steering committee, which will probably receive a number of competing ones from various user departments and the firm's own data processing department. As resources are limited the committee must choose which proposals are to go forward for further consideration. It is therefore vital that all proposals be fully documented before they go before the committee. At this and all later stages in project development most organizations adopt detailed standards for documentation and approval of schemes to ensure that the basic work is performed properly and to assist the review process. The steering committee will discuss the schemes and if unsure they can refer them back for further details. In most cases they will either reject them or, if they seem worthy, set up a feasibility study group.

The feasibility report, when completed, is addressed to the steering committee and should include the following:

(a) An outline description of the scheme, with details of its aims, likely benefit and other reasons for its development.

(b) The findings of the study which could suggest one or several possible alternatives which are thought worthy of further investigation. For example, the group may think a proposal is valid and should be implemented but that it would be costly to develop in house. In such cases they might suggest looking at suitable packages for the firm's mainframe or even possible use of micro-based packages within the department concerned.

(c) Estimates of the costs and benefits likely to arise from the project together with comparisons with the processing method currently in use for this work. The proposed scheme could well affect the firm's requirements for both staff and equipment, so schemes are normally classified as confidential at this stage. If the scheme is later approved it will be very important to brief managers, staff and unions, but at this stage it is only a suggestion and it is important to be able to evaluate it impartially without pressure from various groups who may have their own interests to defend.

If the committee is satisfied with the findings of the feasibility report, it will authorize the setting up of a project development team consisting of systems analysts and user department staff seconded to work with the group. They will be issued with formal instructions setting out their terms of reference, any limitations on their scope, details of time scale, etc. Once it gets to this stage the project is no longer merely a suggestion and analysts will soon be seeking the ideas of staff affected or likely to be affected by it. The scheme can no longer be considered confidential and it is good policy to make a formal announcement at this stage to staff associations, unions, etc. It is better that staff hear what is happening formally rather than on the grapevine. It is vital, however, that details are communicated before the team starts interviewing staff about the project.

STAGE 2: CURRENT SYSTEM INVESTIGATION AND ANALYSIS

The first task of the project team is to ascertain what is currently happening in the area of the investigation and to assess its effectiveness. They must be careful to ensure that they do not approach this part of the work with pre-conceived ideas as to the type of system required. It is frequently found that areas of work that pose serious problems may have developed on an *ad hoc* basis and that after a proper investigation of what is being done and what is required manual methods can be devised to perform the tasks cheaply and efficiently. The aim therefore is to ascertain what the present system is and to identify its weaknesses. Accounting students with large-company audit experience will find this approach similar to some of their own work on systems.

To review the current system, analysts will use similar methods to those used by auditors. These include:

(a) inspection of records,
(b) interviews,
(c) observation,
(d) questionnaires.

Inspection of records

Some organizations produce a great deal of formal documentation on their systems, including organization charts, systems manuals, flow charts, standing orders, etc. Systems analysts can use these to learn how the systems should operate and to assess the formal structure of the department. They say a great deal about what is supposed to happen but the actual procedures and relationships between staff may be quite different. As with auditing, the analyst cannot rely wholly on the formal description of organizations, but must interview staff and observe what actually happens.

Interviews

Interviewing is a useful method of obtaining data when used by a skilled analyst, but he or she must have a clear idea in advance of the information he is seeking and must be careful how the interview is conducted. It will probably be necessary to hold more than one interview in most cases, as a first visit must be used to establish a relationship and possibly overcome hostility and mistrust.

In discussion the analyst will steer the subject matter into the areas he or she wishes to discuss, but must be very careful to avoid any bias towards preformed ideas and must be seen to listen to the opinions and ideas of the interviewee.

A common problem is that employees often contradict one another and frequently give only a partial explanation of what happens. They will almost certainly give their own personal view of what they think happens, which might be seen quite differently by their colleagues. To deal with such problems, systems analysts frequently document their findings and submit them in summarized form to the department for comment. In this way they can finally arrive at an agreed description of current practices before moving on to look at alternative methods.

Observation

Throughout his or her period in the department a vigilant analyst will be observing what is happening and gaining an idea of how things are operating.

It may be possible to obtain agreement to visit a department and formally observe the documents in use and the staff at work. If, however, an analyst is trying to assess the level of work performed, more scientific methods of work study may have to be used, and possibly organization and management (O&M) techniques of work measurement. This takes time and can be costly, so where the results are not critical a simple method of activity sampling is often used. Here an activity is observed at previously calculated random intervals, and each time what is happening is noted, to build up a profile of the pattern of work in the section. It is obviously important that the department is visited during periods of normal activity and that sample visits are truly random; visits at the same time each day might give a very biased view.

Observations can be helpful in affirming or challenging the information previously obtained from interviews and questionnaires.

Questionnaires

The questionnaire is another tool which can prove helpful in particular areas of work. It must, however, be used with great care. It is particularly useful with organizations that have a number of branches and where the team can only visit a limited number of them. In such cases the team may:

(a) interview staff at some branches to ascertain how the system operates locally;
(b) from their findings, devise a questionnaire to be sent to the other branches;
(c) analyse the results and compare them with the findings from interviews and observations at the branches visited.

The preparation of questionnaires is a difficult job because the questions must avoid ambiguity and must not lead the respondent to answer in a particular way. The reader may have tried certain quizzes in popular newspapers that claim to measure intelligence, physical attraction, etc. In most of these one soon sees that a yes answer indicates the better reply to each question or vice versa, and it is hard to answer the rest of them objectively. Professional questionnaires must avoid such bias and in fact they will often ask the same question in different ways within the form, comparing the different answers for consistency. Even after checking by professionals, questions may be read in different ways by various respondents so the questionnaire should be tested on a sample of staff before being used.

A simple questionnaire can be a useful preparation for a later interview, concentrating the person's ideas on the required area and helping to sort out ideas in advance.

Describing and evaluating the present system

Having ascertained what is currently taking place, and with details of what information users will require, the systems analysts must next record these details and identify the strengths and weaknesses of the existing system. This recording may be done in narrative form but, like auditors and O&M staff, analysts have found flow charting to be a useful tool in this area.

Several levels of flow charts are used throughout the life of a project. Outline systems charts of the sort seen in Chapter 5 are used to give a general overview of the system. As the work becomes more detailed and the team comes to program particular sections of the work so more detailed program flow charts and other tools such as decision charts are used. A great deal of work is involved in the development of systems and it is important to obtain a general overview of the process.

STAGE 3: NEW SYSTEM DESIGN

From the previous stage the team will have learned the following information about the current system:

(a) the way it is organized, the work done and who performs it;
(b) all inputs and outputs to the system, details of all forms used and the way that information on them is calculated, together with full details of how they flow through the business;
(c) the volume of work normally processed together with any problems, bottlenecks and details of slack and busy periods; it is important also to identify which parts of the work are being performed well by the current system as these may be carried forward into the new system;
(d) details of users' present requirements for information and their likely future needs from an improved system.

Armed with this information the team can commence designing the new system which will be based on users' needs. As mentioned previously the best method may not always involve a computerized system. For example, a large organization in the leisure industry has recently installed a specially designed pegboard system to deal with their accounting and record keeping across the country at a large number of leisure locations. However, for our purposes we refer to the development of computerized systems in the remainder of this chapter.

Whatever design is chosen the user departments involved should be given the chance to comment on it and to suggest improvements. For this reason a presentation is normally made to the staff concerned which will demonstrate new forms, new screen layouts, proposed new output reports and the planned flow of documents. This does not mean that the system has been finalized; at this stage, the specimen screens and forms are easily set up on the computer and are purely for demonstration purposes. The users' comments will be noted and discussed by the team in arriving at their final system which will be set down in a detailed systems specification.

The work involved in this stage can be split into the following steps:

(a) design of input and output forms,
(b) file design,
(c) systems specification,
(d) programme development and design.

Design of input and output forms
Input   We have seen that various input methods are available according to the type of system in use. This is traditionally an error-prone area of work and good form design and data capture methods can help reduce the incidence of errors in a number of ways.

(a) Certain form design standards may be adopted across applications; for example, customer identifier, dates, document numbers and other identification fields may be placed together in a standard area on all forms. This avoids the need for operators to search for information and helps to speed up input and reduce errors.
(b) Input forms and input software can be designed to complement one another. The input screens will work through data in the order it appears on the forms and the screen layout will be designed to closely resemble the form in use.
(c) Wherever possible the software will validate the content of any field. For example, are letters included in a number-only field or does the amount in a particular field exceed the likely value?

Manual data capture has always been slow and costly so, as technology has developed, new ways of automatic data capture have been developed. We saw how integrated accounting systems reduced the volume of data entry and in our supermarkets electronic tills and bar code readers are used more and more to collect data directly at the point of sale. Similar developments are also spreading into the production area where keypads in the departments are used more and more by operating staff to enter costing and production control data.

Output A great deal of computer information is still output as printed hard copy. However, in more and more cases enquiries are made using a VDU, with a hard copy being produced only if a record needs to be kept.

Too much information can be as bad as (or worse than) too little, because it confuses the user and may hide the trends he or she is looking for. Analysts must therefore pay attention to the form of report produced by the system. Some accounting systems, for example, produce large, complex reports, which are confusing even to an accountant, while their screen report facilities are often far clearer, probably due to the restrictions on screen space. The following points should be considered when designing output forms.

The analyst should endeavour to find what output is really needed. Many systems provide large detailed printouts intended to serve a variety of uses, e.g. to provide information, to strengthen control, or purely as a backup for information on file. With a proper, detailed analysis of user needs it might be possible to replace these with a number of smaller, simpler reports that could both improve efficiency and reduce printing time, with the detailed backup data being stored on a separate data file until required or printed directly on to microfiche.

Interrogation reports are normally designed for on-screen use with the facility to produce a hard copy if required. If users can access these easily and quickly, they will normally come to rely far less on the printed version and may be able to clear most queries on screen. This saves a great deal of printing and avoids the need to circulate full printouts of details on file. In designing such information screens the following points are relevant:

(a) We have commented on the limited space available on a screen, and it becomes cluttered and hard to read well before it is full. Good screen design is therefore important and much thought is needed here. As a result designers have to break screen reports down into manageable blocks. Rather than producing one all-embracing screen showing all details relating to a particular customer, we may offer a set of screens, each dealing with certain related aspects of the record, e.g. personal details, credit details, etc.

(b) Interrogation facilities may be equipped with powerful search facilities to help the operator locate a particular record instead of printing out a whole batch. For example, if the operator is unsure of the account number of a customer, the system may accept all or part of the surname. It will then list the names, addresses and customer numbers that resemble this and the user indicates which of these is required. The appropriate record is then printed to the screen.

(c) Various options exist with screens to help highlight information to the user. Field headings may be displayed in a different colour or in reverse video. This helps to make data stand out from headings, etc. Items on the screen can be made to flash to attract attention, and most machines offer sound facilities to attract the user's attention when an error has been made.

File design

Files are a vital element of any computerized business system and must be carefully planned in advance if they are to operate efficiently. If a slow access method is chosen and the records are poorly arranged, the organization will be plagued with problems and delays for many years. A number of points need to be considered in the design of files.

The file format   A file is merely a collection of similar items of data stored on a memory device. As it stands it has no meaning to the computer, which sees it as a list of zeros and ones and does not know what they represent. The programs that run the particular system impose some order on this data, telling the machine where one field starts and another ends, and what to do with the data found there. The shape of the file therefore depends on the data called for by the programs. The system designer will need to define the file structure at a number of levels:

(a) The overall format of the file must be designed. This shows what type of records will appear throughout the file. Most records will be of the same format, representing similar data items. However, certain ones particularly near the start and end of the file may be of different format, providing information about the file itself such as the total number of records on file or the total value of balances on a ledger file.

(b) The format of individual records must be planned so that the computer can recognize the fields within them. For example, a payroll file record would contain fields for employee's name, works number, address, pay rate, tax code and many others.

(c) With certain computer languages the format of individual fields has to be specified in detail. For example, with COBOL a 'picture' of each field is required, showing the maximum number of characters allowed, whether each may be numeric, alphabetic or either, and the position of the decimal point. This must be planned very carefully, for if illegal values arise in these fields during processing, the system will fail to run. Other languages may not require so much detail at this level.

The analyst must identify which fields, are to become the key fields as it is on these that the file will link data with other files. It follows that these fields must appear in the same format in each of the files with which there will be a link.

The reader should appreciate that the information we obtain from the system comes from an analysis of the data held on the files. If we do not hold a particular item of data on file, we cannot produce data from it. To add fields to files at a later date can be a major exercise, so it is important that systems analysts ascertain from users details of information they would like to obtain from the system in the future. If the necessary fields are included on the disk at the design stage, it may be relatively simple at a later date to amend the programs to make use of them.

File content and usage   This affects several aspects of file design. Some files are relatively easy to handle because the data they hold follows a particular pattern and we can therefore plan the contents and size of the file. Others, particularly data files, are not nearly so obliging. To illustrate this, think of a data file used to hold details of invoices from suppliers, and assume that it is structured so that every invoice represents a record, and personal details and every product line purchased are the various fields. We can then consider some of the problems it poses.

Certain fields such as the supplier's name, invoice number, etc., are outside our control and may vary greatly in length from one record to the next. This poses the problem of how the computer should handle such records. It can be set to handle variable length records but this does complicate the work of the machine somewhat. The alternative is to specify fixed length records and set the field to the maximum size likely to be met in practice. This is rather inflexible and wastes much file space as the fields are padded out with blank spaces on the storage medium. In practice, should a supplier's name be met which is longer than the allocated size, the operator will have to abbreviate it, although the next person to access it may not be aware of the abbreviation used.

As each invoice is to constitute a record on this file we can foresee a further problem. How many fields will appear on a record? We do not know in advance, as it depends on how many lines will appear on the appropriate invoice. One way of solving this is to include a further field on the file, telling the computer how many items appear in that particular record.

It is important to size the filing requirements of the system as this will affect the running of the system. The analyst must ensure that the system can run the current size of file plus an adequate allowance for future growth.

File access and physical organization   The most appropriate access method will depend on the type of application and the demands made on it for information. With a high hit rate application, sequential access will normally be used to claim the benefits of fast updating. A real-time application where retrieval times are important could use random files or, if a balance is needed between access and update times, the indexed sequential method. For a large application involving many departments and large volumes of data a database system may yield greater benefits.

Once the storage method is agreed and the file structure finalized the analyst must look at how the files will be stored on the chosen medium. We have seen how disks can be organized in cylinders to save the amount of head movement.

The type of storage system chosen will have an effect on security procedures in the event of a system breakdown. With tape systems a file cannot be overwritten when updated, so we must create a new copy. If we retain some of the old copies, these can be used as backup copies should damage occur to the current one. However, a disk system overwrites the disk when changes are made. In this case computer staff must *dump*, or copy, the information to another disk at regular intervals. If anything goes wrong, the last backup copy is used and must be updated by running the data of the intervening period to recreate the damaged file.

With real-time applications, the system will have to be off line while a fault is rectified and the aim must be to correct the file and put the system back on line as soon as possible. In such cases the file may be copied at fairly short intervals and a *logging tape* inside the computer will take a copy of every transaction that affects the files. In the event of a system breakdown, the logging file is run against the latest copy of the file to update it to the position of the original file at the time of the failure. The delay is not too serious as this updating is performed at high speed by the computer and many of the day's transactions on such a system will have been enquiries rather than file amendments and will not therefore have been stored on the logging tape. The volume of data requiring updating will therefore be only a proportion of what has passed through the machine.

The systems specification
The end result of the analyst's work is a formal document, the *systems specification*. This is a complex document setting out the full results of the

work. Due to its size and the amount of detail involved only parts of it will be presented to various user groups, etc. However, it is important to have it documented to this level as the analyst may move on to other work or leave the firm and if queries arise later detailed documentation is an absolute necessity. This systems specification performs a number of roles. It will be used to:

(a) present the team's findings to senior management—their adoption of the specification is the authority for the scheme to progress;
(b) prepare the presentations to user staff and managers;
(c) prepare the detailed program descriptions that will form the basis for the writing of the new system.

The systems specification will include the following information:

(a) an outline description of the project, setting out terms of reference, benefits expected, etc.;
(b) the present system description, which obviously cannot be included for a totally new application area;
(c) details of files, outlining all the factors mentioned in the last section;
(d) details of all input and output documents, screen layouts, etc.—copies of the actual documents will be placed on file and the flows of documents should be explained and other useful information included, such as details of document suppliers and likely levels of usage;
(e) detailed explanation of the new system, which may be done through the use of flow charts, narrative notes or a mixture of these;
(f) explanation of external system operations, which refers to the links with the rest of the firm's systems and may involve changes in staffing and equipment or at least alter the present duties of staff;
(g) implementation planning—the system must be properly introduced if it is to gain the support of staff and continue to operate properly; depending on the organization and the size of the system, this can range from a simple paragraph up to a full plan in its own right;
(h) a timetable through to final implementation—the whole aim of the work is to introduce the scheme and have it working on time, so time management is important.

At this stage a number of presentations will be made for managers, user staff, unions, etc., who will all need to be consulted. Their comments, criticisms and advice will be noted and may be incorporated into the system. Once the systems specification has been finalized and approved the project can move on to the next stage—program development and design.

Program development and design

At this stage the systems specification shows the overall system as a series of program boxes to be run in a specified order. The next stage is to turn each of the boxes on the flow chart into a working program. The systems analyst, working from the systems specification, will now produce for each box a detailed program specification showing what the program does and how it will link with others to form the overall system. Some firms totally separate the work of analysis and programming and this will therefore be the official handing over of the project to the development staff. Documentation must therefore be clear and thorough. In other firms the analyst/programmers who designed it will continue to work on the project. However, even here their emphasis will change and it is important to have a document that spells out the general overview.

The program specifications are first reviewed by senior programming staff who will refer back any obvious queries before allocating each to particular staff. They will give a time allowance and retain responsibility for controlling the various projects and for monitoring progress to ensure that they will all be ready on time to be tested together.

Each project programmer will receive the program specification and start to plan the way to approach it, at this stage referring back any further queries. Here again the firm will have their own internal standards on file layout, documentation, etc., which are communicated to all staff and greatly help to reduce the number of such problems.

The program specifications will contain the following details:

(a) general information on the program, identifying its place in the overall system, information on the aims of and reason for the overall system and copies of the systems flow chart;

(b) detailed notes on the work the program has to perform, inputs and outputs to it, full information on the files and their structure, and details of special controls;

(c) timetable for writing and testing the program and details of the testing procedures involved;

(d) details of the hardware and peripherals available to the program.

The programmer who codes the program is normally responsible for ensuring that it works properly. There are various ways of testing, ranging from following on paper the logic of all routes through the program (*dry running*) through to using test data and even live data through it.

A system normally consists of a number of programs and, although each may work quite well in isolation, this may not be the case when they are run together. A proper plan is therefore necessary to ensure that they are all completed on time and can be tested together. At this stage it is useful to run real live data through the system in addition to the pre-prepared test data, as unforeseen snags can often occur with live data. For example, a simple thing like a negative figure may not have been foreseen at the planning stage. This form of testing also allows timings to be taken to ensure that the system will give reasonable response times and be able to handle the volumes of work anticipated.

Once the system is written, tested and approved it is ready to be implemented. This is an important aspect of development, and failure to plan here can ruin all the work done to date. If the system is not properly installed it may fail to operate and will certainly lose the support of users. Implementation involves a great deal of detailed work which cannot be short cut, while at the same time there will be pressure from all sides to get the system up and running and end the disruption it causes.

STAGE 4: SYSTEM IMPLEMENTATION
The commencement of implementation planning cannot wait until the new systems are produced. It must start well before this—we saw mention of it as far back as the systems specification. While the programs are being written the company will have proceeded with implementation tasks such as ordering new forms and equipment, and possibly with the recruitment of certain specialist staff ready for the commencement of the system.

The steps involved at this stage are:

(a) file setting up or file conversion,
(b) controlled running to detect errors,
(c) training and documentation,
(d) hardware and software installation,
(e) obtaining staff, equipment, stationery and other requirements.

The amount of work involved depends on the size and complexity of the system being introduced and whether or not the staff concerned have worked with computers before. A large, complex system may require a detailed plan, and project evaluation and review techniques (PERT) may be used to ensure that it is finished on time and to ascertain tasks that will delay the overall work if not completed on time.

File set-up and conversion
The new system will rely on its files, which may contain thousands of records which are to be processed regularly. Before the new system can operate,

therefore, the master files must be created and all the records set up with the opening data on them. In many cases, e.g. with accounting ledger systems, this task is complicated by the fact that the current file is in constant use.

The ideal way of setting up the new file would be to program the computer to extract the figures needed from the old files and to create a new file from this. However, this requires a program to be specially written and tested for the job and in many cases this is just not possible.

In such cases the file conversion or creation work frequently involves a great deal of manual data conversion either by increased work from the firm's own staff or through the use of temporary staff from a bureau. In the case of our debtors file mentioned above, staff could set up the new accounts on file, ready for the new system. However, a problem arises when they wish to transfer the opening data to these accounts. The current ledgers will be in steady use as staff process debtors under the current system. The work of transferring the opening balances and outstanding invoices to the new ledger could be performed in one of the following ways:

(a) The work could be done during the firm's holiday period or outside working hours while the current files are not in use.
(b) It may be possible to write a program to read the outstanding balances from an old ledger file on to a data file for later processing against the new system.
(c) If these methods fail, the system may 'go live' on the appointed day with all the records on file but no opening figures. All future transactions would be posted to the new file and over a period of time the opening balances would also be transferred in batches, bringing the file up to date.

The normal high error rates in this area are likely to be exacerbated by the additional pressures involved, so it is vital that control is imposed over the work. One useful method is to prepare control totals on the number of items and total values of particular fields. These are then checked against the machine totals after processing is completed.

Controlled running
Rarely will an organization move over directly to a new system without some further period of testing. In most cases they attempt to eliminate as many errors as possible before full reliance has to be placed on the new system. A prolonged period of live running is therefore operated to show up problems in the live data that were not foreseen in the preparation of the program.

There are two main ways of running this period of testing: parallel running and pilot running.

Parallel running   Here the old and new systems are run side by side for a number of weeks and the outputs from the two are compared. Accountants and data processing staff concerned with accuracy of results tend to prefer a long period of such testing but the pressures on operating departments normally lead to it being discontinued after a shorter period. Running two systems side by side obviously involves far more work and pressure for office space; things can be even worse if some staff are being made redundant by the new system and are working out their notice while operating the new system alongside it. Such testing can also help erode confidence in the new system, as the aim is to find differences between the two sets of output and existing staff often see each example found as damning of the new system rather than as an exercise in tracing problems. There is, however, the advantage that should the system fail the organization can always fall back on the existing system while things are corrected.

Pilot running   This is most commonly employed where a system has to be implemented across a number of branches or offices. The system is run first at one site which is chosen as the pilot site. User staff here are assisted by the data processing staff during the implementation period and the two groups work together on the new system. Once it is successfully running staff from other branches can visit the pilot site and staff from the pilot can be seconded to other areas to share their experience. This method is not really suited for firms where staff have no previous data processing experience but in cases where there is some experience the staff become far more involved and work more closely with the development staff. As a result they tend to gain better experience of and seem more likely to support the new system.

Training and documentation

Training is an area of project management that is frequently overlooked or rushed through. However, once the system is fully commissioned the development staff mcve out and the day-to-day running becomes the responsibility of the user staff. If they do not understand what is required of them, the system may well fail to achieve its design aims, not through any inherent weaknesses but due to poor operation.

Training may be performed in a number of ways and at a number of different levels. The systems staff in consultation with the training department will need to identify the training needs and arrange for them to be covered in time for the implementation stage.

The systems staff will need to ensure that proper operating manuals are prepared both for user department and data processing staff. User departments need information on their aspects of the system, e.g. document creation, control procedures, etc. Computer operators must be provided with detailed operating manuals specifying the systems hardware needs and recovery procedures in case of failure, etc.

Other steps
Management will obviously have to ensure that the machinery is installed and that the correct stationery and supplies are obtained prior to the proposed date of implementation. The actual work involved will vary greatly from firm to firm and is therefore not detailed here.

STAGE 5: SYSTEM MAINTENANCE AND AUDIT
Once the system is adopted the development staff still retain some involvement with it, being responsible for maintaining it in an operational state. This includes correction of systems faults and amendments to systems.

Correction of systems faults   From time to time problems will occur when running the system. If these are routine machine faults or power supply problems, operating staff will consult the operations manual and instigate the necessary recovery procedures. If, however, problems result from a systems error, staff will be unable to recover from them; a systems analyst will be called in to take over and will take copies (*dumps*) of the memory contents to find out what has happened inside the machine and check this back to the system and program documentation to trace what has gone wrong. Once the problem is identified it can be corrected but the same level of authorization and documentation should be applied to such amendments as operated when the system was being developed. This is important because without full documentation of all changes staff dealing with future systems errors would face an impossible task. The systems staff may be called out at any hour to deal with problems and, particularly during night shifts, they could be left alone in the machine room for long periods of time. This could pose a serious breach of control, allowing them to make fraudulent changes to programs. As we will see in a later chapter this is an area that particularly worries auditors.

Amendments to systems   The systems staff will from time to time be asked to make improvements to the existing systems. This might be an improvement to provide better information than was previously available or an update necessary to keep a system such as payroll in line with changes in legislation.

Systems maintenance is time-consuming and increases with the growth in the number of systems within the firm (one major bank has 17 project teams who have to maintain over 200 different computer applications). It is claimed that some analysts spend over half their time on maintenance of existing systems.

Computer audit

Accounting firms that audit computerized accounting systems face particular problems and have had to adopt special audit tools and methods to deal with them. We will consider these in Chapter 14 but it should be noted at this stage that both external and internal auditors are users of the system and their needs and suggestions should be fed into the systems development process at an early stage.

Financial audit is only one aspect of the audit of computer systems. Many firms now use specialists within their internal audit function or their data processing department to test a number of factors not normally part of the role of external auditors. Such staff will look at:

1. the systems operations,
2. the standards of system documentation,
3. control.

The systems operations are examined to ascertain whether they are achieving the original aims detailed at the start of the project. This can be quite difficult, and computer consultants have commented that many of the major benefits that arise from applications, e.g. better information or increased control, are difficult to quantify. There are areas where the costs can be measured and compared and the one that most people think of first seems to be that of staff reductions. However, few firms seem to save much in staff costs when developing new systems. Where gains do eventually seem to arise is from the ability of the system to deal with extra work without the need for additional staff.

We have noted the importance of proper documentation and the need for in-house standards for documentation. The internal computer auditors will review the standard of systems documentation within the firm to ensure that these standards are being complied with both for new developments and for amendments.

The area of control merits increasing attention. The incidence of computer crime appears to be increasing annually and errors in computer systems can be very costly. The problem has been exacerbated by the increased use of distributed processing. This has brought a whole set of new problems in trying to safeguard the firm's information as communications transmissions have become vulnerable to interception for reasons ranging from hobby hacking to industrial espionage.

Case study

To illustrate the work described in this chapter we will consider part of the process of designing a sales order and accounting system for the confectionery company mentioned in the mini case in Chapter 3. We can consider this only in general terms, as in reality a great deal of detailed systems work would have to be carried out on this system and it would have to link into the rest of the firm's information system.

INTRODUCTION

The company has for many years produced tobacco products and sold them directly to retailers across the country through their own team of sales representatives. The sales staff fill in a standard order form, at the customer's premises, covering all 110 different product lines (Fig. 10.3). These are later sent on to the company's regional office and stores where the orders are made up and the necessary sales documentation produced.

COMMENTS ON THE CURRENT SYSTEM

Analysts studying the existing system and discussing the needs of user departments across the company have found the following problems.

As soon as the order forms are completed, sales staff move on to their next customer. They do not have time to complete their sales summaries so they tend to complete these in the evenings at their hotel and send them off to regional office twice weekly. The staff themselves require the summarized figures in order to check on their commission, and regional office requires them for control purposes. By the time returns arrive at regional office almost one working week has passed since the orders were taken.

Any delays with the post can therefore have serious effects on the company's business. A recent local dispute in the West country lasted several weeks and, although most orders were telephoned through, the firm did lose several orders and one good customer.

The company has experienced problems with the pricing of goods over the years. Originally the sales representatives did not have to enter price details on the orders; this was done at regional office. However, with the delay in forms reaching regions problems were occurring where goods had been sold on a special offer which had since lapsed. Regional staff were pricing from the most current price lists and customers were naturally annoyed when they checked their bills. Two years ago the order form was amended to allow the salesperson to input prices. Some representatives resent this and only enter the prices of those goods that are on special offer; others enter all prices.

SUGAR PLUM CONFECTIONERY LTD.

Arlington House,
Old Wharf,
Bristol,
BS2 3HD

Customer: *H. R. Kane*
Greenhill Stores
Uptown . Falkirk

SALES ORDER FORM

DATE *20ᵗʰ April '87*   SALESMAN *N° 9. D. REEVES.*

CODE	DETAIL	QUANTITY	CODE	DETAIL	QUANTITY
ABO1	T. mints (pack)	—	BB21	Sports gums (jar)	1
ABO2	T. Fruits (pack)	2	BB22	Hard gums (jar)	3
ABO3	H. Mints (pack)	4	BB23	Jelly tots (tube)	—
ABO4	Fruit drops (jar)	—	BB24	Acid drops (tube)	—
ABO5	little apples (jar)	2	BB25	Hot mints	1

Figure 10.3 Old sales order form

The market is a competitive one and the company has to adjust its current prices to keep up with its competitors. A great deal of time is involved in updating and issuing price lists and details of special offers; these have to be mailed to each sales representative, and once again any disturbance or delay in the mail leads to problems. Because of these factors the company at present changes its prices only once every fortnight. The sales director commented that he would like to be able to do this more frequently to respond to changes in competitors' prices.

Once the orders arrive at regional office they have to be typed on to an internal order form, which is used to notify stores, sales department, etc. The firm did experiment with special order forms allowing the representative to produce more copies and thus save time. However, the quality of the extra copies was very poor and led to a high volume of telephone queries and further delays.

This work introduces a further delay in fulfilling the order and, with the forms being received twice weekly, staff in the department face peaks and troughs in the typing work at various times in the week.

NEW SYSTEM DESIGN

The design team has suggested that a new sales ordering system should be designed as part of the new integrated management information system and their suggestions include the following.

Regional offices will run their own sales and stock accounting systems on local minicomputers, networked to the head office mainframe. These will produce all the sales order and processing documentation and will update stores records, customer accounts, etc., with information received from the sales representatives (Fig. 10.4).

To speed the data flow from sales staff in the field they recommend the use of small, hand-held microcomputers which can transfer data to the regional office each day. Their system would operate as follows.

Details currently included on the order form will be programmed onto these micros, one of which will be carried by each sales person. At the customer's premises the representative will first enter the customer number. The machine will then list the product lines, showing current price details and allowing the number ordered to be entered.

Details of the order will be stored in the machine memory. At the end of the day the micro will be connected to a telephone line and the data transmitted through to regional office. Thus all orders will arrive at regions at the end of the same day.

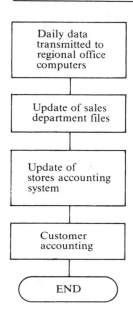

Figure 10.4 Integration of the sales order function with the overall system

Transmission completed, the regional office is then able to transmit its own data back down the line to the micro. Price changes will be transmitted and will amend the price table in the micro each day. Messages can also be sent and the summary figures from the previous day's orders sent to the appropriate salesperson. This will allow very flexible pricing policies, not possible with the previous system.

The responsibility for pricing will revert back to regional office, where the computer will price goods at the price offered to the customer that day.

The day's data will be processed overnight at regional office and the following morning stores staff will arrive to find copies of the day's orders awaiting them on their own printers. Sales staff will be able to access up-to-date data on orders received but these will not be printed out for them. They will have all the details they require on the VDUs.

INPUT DESIGN
There are no input forms in this part of the system as we have moved to a form of system where the data is captured at the point of sale. It is then transmitted directly to the regional computer for processing.

There is no need therefore to design an input form. The system will, however, have to include validation checks in order to reduce errors. Once the salesperson has left the customer's premises it is difficult to check on a query without bothering the customer. We must therefore ensure that the customer number is a valid one at the time of entry and that the number of any item ordered is reasonable. One way of checking the customer number is to have the computer transmit to the micro the numbers of all customers to be visited the following day. The machine could then check customer numbers input against these.

The regional office computer will also, later, check that the customer numbers agree with those on the master file. The system will also have built-in checks to detect corruption or loss of data in transmission.

FILE DESIGN

The question arises as to whether to use tape or disk files for this system. As data is processed overnight, the stock files at the regional office will probably be processed serially to save time. These details then have to be integrated with other parts of the system and may be used to answer queries. The firm is therefore intending to hold its main files on magnetic disks.

FILE FORMAT

The original data is stored in the battery-backed-up memory of the micro issued to each salesperson. It will be held here until the day's business is concluded. The amount of memory available is very limited. As most customers will purchase only a proportion of the product lines the machine will hold only the barest details of the transactions (see Fig. 10.5). This will include the date, the saleperson's number and the amounts of product lines actually ordered. Other details such as price do not have to be stored on this file as they can be picked up from the stock files at the regional office. The length of the record for each customer will depend on the number of lines ordered.

At the regional office a large stock master file will hold details of stock balances, product lines, etc. A pricing file will hold the current prices of all lines and will be updated regularly. These files will be run against the data file in order to:

1. produce dispatch notes, invoices, etc.,
2. update the stock records,
3. update the debtors ledger,
4. provide detailed sales analysis and sales returns for sales staff, etc.

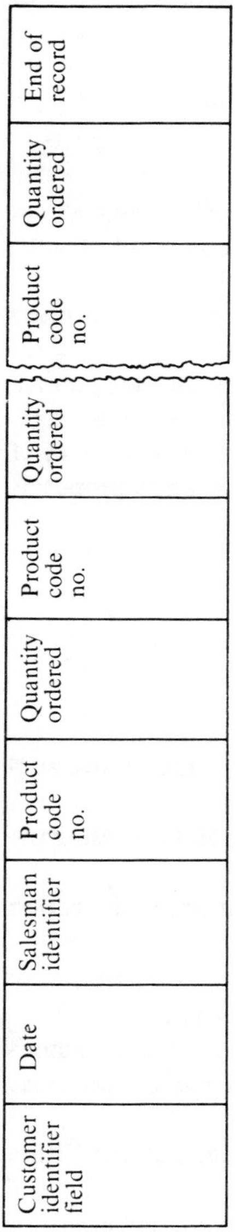

Customer identifier field	Date	Salesman identifier	Product code no.	Quantity ordered	Product code no.	Quantity ordered	Product code no.	Quantity ordered	End of record

Figure 10.5 File record structure diagram

Summary

1. Finding suitable applications software poses a problem for all computer users.
2. The choice lies between:
   - developing one's own systems (bespoke software), or
   - purchasing a software package.

   The current chapter addresses the former solution.
3. Systems analysts are charged with developing the new systems and managing projects. A large proportion of their time is also spent on supporting the firm's existing systems.
4. Accountants, because of their role as information providers, are often involved in the development of new financial systems.
5. Most organizations place the general computing policy under the control of a computer steering committee. This normally includes senior management staff, the DP manager, senior systems staff and representatives of the various user departments. Their role includes screening new proposals and monitoring progress of approved schemes.
6. The stages in developing a new system are:
   - the feasibility study,
   - present system investigation and analysis,
   - new system design,
   - system implementation,
   - system maintenance and audit.
7. A feasibility study assesses the probability that a scheme may prove successful. If not, it is not worth proceeding further.
8. The first task of the project team is that of investigating and analysing the current system. This normally involves:
   - inspecting records, including all formal documentation, organization charts, systems manuals, flow charts, etc.;
   - interviewing staff in order to reach agreement on the description of current practices before moving on to look at alternatives;
   - observing the department in operation, using either scientific methods of work study or techniques such as activity sampling where accuracy is not of paramount importance;
   - using questionnaires, which can prove useful in organizations with a number of branches, but must be used with great care.
9. The system analysed must be fully recorded either in narrative or, preferably, in flow chart format. It can then be evaluated to identify strengths and weaknesses.

10. The analysis of the existing system should identify:
    - the way it is organized, the work done and the responsibilities of staff;
    - all inputs and outputs, showing details of all forms in use, the way that information fields are used and the way the forms flow through the system;
    - volumes of work normally processed, and any problems, bottlenecks, details of slack and busy periods, etc.;
    - details of the user's present information needs together with perceived future needs from an improved system.
11. It is common practice to arrange a presentation to user departments to demonstrate the new forms, screen layouts, proposed reports and document flow. This gives users a chance to comment on the proposals and suggest improvements. Their comments will be taken into account before the new system is finalized.
12. Work involved at this stage falls into the following classifications:
    - *Design of input and output forms* Form design is important and can assist acceptance of the system by users and help reduce processing errors.
    - *File design* This involves planning both the file structure and the record formats. Poor file design can lead to the system failing to meet the requirements identified.
    - *Installation planning* This is an important area of work to which insufficient attention is often paid. As the system nears completion the pressures to get it running increase.
    - *System maintenance and audit* These continue after the system has been successfully implemented.

11

Acquiring a packaged system

Introduction
In the previous chapter we considered the work involved in the planning and development of a computerized system. Most of this work is performed by experienced data processing professionals and although the accountant may have an important role to play, as an important user, he or she will not normally take the leading role in this type of work. When it comes to acquiring a packaged system, however, the accountant is far more likely to take a leading role. In small and medium-sized firms there will normally be no specialist computer staff and the accountant, as the information manager, is often seen as the natural person to lead such a project. Very small firms will not even employ an accountant and may be unsure as to where they can obtain this type of assistance. A natural resource to turn to would be the accounting practice that prepares and possibly audits their annual accounts and, once again, accountants will be asked to take the lead in such projects.

In this chapter we will concentrate particularly on the small firm using or intending to use minicomputers or microcomputers and packaged software. We have noted already that large firms also make use of packages and of smaller computers but in such cases the data processing staff will normally act as advisers.

There are many examples of small firms that have turned to their accountants and have received good advice. One wonders, however, if this is generally the case. The professional training of accountants is designed to provide expertise in accounting and, through their auditing work, they gain a specialist knowledge of control aspects often across a number of different firms. These are important areas of knowledge for advising small firms intent on computerizing their businesses. The accountant's main weakness, however, lies in the area of computing itself. The professional syllabuses have included elements of computer studies for many years but these have been very descriptive by nature and only recently have they started to become more practical, and we still have a long way to go.

Accountants employed in industry and commerce had little choice but to take on this type of work when asked by their employers or in order to solve problems in their own workplaces. In the profession, things were not so clear cut. Some firms saw computers as a way of increasing their fee income and range of services and have provided such advice over a number of years. The large accounting firms in particular have become a major force in this market and even very small practising firms have grouped together to provide such advice to their clients. Despite this many firms have still failed to take up the challenge and either do not offer such advice or at least fail to inform clients that they do so, and as a result many small clients have turned to other sources for advice. This may have been a loss to both the client and the accountant. The practice will have lost both income and the chance to improve client loyalty while the client may have been forced to rely on sales staff for advice which is often biased and pays little attention to the particular needs of their firm.

In this chapter we consider the work at each of the main stages in identifying and acquiring a packaged solution to a business problem.

The main stages in acquiring a package

The decision to computerize a particular aspect of a firm's business may arise for a number of reasons. For example, they may be unable to process the work in reasonable time, or may require information which is not available at a reasonable cost using their present system. The firm may already have a computer or may be considering the purchase of computer equipment specially to run this software, when selected. As we are dealing with systems that have already been written, certain details such as file design will not be relevant, having been decided when the system was written. The emphasis in this type of work is on the data that can be handled and the information possible from such systems. Despite this, much of the approach outlined in Chapter 10 can assist the firm seeking to obtain a package suited to their particular requirements. Figure 11.1 illustrates the main stages which will be considered in more detail below.

STAGE 1: IDENTIFYING THE FIRM'S REQUIREMENTS
The purchase of a ready-written package in such firms will normally save development and testing work, which are very costly and time-consuming. However, the buyer must realize that many areas of work such as screen design, file design, etc., will have been finalized by the designers and the user will be unable to change them to fit different requirements.

The software will be purchased to solve a particular set of business problems and, as before, it is important that time be allocated to identify and explain those problems and ascertain the needs of the staff who will use the system.

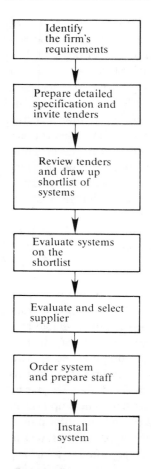

Figure 11.1 Stages in acquiring a package

This may seem obvious but many firms have bought packages only to find that they have special needs which that particular software cannot provide for. In other cases one member of staff such as an accountant has taken on his own back the task of finding the software and then expected colleagues to alter their work to fit into the new system. No single user, however important, has a monopoly on knowledge or ideas and it is vital to ensure that all users are able to contribute towards the decision-making process. Probably the best way to do this is to adopt part of the approach used in systems development. A small computer steering group can be set up to plan and monitor the scheme. Once again this will contain senior staff, both to keep them informed and to lend authority to the work of the group.

As previously mentioned, the accountant and accounting staff are likely to be actively involved if there are no specialist computer staff. If they are not felt to have the necessary time or knowlege, consultants will normally be hired to help the firm work through the necessary stages and to advise the working group. A number of private consultants now offer their services in this area. The firm should ensure that the one they use is a general consultant and is not in fact tied to one particular software supplier. This problem of obtaining independent advice prompted the National Computing Centre to set up a network of microsystems centres around the country at which clients can obtain independent advice at a reasonable cost and where they are able to try out various machines and software systems, free of commercial pressures. Some independent consultants have even started a scheme of computer matching using their own databases of machines and software. The client fills in a questionnaire identifying his or her particular needs and this is then input to the computer which will produce a list of the products and suppliers that appear to meet these needs.

The steering group will discuss the project with the various user staff and attempt to identify both the problems and the advantages of the present system, present and likely future information needs, etc. At the end of their enquiries they will assess their findings and decide whether or not a computerized system offers the best solution. Too many groups assume from the start that this is the case and then proceed to try to justify this assumption. In practice, groups often find that their systems have grown in a piecemeal way over several years and only when problems arise and the system fails do they seek to ascertain whether there is a better way. When the system is analysed by the steering group they often find that what at first appeared to be a major problem can be solved by reorganizing the present manual system to deal with the new conditions.

Where it appears that a computer will be needed for the first time, the steering group will eventually have to produce a list of the equipment to be acquired. Many groups make the error of treating this as their primary task, but this approach is not good as it in effect tackles the problem the wrong way around. The first priority must be to define the firm's problems and needs— only then can they start to see what they need. At this stage they should not be concerned with detailed considerations of the type of machine; it is far too early for that. They cannot fully ignore the hardware side but the questions that arise should be far more general ones such as whether the firm will need multi-access to the system or if a stand-alone machine is likely to suffice. In considering these points they will need to look to likely future expansion as well as current needs.

They must ascertain the volume and type of inputs and outputs to the system, the number of live records held on file and any non-standard requirements they may have, e.g. special invoices for particular customers. All these points will need to be raised at a later stage when they seek to assess the packages that are offered by various suppliers.

When this stage is complete they are ready to move on to the preparation of a detailed specification document which will summarize the work they have done and will be sent to possible suppliers.

STAGE 2: THE SPECIFICATION DOCUMENT

As with any important purchasing transaction the firm will invite various suppliers to tender on price, quality and delivery. This process should also be followed when seeking suitable software. However, in this case price will be only one of the factors involved and more weight may be allocated to the others. The firm will not only try to ascertain the suitability of the software but also the reliability and competence of the supplier. Some suppliers will hardly bother to reply, sending standard details of the products they offer and letting the customer sort out the details, while others may contact the firm asking further questions of their own. This stage can therefore provide a guide to the degree of commitment and help that may be expected from the supplier later.

The document they send out will include the following information:

(a) A brief outline of the firm is needed, explaining its structure, e.g. number of branches, the business it does. In this section they will aim to provide general details that may affect the type of package chosen. It can be difficult at this stage to find a reasonable balance between brevity and the amount of detail needed to assess the problem.
(b) A short description of the work areas to be computerized should be provided. It is useful to outline briefly how these are handled at present.
(c) Clear details of the volumes of input, output and storage required to run the system should be provided. These allow the supplier to estimate which level of system the customer is seeking and are very important. It is wise also at this stage to include an estimate of the level of growth that may be expected over the next few years as the firm will not wish to acquire a package that they are likely to grow out of very soon.
(d) If the firm already owns hardware and plans to run the new package on this, it should provide details and make this restriction clear at this stage.

(e) Details of any features they particularly require should be set out. For example they may insist that files are able to provide up-to-the-minute information throughout the day. Any non-standard requirements such as the invoicing requirements above should also be stressed in this document.

(f) As future users of the system, the firm's auditors should have been consulted and will probably have stressed their needs for certain controls or audit trail facilities. These control requirements should also be listed in the document as they too will influence the choice of package.

The specification will be sent out to a number of dealers who appear competent to supply such systems. They should be asked to reply by a certain date so that the review process can commence. It is quite common for several firms not to reply and if nothing is heard from firms that are thought to be particularly good it is advisable to telephone and speak to a senior member of staff, drawing the document to their attention.

STAGE 3: REVIEWING THE QUOTATIONS
Once all the quotations are in, the working group will have to work through them and produce a shortlist of suppliers who will then be approached and asked to demonstrate their product. At this review stage there are a number of things that will need to be considered.

Obviously the group will want to ascertain what importance has been attached to the queries raised in their document and what replies have resulted. Some firms will have specifically answered these while others will have paid scant attention to them.

The need to estimate future growth was mentioned above. Some suppliers will point out the ways in which their product can be adapted as the work increases. Most accounting modules today can be integrated with other modules by the same supplier to provided an integrated system. While most suppliers will no doubt stress this facility, if this type of development is likely to occur the steering group should, at this stage, evaluate the other modules that bolt on to form a full system. Having committed themselves to one product they do not want to find later that the other modules when purchased do not offer the sort of facilities they require.

Some software will allow the firm to run several sets of data under the same programs and this is very useful to a firm intending to open branches or create a divisional structure.

The task of assessing the actual product can be quite difficult. There are no basic standards to which accounting software must comply and although there have been attempts to create such standards, to date they have not been successful. There is currently a scheme for professional bodies to sell a 'seal of approval' to software developers if their product passes certain tests. In addition a number of guides such as that produced by the information technology committee of the English Institute may prove useful to the accountant in this area.

The group will certainly need to look at the way the products are claimed to deal with the needs identified in the original specification and it is likely that a large proportion of products can be ruled out at this stage. Eventually the steering group must arrive at a shortlist of two or three products that they wish to evaluate in detail.

STAGE 4: EVALUATING THE SYSTEMS SHORTLISTED

The group will now have to contact the suppliers of shortlisted software, asking them to demonstrate their product and provide any further information required. In most cases this will involve a demonstration by the supplier at his premises. It is vital that the group meets and identifies beforehand what it wishes to gain from any such demonstration; otherwise they will be in the hands of the salesperson and are likely to be shown the aspects he or she knows and normally demonstrates. They will be very unlikely to see any of the weak points and unless they ask may not see how it tackles their particular problems. Points to watch include the following.

Ask to see the system set up and running with some of the firm's own data. If this is not done, the group will see the supplier's own data run on files that are already set up. This may well hide a number of problems. For example, certain products may require the use of both their own and the machine's operating systems to set up disks for the files.

The group should ask to be shown the facilities it has identified as being important to it. The response to such requests can prove interesting, as sales staff are frequently not acquainted with these aspects of the system. To demonstrate these the dealer may need to call on other support staff and the way this is handled may give the customer some insight into how well the dealer will be able to give support, should problems arise later.

The capacity of the system to handle the firm's work is vital and often rules out a number of products. The firm will need to discuss this with the supplier and obtain assurances that it is able to cope and that the required response times will be achieved.

The dealer should be able to give some idea of the size of the user base, i.e. the number of copies currently sold. Most dealers will also provide customers with the names of local users who are willing to be approached and who will give their opinions on the system in use.

It is at this stage that the steering group will need to become interested in the detailed hardware requirements. They will now have seen one or more systems that can handle their work and they will need to acquire equipment that is capable of running these. With the adoption of standard operating systems such as MS-DOS and the move to IBM-type microcomputers the choice of machine is normally far less important than it was in the past. The purchaser will therefore seek a machine that is able to run the chosen software and that can be expanded to meet future needs.

Time can be well spent reviewing the documentation that accompanies the package when supplied. It should be very detailed but clearly written so that staff can set up and run the system. It will also give details of some of the particular system features the steering group wishes to see demonstrated. Today an increasing number of programs include on-screen help facilities which reduce the need to rely on the written manual, and the firm will be particularly interested in ascertaining how user-friendly each package is. Many systems also include a tutorial disk to help staff become acquainted with aspects of the system.

Most systems today include some form of report-generating facility, allowing users to generate a range of reports to suit their business. The group members should ask to see this used to set up a report at the demonstration as they will wish to assess how easy it is in use and the degree of flexibility offered in this important area.

The importance of control was stressed above, and the steering group will wish to assess the controls in action. For example, with good packages the user is made to create audit trail reports and backup disks before the system can be closed down at the end of a period. Some systems take the user through this in a very simple manner while others assume a level of knowledge that many users may not have.

These demonstrations are time-consuming but they are an important part of the procedure. The microsystems centres mentioned previously play a very useful role here as they allow users at a very low cost to gain experience of particular packages away from the pressures of a sales showroom, using their own data in the test.

The end result of this work should be a better understanding of the benefits and weaknesses of each system on offer. This should have reduced the list of software to just one or two packages and the next important stage is to evaluate the dealer from whom the system will be purchased.

STAGE 5: EVALUATING THE SUPPLIER

Once the package is purchased it must be installed and made to work in the firm's own application. In some cases this is relatively painless while in others a number of problems can arise. Where can the customer then turn for help? Consultancy fees are high and help may be required at short notice when a firm's accounting system is on stop. The dealer who supplied the system is normally the first line of assistance; he or she supplied it, has staff trained in it and worked through the original specification and advised it. The role of the supplier is therefore very important and this is why we have referred so often to the supplier in the preceding sections.

The market for general business software today is highly competitive and many packages can be purchased by mail order at discounted prices. This has placed great pressure on the local dealers who try to provide a high level of support to their customers. It is noticeable that after a free market policy for several years an increasing number of software houses are returning to selling their business packages through registered dealers who must undertake to support the client.

The two main areas in which people look to their dealers for support are training and system maintenance. Some dealers will include a certain amount of basic training in with the cost of a major package. However, the competition at the level of microcomputer-based packages has meant that this is increasingly an extra that must be paid for. We will discuss training in more detail at the next stage.

Systems maintenance is also an area that is increasingly being charged for over and above the price of the package. With reduced profit margins on the product, dealers increasingly find it uneconomical to spend time reviewing a user's needs before purchase and then in holding his or her hand afterwards. As a result many offer several levels of support with an appropriate charge for each. The amount charged will cover the issue of updates to the programs, e.g. to reflect tax changes, and the offer of assistance with the customer's problems.

The steering group will need to ascertain what customer support is offered with the product and what is available at an additional charge. It is therefore vital that they try at this stage to satisfy themselves as to the competence and reliability of the dealer. It was suggested above that the group contact existing users of the product; this could also provide a chance to discuss the level of service that other users have received from the supplier.

The dealer must be made to set out clearly what services are being offered in any agreement. This could range from the number of a telephone hotline (which may be constantly engaged) through to on-site assistance with implementation and other problems. The dealer's experience with the package is vital and the steering group should not hesitate to ask how many installations they have handled, the size and experience of the staff and the services they offer. A good supplier hardly needs to be pressed on these points but is only too keen to show prospective clients around and stress the professionalism of the staff.

If an agreement is concluded for the dealer to maintain software or hardware on site, the contract normally stipulates the maximum acceptable response time. For example, a dealer will normally charge more for a short response time (e.g. the same working day) than for an agreement with a longer permitted response time. It is a good idea to ascertain where the support staff are based, as it is normally better if they operate from a local office.

If an efficient supplier is chosen, a good working relationship should last for many years as the supplier will get to know the client's business and be able to help and advise on upgrading the systems if and when this is required.

STAGE 6: IMPLEMENTING THE SYSTEM

We saw in Chapter 10 that it is vital to plan the implementation of the scheme well before the software and hardware arrive. Much of what was covered there is also applicable here. For example, it will be necessary to start certain jobs before either software or hardware arrives. Computer supplies such as printing paper, forms, floppy disks, etc., will have to be ordered and any necessary cabling or ducting will need to be installed for the equipment.

New coding systems will be required to operate accounting systems and this can involve a great deal of work covering most sections of the firm. It can lead to major delays if work of this nature is not tackled in advance of delivery.

So far we have said a great deal about both hardware and software but we have not mentioned the other important resource, people. The firm will have to identify which staff are to be involved in running the new system and arrange suitable training for them. This frequently poses more of a problem for small firms who have no specialist computer staff. There are several ways of organizing training:

1. self-training,
2. learning from existing operatives,
3. external training courses.

Self-training seems popular with far too many organizations these days. Staff are given the machine and systems manuals and expected to learn for themselves. This often appears attractive as there is apparently no monetary cost to the firm. However, the standard of most hardware manuals and the complexity of many of the software systems currently available mean that all but the most committed of staff will soon be totally demotivated by this approach, particularly if they are also expected to carry out their normal work at the same time. This approach can lead to high staff turnover and late commissioning of systems and in the long run can prove very costly to the firm. It can also develop in the staff concerned a feeling that they had to learn the hard way and do not therefore see why they should pass on this hard-gained knowledge to others.

Where a firm already has a computer system up and running, new staff can learn from the existing operatives. This does reduce costs but it can slow down the speed of working while instruction takes place. The trainee operator will see only the parts of the system that the existing operator has mastered, complete with any bad habits, and this form of training may not therefore be fully effective. There is also the problem that such on-the-job training often leads to a large number of interruptions.

The ideal way of training operators is to send them on a proper course away from the workplace. This will show them a wider view of the software without interruptions and, despite the cost of such courses, may prove cheaper and more effective in the long run. These courses are run by a variety of firms; software suppliers and in recent years many colleges have started to offer these services on a commercial basis.

A further difficulty can arise in choosing who to send for such training. Obviously staff who will be responsible for the day-to-day operation of the system need to be trained but if they move on to another firm there could well be no one else able to take over the work until new staff are recruited. It may therefore be better to train extra staff or at least to allow others to gain experience from the trained operators, supplementing this with formal training if and when they take over the work.

As with larger systems there is the problem of creating the original files and transferring data to them. The solutions used are similar to those listed in Chapter 10. Once again parallel running will be needed and the problems posed are the same as in the larger firm; however, the smaller number of staff available may make these far more acute.

The steering group must recognize that the new computer package must link with the rest of the firm's system, much of which may still be maintained manually. It may be necessary therefore to design new input forms, and prepare internal manuals and guidelines, e.g. on file retention, security aspects and time schedules.

Once the system arrives the staff and equipment should be ready to start file creation work. A detailed timetable for installation, testing and adoption should be prepared by the working group, the members of which will be responsible for monitoring its progress.

It can be seen therefore that although the system is actually written and tested by an independent supplier the purchaser still has a great deal of systems work to perform. If all goes well the result should be a system capable of meeting the firm's detailed requirements for many years.

Summary

1. This chapter considers the work involved in the acquisition of a packaged solution to the firm's data processing problems. While certain aspects of the design work are outside the control of the user firm, they still have to perform much of the work described in Chapter 10.
2. The stages involved were identified as:
   - identifying the firm's requirements,
   - preparing a detailed specification,
   - obtaining and reviewing quotations from suppliers,
   - evaluating the most likely systems,
   - evaluating the supplier,
   - ordering and installing the system.
3. If the firm is to acquire a package that is capable of serving their needs for a number of years, time must be spent documenting and specifying those needs. A steering group is normally set up to perform this work. The accountant and accounting staff are likely to be involved with this work and outside consultants may be employed to advise the group.

   Their findings are summarized in a specification document showing what they require from any proposed system.
4. The specification is sent to a number of suppliers who are asked to respond with suggested systems and tender for their supply.
5. Once the quotations are reviewed a shortlist of packages is produced and these are then evaluated at demonstrations and through further discussions. At this stage the firm will become affected by software decisions as equipment must be able to run the chosen package.
6. The post-delivery role of the supplier can be important in many cases. Part of the process involves assessing that organization's capability and agreeing the level of support that will be offered.
7. Implementation of the system must be planned and managed carefully. Much the same problems are faced here as were described in Chapter 10. Small firms do, however, face special problems in training and implementation due to the small number of staff available.

Part 5

Control aspects and audit

Part 3

12

Security, privacy and fraud

Introduction

For centuries business and government organizations have collected data on employees, customers and suppliers, and there has always been the risk that criminals might break in and steal or damage these records. Why then do we hear so much discussion about data security, privacy and fraud now that such records are stored in computerized systems? The advent of computers has highlighted a number of problems which existed with manual systems but which are now far more serious given the power of electronic systems.

The nature of what is stored has changed. When data is stored in a manual system it is bulky, and time and effort are required to convert it into useful information. Computers, however, hold their data in far more compact form and if illegal access can be gained far more useful information can be extracted. Today's thief may also operate in a very different manner. No longer does the businessman turn up in the morning to find a door forced open and papers strewn over the floor. Today he may not even know that information has been extracted from his system; it is possible to pick up and interpret signals from a VDU many yards away and if that fails there is always the latest scourge, the 'hacker'. For years business users have paid out increasing sums of money to acquire ever better locks to keep their machines safe inside their hi-tech fortresses, yet now those same systems are prey to intruders who gain entry via the telephone lines (and some of them are still at school!).

We have seen how integrated systems bring together the work of several departments. Unless this is carefully planned, firms may see a weakening of their security systems as an increasing proportion of the work comes under the control of a small group of specialist staff, with very little direct supervision of their work by others. This can provide far more opportunities for fraud or may mean that errors are not picked up. In this section of the book many references will be made to fraud in computerized systems. It should be stressed, however, that internal control in all types of accounting systems exists to combat errors as well as fraud. In fact the average business is likely to lose more through errors and carelessness than through fraud.

Once firms computerize their systems they come to rely very heavily on the machine and alter their organization and way of working to reflect this. For example, if most large firms were suddenly deprived of their systems they would be hard put to prepare their payroll manually in the necessary time. Add to this the fact that much of the firm's data is now centralized on the computer, and it can be seen that large organizations are highly vulnerable to any accident affecting their systems. Three areas that have posed particular problems to computer users in recent years are those of computer fraud, general security and privacy. We shall now consider each in more detail.

Computer fraud

The traditional British hobby of writing to the *Times* claiming to have heard the first cuckoo seems to have been superseded, at least in the accounting press. Learned researchers these days seem to vie with each other to write in claiming to have estimated the total amounts lost through computer fraud. The authors have seen figures from £145m through £300m up to £1500m per annum printed as estimates of the annual loss world-wide from general frauds. The truth is that no one actually knows, and it is impossible to measure the figure as a great deal of fraud goes unreported, particularly in the UK. Some of the causes of this are the following.

In the UK there is no legal responsibility on firms discovering fraud to report it to the police, while in some other countries such as the USA this must be done. However, even in the USA the FBI have claimed that only one in every 22 000 people who use computers for criminal purposes is prosecuted. It certainly appears that much of the fraud detected in the UK is never reported. Add to this the frauds that must go undetected and the difficulties of estimating the total losses can be imagined. Apparently many firms do not report the fact that they have been defrauded because the investigation that follows is costly and time-consuming. Documentary evidence going back many years is often needed, and a detailed investigation is needed to calculate the extent of the fraud.

Even when the police have prepared a case there is a high possibility that they will fail to gain a conviction. The onus of proof lies with the prosecution who must prove beyond doubt the guilt of the accused, not just that a crime was committed. The court will not accept as evidence items generated by the computer, but requires that this evidence be corroborated by staff of the firm. The very nature of the crime means that such corroboration is hard to produce. One wonders also whether the injured party feels the penalty imposed on the miscreant will be worth the effort. Early in 1986 the press reported the conviction at the Old Bailey of a female bank clerk who raised suspicions when she was seen driving a Range Rover and other vehicles which were well outside the range of her income. Enquiries showed she had used the bank's computer to steal almost £280 000 in two years; her penalty—two years imprisonment, one of them suspended. It is interesting to note that she defrauded an American bank (otherwise it is highly unlikely that the case would have come to court).

Fraud cases are tried by a jury and it is sometimes claimed that many jurors are unable to follow complex fraud evidence. The defence is also allowed to challenge three members of the jury for each defendant, a right which can be abused. It is claimed that one tactic of the defence is to try to confuse some jurors by calling for large amounts of detailed written evidence which may not be justified by the case.

These problems apply to all fraud not just to computer fraud and as a result a committee under Lord Roskill was asked to consider how the process could be improved without threatening personal liberty and justice. They reported in the first half of 1986 and made a number of suggestions. They wanted to remove the right to challenge jurors but to retain the jury in all but complex fraud cases. In the latter cases they suggested the use of a tribunal consisting of the judge and two lay persons selected at random from a panel of experienced persons. Early reactions from certain parts of the legal profession accused accountants and computer specialists of supporting these proposals purely for their own gain and argued that they did not want to trust justice to so-called experts.

This topic will no doubt prove to be a problem for some time as lawyers try to find a way of balancing the rights of individuals with the need to convict and deter criminals. Surely, however, something has to be done. We live in a society where the level of burglary has led to the creation of neighbourhood watch groups and larger numbers of police on the streets. Yet the overall annual value of fraud is thought to exceed the total of burglary plus car theft. However, the attitude to this white colour crime is totally different and another of the Roskill committee's suggestions was that in future fraud jurors should have sufficient knowledge of the English language to be able to read and write using it!

A high proportion of businesses attacked by computer fraud are in the banking and financial services sector and the amounts involved are often very large, possibly involving the transfer of funds across international frontiers. The firms involved, being in a position where reliability and trust are very important to their public image, are often very reticent to prosecute. Hence the comment above concerning the American bank; if their own law had not required it one wonders whether they would have been willing to have their name publicized in that way. Some such institutions have argued that another reason for not wanting to disclose such frauds is the fear that the amounts involved and the degree of public interest in this type of crime may lead to cases of 'copycat' fraud.

There may be some validity in the latter argument, as people who can cheat the computer are often seen as some form of modern-day Robin Hood. We may well chuckle when we see in our morning paper that fake runners entered the 1986 London marathon wearing teeshirts carrying very good fake bar codes taken off food packets. The computer system read the numbers in and realized they were not genuine but the results for genuine runners were delayed by several hours. It may still seem relatively harmless to read of the young man in London who used his home computer to hack into Prestel and send a bunch of flowers to his girlfriend. He was the first hacker successfully prosecuted in this country and it cost him a fine of £50 under the Forgery and Counterfeiting Act. If we remember that systems like Prestel are being used to develop home banking systems that will give access to people's personal funds (albeit with different controls), we start to see this type of activity in a far different light.

We certainly have a situation at present where the perpetrators of very large frauds are often not prosecuted, and at least one has moved on to offer his services as a computer security consultant on the basis of his experience.

It can be seen therefore that white collar crime is viewed quite differently from traditional crime and, although no true measure of the amounts involved is available, many authorities fear that computer fraud in particular is a growth industry. As a result the information technology group of the ICAEW (The Institute of Chartered Accountants in England and Wales) has set up a working party to look at the main areas threatened, and to advise on how to prevent fraud. Surprisingly, however, a recent survey carried out by one of the larger accounting firms found that most respondent companies did not greatly fear this type of crime. Even when approached a second time and questioned specifically on this point few rated it as a major worry.

A number of surveys have been carried out on computer frauds, and they suggest that a high proportion of the cases found are really traditional types of fraud but with the computer being used to help cover it up. For example, fraudsters have manipulated input such as expenses claims for many years. If they do this with a computerized system does this suddenly become a computer fraud? This type of crime appears to be very common still but computers can be made to help cover it up, e.g. by printing out different figures, leaving the ribbon out of printers, etc.

The number of cases where the computer itself has been made to perform the fraud seems relatively small, but such crimes are often cheeky and certainly catch the attention of the media. Once again their treatment of the subject at times hardly makes it appear as the crime it really is. The media have coined colloquial names for the various types of fraud including the following.

Salami fraud

'Salami frauds' refer to those cases where a very small amount of money is misappropriated from each transaction. This sum might be less than 1p but as it is repeated on each of the transactions processed it can provide quite a large return for the originator. The fact that the individual amounts involved are so small means that they are less likely to be detected by casual observation and should anyone query them the plausible explanation is to say that they are rounding adjustments—because while money figures are presented to two decimal places computers work to many more and must round off the figures. The perpetrators normally transfer these small slices into other accounts under their own control against which they can draw money.

The Trojan horse approach

One way a programmer may defraud a business is to place a special section in the program which will be run only in certain cases, e.g. when his name appears on a document, or when a very large value transaction occurs. Apart from these special occasions the programs will appear to operate normally. However, the offending section lies there unused awaiting its next chance. Not surprisingly the press have labelled this a Trojan horse approach and it can be very hard to detect once the system is up and running.

Hacking

Most people today have heard of the problem referred to in the press as 'hacking' which started among US home computer owners and students. At first it was seen as an intellectual challenge to break into computer systems by detecting the access telephone numbers and the passwords that protect the system. Those hackers frequently looked around inside the host system they had attacked and often left electronic graffiti, i.e. messages showing they had hacked the system. This could prove a costly nuisance as it damaged certain records and involved the host firm having to work back and recreate its files. At first the hackers were seen as harmless and labelled as 'whizz kids' by the press. In the USA one professor awarded an A grade to a student for achieving it. However, it was soon realized that hacking could be used to perpetrate fraud and this has now taken on a different aspect. Claims were made that hackers could break into the DVLC computers at Swansea and would remove drivers' penalty points for a fixed fee per point, though this has been denied by the centre. Other hackers have been convicted of penetrating the Prestel system and are said to have left a message in the Duke of Edinburgh's private mailbox.

Time bombing

Another problem has been referred to as 'time bombing'. Here a programmer inserts a piece of code into a system which will be operated in the distant future only if a defined event occurs. The standard example given is of a payroll system where the code is designed to destroy the master file if a record is processed showing that the programmer involved has been dismissed. Cases have been reported of programmers inserting such bombs and after leaving the firm, trying to extort money on the threat of activating it.

Time bombing has actually been used as a protective device in some commercial programs which are hired out rather than sold. The idea was that the user would, on payment of his annual fee, be given a code to insert, but if this was not done the system would flash several warnings before destroying the customer's data and ceasing to work. A case was reported in the computing press of one such software firm that went into liquidation owing a great deal of money. To avoid pressure and publicity the owner went into hiding. In the meantime, users across the country were asking the authorities to help trace him as their machines were flashing up warning messages and threatening to destroy their systems.

Whole books could probably be written about computer fraud but in a text such as this we can only briefly touch upon the problems involved. In the case of accounting applications it has always been part of the accountant's role to develop control systems. Once again it should be stressed that accounting control systems are created to prevent both errors and frauds, and though frauds hit the headlines, errors are probably a far greater problem. It is also interesting to note when reading the reported cases of fraud how frequently these could have been prevented by the proper application of basic accounting controls.

Computer security

We noted above how firms come to rely increasingly upon their computers and may therefore be highly vulnerable if any major disaster deprives them of the machine's services or if they lose their data. To combat this threat, managers need to identify the risks that face them and plan in advance how these may be overcome. Their computer security plan should cover a wide range of possibilities, trying to estimate the possible risks and their likely results. From this they are able to look at various remedies and identify those which are commercially viable given their own particular level of risk. The areas they need to consider include the following.

PHYSICAL LOCATION AND ACCESS
Computers are delicate and valuable pieces of equipment and must be protected from damage. Some machines may require a special environment, e.g. air conditioning and protection against smoke and fire.

About 10–20 years ago firms liked to inform the public that they had purchased computers, and early machines were often installed in glass-sided viewing rooms where the public could view them. This is far less common today as businesses have come to recognize their computers' vulnerability and the need to avoid any form of interference with them. The reader might wonder just who would interfere with a firm's computers. Apparently a case is reported in the USA of a member of the public who attempted to shoot a computer with a hand gun, and in Europe several terrorist groups have attacked computer centres and claim that this is a useful way of achieving part of their objectives. The power to disrupt an organization by removing its computers was shown during the industrial action by British civil servants. The blacking of work by computer staff led to problems that were greatly out of proportion to the number of people or the action involved and in at least one establishment attempts by other staff to operate the equipment led to some embarrassing failures.

The location and design of the computer centre has also taken on a new importance in recent years. For example, with increased problems of vandalism, access for night staff, etc., the traditional city centre location may need to be reviewed and heavy security measures may be required to reduce access, limiting it to authorized persons. Inner city locations may require heavy security measures.

Companies must also be aware of any local factors that might lead to problems later. For example firms in the Los Angeles area of the USA know that the San Andreas fault could create problems for them, even though their own building may have been designed to resist earth movements. Any problems in that area could affect their power to communicate with other branches of the company. Within buildings computer systems are very rarely sited below ground level unless special precautions are taken to avoid possible damage from natural flooding or from flooding resulting from fire-fighting activity on a higher floor.

Access to computer equipment is normally restricted only to those staff whose duty it is to operate the machine. They are normally given special passes and electronic keys which allow them access to the computer room, and if systems programmers or others need access, e.g. to deal with system queries, special permission is required. In large computer-based firms all staff and visitors may be required to carry photographic passes. Staff passes frequently carry an electronic code to open certain locks and allow them access only to the area they work in and to communal areas such as a staff lounge or canteen. All visitors in such buildings will have to be escorted by an employee before they are physically able to pass through the building.

Computers are totally reliant on electric power and unless special equipment is used they will be susceptible to power cuts, fluctuations in voltage, etc. Sophisticated control equipment is normally used in large installations to sense power fluctuations and compensate for them or switch in alternative power supplies.

SECURITY OF DATA

The new Data Protection Act places upon firms a responsibility to safeguard personal data and ensure that it is not wrongfully disclosed. An organization may be fined and subject to damages unless it can prove that it took reasonable care to safeguard such information. This will require a whole range of controls to prevent illegal access and many organizations are designating someone as data protection officer to monitor this. Some of these controls will be detailed in Chapter 13.

BACKUP AND MAINTENANCE

Despite taking precautions, problems mentioned above could result in part or all of the system being out of use at some time. A good management team will identify the range of problems that could occur and assess for each of them the degree of risk that is acceptable. For example, they may be able to accept the full system being out of commission for up to three days but no longer, while problems with particular peripherals might be less sensitive and could last for a longer period without causing major problems.

The next stage is to plan the action needed to reduce the problems within these limits. The firm will need to look at maintenance contracts and arrange for a level of cover offering the required response rate. With large machines engineers will attend to deal with the fault, and they may promise attendance within 24 hours or less. With microcomputers maintenance firms do offer similar deals but they may need to take the machine away for repair.

In cases where repairs will take some time the firm needs to plan some form of backup while the system is out of commission. Some insurers who cover large mainframe systems have set up special secret centres with backup machines that can handle client data in the case of total collapse. Other companies may be able to agree reciprocal support with another user of the same machine. With popular makes of microcomputer it may be possible to borrow a replacement machine from the repair firm, or to lease one for short periods from specialist hire firms.

Data protection and privacy

In the late 1960s a friend of the authors was billed by a finance house for a further instalment of a hire purchase contract which he had paid off. The finance company threatened all sorts of dire legal consequences until the customer produced documents proving that they were in error, after which a grudging apology was offered. The fault lay totally with the finance company and their poor accounting system. However, the customer was very concerned because at that time people were unsure where credit rating agencies obtained their credit rating information on individuals. It was known that finance companies frequently passed on lists of people who they believed had failed to pay them money, and he was unsure as to whether this incident of alleged failure to pay had been passed on and would prevent him obtaining credit at a later date. Pursuing the matter with the finance company was not very helpful as at that time they were not very keen to discuss this aspect of their work. He had paid his bill before it was due, the company had made the error, yet he was left wondering what would happen in the future.

At that time similar doubts were being raised by many people across the country and a general debate started about data protection and privacy. People were particularly concerned about the following:

1. *Privacy* The customer in our case had a private agreement with the hire purchase company and passed on to them private details of his income, outgoings, etc. Did they have any right, therefore, to pass this on to another user without obtaining that customer's permission, especially to a firm that made a living from collecting such personal data?

   Many people argued that they did not have such a right. However, others argued that the business community in general should have a right to obtain such details because if businesses could not obtain details of non-payers they would make losses which would be passed on to other consumers in the form of higher prices.

2. *Data protection* The data held by the credit agency would affect a person's chances of obtaining goods and could cause a great deal of trouble. Should the subject therefore have the right to find out exactly who held files on him or her; be able to view their content; be assured that such information was not used improperly; and have the right to have incorrect information amended?

In the early days therefore interest in data protection and privacy in this country was focused mainly on private computer systems. However, as the debate developed people became aware of how much personal data was held on them by various government information systems. This was not a new development, as data had been held by such bodies for many years. The fact that such data was now held on computers was the main cause of the concern.

If such computers could be linked, it would be possible to collate data in a way not previously possible and the result could have adverse effects on personal privacy. With this in mind attention turned towards government rather than private systems and a great deal of concern was shown on the ability of government departments, security agencies, etc., to tap into other computers and collect personal data from them.

By now the reader will appreciate that to match data a key field is required which allows links to be made between the two sets of records. This key must be unique or confusion and misinformation will result. They could not, for example, match on names, as there is much duplication in this area. Probably the nearest thing we have to a unique key is the national insurance number, which is allocated to most employees, or the national health number allocated to every citizen. However, these items are not stored on all computer applications. Some other European countries allocate every person a unique citizen number which is used for social services, education, crime prevention, etc. The use of such a code would allow a fast search to be made on a person across many computer systems. Some civil rights groups argue that this would be a severe infringement of civil liberties, but this is countered in the countries using it by the argument that it is quite the opposite. They claim that this personal identifier allows the individual to prove his identity and claim the rights of citizenship.

Various groups in this country have raised the spectre of more widespread links between state computer systems in the UK, but we are constantly assured that it does not and cannot happen here. In the light of this it is surprising to note that an article in the accounting press in May 1986 alerted some Members of Parliament to a clause in a bill which would have allowed

DHSS officers to obtain information concerning small traders on demand from the Inland Revenue, despite the latter's formal promises of confidentiality. As a result of pressure in the House this clause was eventually changed.

Britain was one of the pioneers in the area of data privacy and the advice of the Lindop committee was generally well accepted and provided ground rules for work done in other countries later. Despite our early start, legislation was not forthcoming for many years and other governments moved ahead of us. When the EEC decided to implement such legislation throughout the community, the UK government had to bring in legislation to prevent Britain becoming a 'data haven' which would have affected our trade by preventing the flow of information from countries with data protection laws. The present act was therefore drafted purely to allow this country to ratify the EEC work and does not go as far as many people had hoped.

The act has created the post of a data registrar who is required to keep a register of all personal data users, and it is an offence to fail to register. It also imposes the following rights and duties:

1. Data users must obtain the data they use legally and fairly and must hold it only for lawful purposes. These purposes have to be registered with the registrar and the data users must not disclose the data for any other purpose.
2. The data held must be relevant to the purpose for which it is held and must not be excessive. It must also be kept up to date and accurate and may only be stored for as long as is necessary for the registered purposes.
3. The data subject has rights of access to the data held on him or her and may have it corrected if it is wrong.

Summary
1. Computers have created particular problems which managers must be aware of and must plan to overcome. These include the following:
   - Systems may be entered electronically and the contents removed or damaged. Theft may occur without the user even being aware of the fact.
   - Centralization of ever more work on the computers can lead to a breakdown in the controls that normally operate and which are based on a proper division of duties between staff.
   - Heavy reliance placed on computers by many firms makes them vulnerable to any damage or breakdown.

2. The true level of computer fraud is unknown but most authorities fear that it is on the increase, with some such frauds involving very large amounts.

   British law does not require firms to report frauds when they are detected. The police forces are encouraging them to do so and are starting to improve their own training to deal with it. The legal procedure, however, is very complex and the chances of a conviction appear low. Even on conviction the approach to white collar crime is quite different from that to other crimes.

3. Many firms, particularly in the financial services sector, are unwilling to prosecute offenders. This is partly due to the adverse publicity it will bring them and partly to avoid the incidence of copycat crimes.

4. It is difficult to distinguish between computer frauds and frauds committed where there is a computer system. Reports suggest that many of the frauds detected are traditional in nature and proper application of general accounting controls would prevent the occurrence of many of them.

5. The frauds that appear in the headlines are those where the computer is used as a major tool of the fraud. These have been labelled by the press as time bombing, hacking, Trojan horse, salami frauds, etc.

6. Managers cannot afford to wait until things go wrong to look at emergency procedures. They need to define a security policy beforehand. This involves identifying the likely risk areas and the probable costs. Given this information they are able to look at possible remedies and identify those that are economic given their level of risk.

7. The computer privacy debate started to affect consumers in the 1960s and concern was focussed on private computer systems but later moved far more to public sector systems. Despite an early lead in this area no legislation was passed in the UK until 1985 when it was required to bring us in line with a European initiative. The resulting law did not therefore go as far as many people hoped. It set up a registrar, required firms to register their information and the reasons for holding it, and gave data subjects the right to challenge the data.

13

Internal control in computerized accounting systems

Introduction

The subject of control is so important to accountants that we have already referred to it many times in previous chapters. In the current chapter we consider the type of controls normally found to operate with accounting systems.

Senior managers lay down the general policy of the business and must then leave it to their subordinates to achieve those aims. They do not, however, abrogate their responsibility, as they will be constantly monitoring the progress of individual departments using information provided by various control systems across the organization. These controls are known generally as 'internal control' and cover the whole of the business. All departmental managers are responsible for imposing internal controls on their own specialist area, hence the firm will have stock control, production control, quality control, accounting control, etc. In this chapter we are particularly interested in the latter type of control, i.e. accounting control.

If it is to operate properly a full accounting control system must have the following basic features.

There will have to be a full and clear division of duties which must be communicated to all the staff involved. This allows responsibility for every aspect of the work to be allocated clearly to individual members of staff so that everyone is aware of where particular responsibilities rest. In this way there can be no ambiguity over any work and the person performing it knows that he or she will be held solely responsible for its proper performance. We shall see this form of control below under the general heading of organizational controls.

All jobs have to be split down into component parts which are then allocated to different people, thereby ensuring that no individual is given full control over a complete area of work and that every person's work is automatically checked by another. The existence of these internal checks means that if a staff member makes an error or attempts to commit a fraud there is a good chance that it will be detected by a colleague.

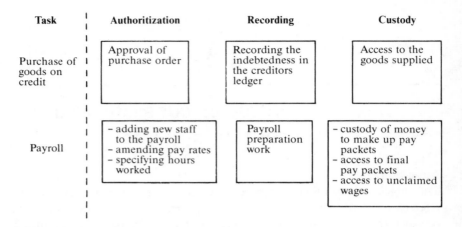

Figure 13.1 Division of duties

If this internal check is to be effective, the work must be divided according to a plan, not in an arbitrary manner (see Fig. 13.1). It has been found that most jobs can be divided into three main types of work:

1. authorization duties,
2. recording duties,
3. custody duties.

For example, the task of purchasing goods on credit could be analysed as follows:

1. *Authorization* This is done when the order is approved, normally by the buyer.
2. *Recording* This is performed when the invoice is entered into the ledger, creating the record against which payment will be made. This is performed by the ledger clerk.
3. *Custody* This involves the physical control over the asset involved, i.e. the stock. This is the work of the storeman.

For maximum control it should be ensured, as far as possible, that no one person performs forms duties from more than one of these classes. The above example separated the work of the storeman, the ledger clerk and the buyer who each acted as a check upon the others. Separation of duties along these lines greatly reduces the chance of errors remaining undetected and will also

help to reduce the risk of fraud. Note that it will *not* make fraud impossible—
no system could claim that—but for fraud to succeed, collusion between staff
will be necessary and this fact will make it more difficult to perpetrate.

A further restriction which needs to be borne in mind when allocating staff
duties is that a person should not be made responsible for checking the work
of his superiors. If this were the case, control could break down owing to the
difficulties involved in staff at this level challenging the work of their
own boss.

With manual systems this separation of duties was reasonably easy to
achieve. However, with the development of computers, an ever-increasing
proportion of the work is being performed on the machine and this has led to
the development of different forms of controls in this area.

Business is constantly changing and as firms expand, reorganize,
amalgamate, etc., their internal control procedures may quite quickly become
out of date and fail to meet the needs of the business. Even if the formal
controls are relevant to the firm's needs, staff will frequently fail to carry them
out unless they are regularly monitored. In fact many of the frauds detected
in the business world would have been prevented if staff had carried out
prescribed internal controls. To ensure compliance and to keep procedures up
to date, many firms employ internal auditors to act as their 'eyes and ears' in
this area. They visit all parts of the organization and report directly to
management, informing them of what is happening and advising them of the
need for new control systems.

Internal control in accounting systems

For the purposes of our study we will classify the main controls under the
following headings.

Organizational controls arise from the way that departments and work are
organized to meet the demands of the job. As we saw above, they involve the
splitting up of work to ensure cross-checking and shared responsibility
for tasks.

Even with computerized systems the people who work within the system are
important and must be properly organized and controlled. In fact they are the
part that is most likely to lead to problems. The computer centre, like all other
departments, therefore needs a proper system of organizational controls.

Systems development controls are designed to ensure that new systems are
properly developed and documented from their inception through to their

final installation. You will find that many of the control procedures highlighted in this section were described in context in the chapter on systems development.

Processing controls are carried out at all stages of processing from input through to output. They are the controls that most students tend to think of first when discussing computerized systems. However, a good control system will need a mix of all three types of controls.

We shall now go on to consider each of these subgroups in more detail.

Organizational controls

These consist of detailed procedures for ensuring the smooth day-to-day running of the business and include the general classifications outlined below (Fig. 13.2).

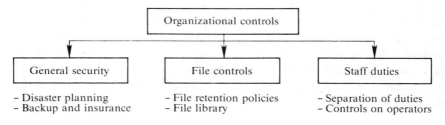

Figure 13.2 Organizational controls

GENERAL RULES FOR SECURITY

These were introduced in Chapter 12 under the heading of computer security where we saw how firms lay down procedures to deal with systems faults, machine breakdowns, fire, power faults, etc. It is not sufficient merely to plan for such contingencies; it is vital that the plans are set down in the form of detailed manuals and communicated to the staff concerned. It is too late for staff to start learning the procedures when an incident occurs, so action is needed to ensure that staff know the procedures and have the manuals and checklists available if and when things do go wrong. Firms are required by law to hold fire drills and they would be wise to prepare equally well for other disasters. Internal auditors often play a useful role in assessing the degree of readiness in these areas.

The reader is already aware of the need to organize suitable machine backup facilities to cover any period of disorganization following an incident. However, this precaution will be of only limited use if the main files and application programs are damaged along with the equipment, e.g. by fire or flood. It is a wise precaution, therefore, to arrange that copies of particular files be regularly stored at a safe location away from the computer centre. However, this must not compromise the general procedures on file security or allow people to gain unauthorized access to them. Some firms lodge copies with their banks and a number of security firms offer a service that will collect files at set periods, store them at safe premises and return them to be overwritten after a specified retention period. This leads us into the general area of file controls.

FILE CONTROLS

New users of microcomputer-based accounting systems are frequently surprised by the number, and hence the cost, of the diskettes they need to run their systems, and with larger systems the problems are proportionately greater. All firms must therefore plan how they will control their files, to ensure that they are neither lost nor accidentally overwritten.

Files normally contain special records which identify them to the computer and provide the program with details of the number of records, control totals, etc., on the file. Using these facilities computer programs are normally able to check that the appropriate file has been loaded and if this is not the case they will issue an error report.

When a system fault occurs during a computer run, the working versions of master files may be corrupted. The only solution then is to turn to a backup copy of the file and process this, bringing it up to date as a replacement. We have already seen that tape files produce a new backup copy every time they are updated and firms normally retain three generations of these on what is called the grandfather–father–son principle:

1. Assume a firm starts with no backup copy. The tape produced at the end of the first day's run is retained and is the current 'son' version.
2. The second day's run produces a new tape which becomes the new 'son' and the original tape is now a second-generation 'father' file. Should the system fail the operator would turn to this and process the day's transactions against it to bring it up to date and use it instead of the damaged file. However, if there were no problems no further work would be done on this tape.

3. On the third day the original file becomes a 'grandfather' and is in the last stage of its life. Following the next day's processing it can be overwritten as there are now a full three generations of more recent files.

In larger firms a specialist computer library is normally created, under the control of a file librarian, and all files are stored here when they are not being processed and will only be issued for authorized purposes. With batch systems the various applications are run to a strict weekly timetable and the librarian will have the appropriate files ready when they are scheduled to be run. The times of issue and return are usually recorded, and if the files are held for a longer period than expected this will be investigated to ensure that they have not been tampered with. This type of control should make it far more difficult to intercept the tapes and interfere with or copy them.

Controlling all the files in a large system can involve a great deal of work, so the task is frequently mechanized. Automatic tape library (ATL) equipment is available which uses robotic technology and is controlled by the computer. It can select reels, and mount and dismount them from the drives. Such equipment starts with smaller units containing four tape drives and off-line storage space for 900 reels of tape; larger units are available to handle up to 8000 reels.

DIVISION OF DUTIES

Internal checks have been used in accounting systems for many years and do not apply solely to computerized systems. The normal division of work into authorization, recording and custody duties is still applicable with computerized systems. However, to obtain a proper division along these lines the accountant will need to look at the work performed by user departments as well as that of the computer centre.

With more integrated systems, however, this becomes increasingly difficult to achieve as many user tasks are automated and brought into the computer centre. For example, when dealing with cheque payments the computer has produced lists of outstanding creditors for many years. However the authorization (signing the cheques) and the custody of the signed cheques used to take place outside the computer centre. In recent years an increasing number of payment systems have offered cheque printing facilities, using presigned cheque forms. Here both the authorization and custody work have been brought into the computer department to join the recording work traditionally performed there.

In such cases accountants have had to identify alternative controls upon which to rely. For example, with such a payment system a control would be placed over the number of cheques used every time. This would be supplemented by a regular reconciliation of suppliers' accounts with the statements received from them. Strict controls would also be imposed to prevent computer department staff entering new suppliers' records on the master files, a common way of covering illegal payments.

It is also important to look at the way duties are divided up within the data processing department. The staffing diagram on page 240 showed the division of staff between the operations and development sections and, ideally, the two types of staff should be kept separate.

The console terminal in the computer room poses particular internal control problems as it gives the user direct access to the system to start up, close down and correct problems with the machine. If misused it could be a dangerous tool, allowing illegal amendments to be made to the system, and it is vital therefore to control access and ensure that only operations staff may enter the main computer room during normal processing. Senior systems staff, in particular, pose a problem as they have a detailed overall understanding of the system and if they were able to gain access to the machine during routine processing a serious breach of security could occur.

A range of controls is imposed specifically on the computer operators to prevent both errors and fraud. These include the following:

1. They should not be involved with any other aspects of the processing work, apart from running the equipment. In particular they must certainly not have access to any of the source documents nor to any manually maintained monitoring systems. If this were allowed, the two sets of records could be altered to cover any errors or frauds.
2. They should not be allowed to perform the function of the file librarian; otherwise they could bring any files they wished into the computer room and amend them on the machine at their leisure.
3. For every application run on the system there should be a proper operating manual laying down the detailed procedures to be followed in the event of error, failure, etc. Without this, major problems could occur. For example, the firm cannot have conscientious operating staff trying their own methods of recovering a system that they know little about.
4. To further restrict their access to the console, etc., it is normally laid down that at least two operators must be on duty at all times. If the same staff always work together collusion is more likely to occur and therefore duties

are normally rotated so that the same staff do not always work together on a shift.

5. The importance of the console terminal is stressed by the fact that we must return to it yet again. In many systems all operator interventions are printed out on a log and the reports so produced provide the data processing auditor or the computer manager with a good insight into what has been happening. The log must be examined regularly by staff such as these with the technical skills to interpret it. This will then act as a deterrent to any operator interfering with the system, for all operators will know that interventions will be logged and therefore be detected unless the record is removed from the log.

To prevent this happening the following further controls normally operate:

1. Each message is numbered sequentially and this number is printed on the log along with the message. Without this facility messages could be removed without detection, but this simple control prevents that.

2. In many installations the operators are physically prevented from gaining access to the log printouts. The simplest method is to place a perspex cover over the terminal which allows the user to read the messages but not to handle them. When the paper needs changing, however, a senior operator or manager will have to be called to unlock it and remove the old log.

Development controls

As the system analysts and programmers perform the detailed work on the system, they are the people with the skill and the access to the files, etc., needed to incorporate technical frauds (see Chapter 12) into the new system. This is a notoriously difficult area to control fully and the main form of control involves submitting programmers' and analysts' work for detailed supervision and review at all stages of development and then keeping them away from the system once it is approved and running. Even with this level of control in the system it must be recognized that senior systems staff are in a position of trust, and misconduct at this level could be difficult to detect. With this level of trust involved, the firm must obviously be as careful as possible in the recruitment of such staff and must enquire carefully into their background and experience before appointing them. It is also important to change passwords, etc., in order to bar access to such staff as soon as they leave the firm.

Most companies allocate development work to special teams and adopt internal standards regarding the degree of and approach to documentation and programming. Regular reviews are performed at all stages by the team leader, whose formal approval is needed before staff may move on from one stage to the next. As documentation is of the utmost importance this approval will not be given unless all documentation is completed up to standard and the team leader is satisfied with the work performed.

For control purposes it is preferable for the systems analysis work to be separated from the detailed programming and testing; this provides a further level of internal check as the analyst would be likely to query any unusual work by the programmer and vice versa. However, this separation cannot be made in all organizations.

The file conversion and/or creation task in particular is an area where control is vital. At this stage of the project a great deal of money and time have been invested and certain political battles have been fought and won. However, no return has yet been seen from all this. There is therefore always pressure at this stage of the project and this, coupled with the amount of work and the eagerness of managers to see results from the new system, can lead to a high error rate at the data conversion stage. The aim must be to reduce to a minimum the number of errors finding their way into the new files, and the main control will involve the creation of control totals over the number of records, the amounts involved, etc. If time allows, a full printout of the new file can be taken and compared with a printout of the old file, item by item. This is the final check. However, in practice most files are too large for this to be done in the time available.

The final level of control over development occurs at the parallel running stage and the firm's systems development procedures should not allow the system to be accepted until it is fully tested and approved. The final systems approval must be given in writing after which the system, as specified, becomes the firm's official one. A basic copy should be lodged in safe storage away from the computer section both for security and for possible later comparison with running versions to detect alterations. Any amendments made in the future will have to be authorized and documented to the same high standard outlined above; if this were not the case, all the development controls could be short-circuited by frauds and errors entering the system at this later stage.

Processing controls

Today's computers are very sophisticated and the hardware carries out a great deal of detailed testing while operating. For example, it regularly tests peripherals to ensure that they are on line and working properly. These controls are built into the system by the hardware manufacturer, so they do not form a part of our overall system of controls. In fact, users are unaware of most of them. They do, however, add to our confidence in the hardware, which is a basic item in assessing the level of confidence we may place in the system.

Processing controls can be introduced into all parts of the system from input through to output. With batch systems there are established controls on inputs, based on prelisting the batches and later comparing the batch control totals with those produced by the computer; any difference between the two sets of figures indicates that an error has been made. There are three types of control figures which might be imposed on a batch of documents:

1. *Document count*   This involves counting the number of documents in a batch; it helps to prevent the omission of a document or the insertion of an additional one. When dealing with cash receipts it can also help to prevent and detect the crime of 'teeming and lading' where a sum of money is misappropriated and the theft is covered by splitting up later receipts and posting them to several accounts.

2. *Control total*   This involves totalling the *value* of the transactions in the batch, e.g. total sales in a batch of invoices. Using such figures is very similar to the procedure accountants have used for many years in the preparation of control accounts.

3. *Hash totals*   Computerized systems will often use totals which in themselves appear to be meaningless, e.g. the total of all customer account numbers in a batch. The total here has no meaning in itself but if the total figure taken from the batch before posting disagrees with that produced by the computer an error has occurred in the processing. In our sales invoice posting example this would indicate that some item(s) have been posted to the wrong account.

The combination of these three types of control figures imposes a good level of control on the processing of such batches.

With real-time systems data is input directly by the user rather than batched and these controls are no longer possible. Such systems have to rely far more on the validation of input data by the program. These validation checks may include checking that the value of particular fields falls between reasonable parameters, checking that a numeric field does not contain non-numeric characters, ensuring that all the information required for a particular record has been entered, ensuring that a particular record exists on file, etc.

Another form of control frequently used on input is the check digit. Code numbers such as customer numbers and employee payroll codes are used widely on computers. To the outsider a code number output by the computer may appear to be a six-digit code and it might be assumed that any other six-digit code would constitute a valid input. However, if a check digit is in operation, only five of those digits will actually constitute the code number, the other digit being the check digit. This is calculated by a complex formula stored in the machine which takes the remaining digits and calculates the appropriate check digit value for that code. If an operator accidently transposed two figures of the code, the check digit would no longer be valid and the machine would signal a check digit error. In addition to detecting such simple input errors the use of such check digits helps to make it more difficult for people to create fictitious records.

Once data is accepted by the machine, the progams will continue to check it during all stages of processing to ensure that it is not lost or corrupted. The machine controls will be supplemented by additional manual ones. One useful form of manual control involves the user departments maintaining totals of all changes input to a particular computer run. Using control totals from the previous run they can adjust these to arrive at the new totals that should be produced by the computer. This process again resembles that used in the preparation of control accounts. One area where such controls are often used is with payroll applications:

1. Staff know the total gross pay figure shown in the last payroll.
2. To this they will add the gross pay of all new employees commencing and deduct the gross pay of all staff leaving during the current period.
3. The resultant figure will be the total gross pay which should appear in the next payroll when it is produced and any differences between the figures will have to be fully investigated.

The final processing controls occur at the output stage as information should be available only to those staff authorized to receive it. With printed output this was not difficult but it can be far more of a problem now that staff are able to contact the computer directly from terminals. In such cases access to remote microcomputers and terminals is an important aspect of control and has created a number of particular problems to which we will now turn our attention.

Problems of passwords and access

When computing was done mainly in batch mode on mainframe machines it was relatively easy to control access because work had to go through several levels of control in the computer centre before it went on to the machine. The introduction of distributed processing has brought terminals into branches and depots where there are no specialist computer staff and where there is little or no control over them. The increasing use of networked micros linked to the mainframe now poses similar problems on an even wider scale. Add to this the problems of access by hacking, i.e. illegally dialling into a system, and it can be seen that such users must do all that they can to restrict access to their system. The following controls can help to combat such problems.

PASSWORD CONTROL

Passwords have been used for many years to deny access to unauthorized users. They are a very common form of control and provide a useful first level of control but full reliance should not be placed on them alone because they have serious weaknesses. When passwords are used the following points should be considered.

It is important to ensure that they are changed regularly. A number of security breaches have occurred, even on police computer systems, because passwords were not changed when staff left the firm. While this can be dangerous at any time it can be even more so where an employee has been dismissed and may seek revenge against the firm.

Multilevel passwords are frequently used in larger systems. Those allocated to senior managers may allow them access to most parts of the system and may allow them to update information on the files. Lower level passwords will allow only restricted access to certain parts of the system and may only allow the user to interrogate the system. Some systems use a key to turn on the system, with the user's identity code stored on the key. The act of turning on the machine informs the system of the user's identity and official status and he or she will then be asked to input a personal password. An unauthorized user would need to obtain both the key and details of the personal password in order to gain access to the system.

Where passwords are used to log on to a system a two-part code is frequently used; the first section identifies the user and the second acts as a personal password. This type of code is used to control access to a number of public systems. In some of these cases the logging-on software is so user-friendly that it appears to have been designed to assist people to gain illegal access. Such software sometimes validates the identity code character by character and rejects the input if this is incorrect, which can indicate to the user the number of characters in the log-on code and make it far easier to break. It would be far better if the user was required to input the whole code and press the return key before the validation began. In such cases the user does not know which stage went wrong and the code in effect becomes one large password rather than two smaller ones which are easier to decode.

Several very common human weaknesses often reduce the power of passwords to protect a system. Firstly, people fear they will forget their password so they write it down on a piece of paper which is often stored in their desk or on a wall where it can be seen by others. Secondly, they often choose words or numbers they believe will be easy to recall such as the names of pets or of their children or numbers such as 22222. It is little wonder therefore that hacking has become such a popular pastime.

When an invalid password is entered, the system normally indicates this and asks the user to try again. This is done to assist users who make an error inputting their details. Some systems repeatedly ask the user to try again. However, a genuine user does not need this facility and after two attempts the system should cut off the terminal and flash a warning message on the log in the main computer room. Unless this happens a user can program a microcomputer to try various combinations of numbers, at high speed, until access is gained.

Keeping passwords secret can be quite a problem so most systems 'echo supress' the password when it is typed in; that is, they do not print it up on a screen or printer. However, there have been cases where lists of highly confidential access phone numbers and passwords have been left on screen in offices and open to public view throughout the working day. Surprisingly, simple breaches of basic controls such as this lead to far more computer fraud than do highly complex schemes.

Senior systems staff are able to obtain a printout of the current passwords stored on the password file. This facility is a necessary part of their job but it could be very dangerous in the wrong hands so its use must be very carefully controlled. Any password control over this facility must be changed immediately any of the staff involved leave.

ACCESS CONTROLS

The following steps should be taken to control access to microcomputers and terminals:

1. The machines should be placed in a secure room which can be locked when they are not in use. In addition to locks on the door there is an increasing market in security devices for the equipment itself. Some keyboards have a small lock to disable the keys, and attachments are now available to lock the disk drives or the power supply to the machine. These provide additional security as cleaners, maintenance staff, etc., will need to gain access to the room in addition to users.

2. The room in use should allow a clear view of anyone using the machine so that other staff can see if an unauthorized person gains access or if a person is spending an undue amount of time on the machine.

    Although other staff should have a general overview of the room, care should be taken to ensure that they cannot actually view the screen and its contents; in this way they might observe the logging on routines, etc.

3. It is also bad practice to leave operating manuals, code lists, etc., around the room or on the notice board as this again can assist the illegal user attempting to gain access to the system, particularly out of working hours.

4. To avoid problems of illegal entry some systems now require the user to log on, after which the main computer will close down the line and then phone back to the terminal concerned. This is done to ensure that the user is actually working on the terminal or micro that the system has been informed is being used. This is just one of the controls that have had to be designed to fight the menace of the hackers. Whenever data is transmitted across a line in this way security is now quite a problem and something must be done to protect it. An increasing number of users now transmit sensitive information in coded form, the recipient's machine translating it back before it can be used at the other end. Devices are now available to encode information on business personal computers such as the IBM PC. These can encode all data held on the machine's files and may help combat the poor level of control on such machines.

5. Some terminals will only be allowed to interrogate the system, the computer being programmed not to accept file amendments from them.

6. Some systems are programmed to turn off a terminal after a certain amount of time if no use has been made of it. This reduces the chance of a person gaining illegal entry through a terminal left on line by a negligent user.

7. Some large public systems have operating system software that monitors the use of terminals, etc., and logs a warning message on the systems manager's own file if it detects unusual activity by any user or in any part of the system. Unfortunately the hacking fraternity are aware of this type of control and seek to gain access to this particular file to remove the message that could help incriminate them.

Microcomputers do not have such sophisticated operating systems as minis or mainframes so access to programs and files is far easier. In such cases the controls over physical access are vital and all floppy disks should be removed and stored safely away from the machine.

Summary
1. Internal control is the responsibility of all managers, not of auditors. It operates in all functional areas and accounting controls are just one specialist aspect of internal control.
2. An effective internal control system will require the following three basic features:
   - a clear and detailed plan of the organization setting out the extent of individual responsibilities;
   - a proper separation of authorization, recording and custody duties so that no person has full control over a major area of work and the work of one person is automatically checked by others;
   - regular checks and appraisals of the system by management or their internal auditors.
3. Employees should not be asked to check and report on the work of staff senior to themselves.
4. Even with computerized systems, controls over staff are still vital as they are often the weak link in the chain. As an increasing amount of accounting work is taken on to the computer, so the traditional division of duties is harder to achieve and managers must therefore seek other controls over particular areas of work.
5. The basic types of controls in a system are organizational, development and processing.
6. Organizational controls cover:
   - general security,
   - file control,
   - division of staff duties.

   Special attention must be paid to controlling the console terminal.
7. Development controls basically involve adopting strict internal standards at all stages of development and ensuring that these are enforced at all times.
8. Processing controls are applied to all stages of processing from input through to output.
9. Although passwords are widely used to control access to programs they have a number of weaknesses and too much reliance should not be placed upon them.
10. Physical access to terminals and micros is the first stage of control and a whole range of security products is available to assist in this area.
11. A great deal of computer abuse can be stopped by regular attention to the basic security rules. 'It's not exciting but it works!'

14

The role of the auditor

Introduction

Auditors are experts appointed to review a system and the information it produces and then to report their opinions to the people who hired them. This description highlights several important points:

1. The auditors' basic role is to form an opinion and then to report that opinion to those who appointed them. This means that it is not they who are responsible for setting up the system. They are in fact merely one user of it, and as such they will require certain things from it which should be made clear when the system is first planned and developed.
2. In arriving at an opinion on the accounts or other information, auditors will never be able to check all the work that has passed through the system. The most they can do is to sample-test some of this work and satisfy themselves that the system itself checks for errors. The system producing the information is not under their control and they cannot therefore change it. If they feel that it cannot be relied on to produce good information, they must report the fact. As a service to their clients, and in order to assist future audit work, they may suggest improvements but they do not have the authority to make changes to the system.
3. Auditors may be employed by various groups of people. In the case of a company, external auditors are employed by the shareholders and report to them on their interests in it. Internal auditors are employed by management to help in their task of imposing and monitoring internal control systems. They report back directly to management and will carry out the detailed work needed to satisfy them that all aspects of their systems operate properly.

In the past auditors placed a great deal of emphasis on checking the detailed transactions passing through the system and on recreating the information from it. However, with the growth of business this soon became impossible, and they had to move to a 'systems-based' audit approach. With this approach, auditors check that the accounting system itself includes a sufficient level of controls and then test that these have been operating properly throughout the audit period. Audit tests such as this, designed to check the operation of controls, are known generally as *compliance* tests. If the control system appears sound, only a small proportion of the auditors' time is spent actually checking the content of the final reports; this type of testing is termed *substantive* testing. If they find that the system controls have been operating properly and that the figures produced appear reasonable, they will be able to place far more reliance on the results than they could have done by merely following large numbers of transactions through the system.

The introduction of computers into accounting brought a number of problems both for accountants and auditors.

As we have already noted the increasing amount of accounting work being centred on the computer and the data processing department has made the traditional division of duties difficult to enforce.

Records are normally stored in magnetic form and are susceptible to damage from heat, damp, dust and magnetic fields. It is important therefore to store them away from such problems and to keep backup copies.

Until the early days of mechanical accounting, transactions had their own individual identity and were easily traced. With mechanical and, later, electronic processing documents were handled in batches and lost this individual identity. This plus the fact that no attempt is normally made to sort transactions until they are entered into the machine can make it a difficult task to trace a source document in some cases. Today we cope fairly easily with this but in the early days it was a major concern for auditors in particular.

A far worse problem was the loss of audit trail with computerized systems. Manual systems had always allowed the user to follow a transaction through the various stages of processing and check that it had been included. Some computer systems allow users to follow items into the system, but after that they lose sight of them as they are likely to be overwritten on a disk file. This has become an increasing problem as firms move over to real-time distributed systems, and in such systems it can be virtually impossible to look back at particular items and try to ascertain what the system did with them.

Approaches to auditing
Faced with these problems early computer auditors at first tried to 'audit around' the computer (see Fig. 14.1). This approach viewed the computer as a simple recording machine and auditors would follow the transactions of a period into it. They would then ignore what happened inside the machine and try to ascertain what should have happened to the data. They would then process it manually and compare their own results with those in the ledgers, etc., output from the system. This was rather crude and while it might work

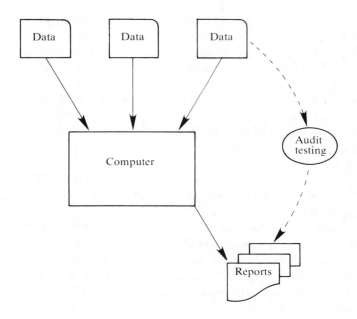

Figure 14.1 Auditing around the computer

with simple small systems it soon becomes impossible with larger systems due to the following:

1. Today's large business systems handle so much data that the sheer volume of data being processed by the machine makes it impossible to check in this way even a small portion of one day's processing.

2. As systems have developed so computer programs carry out ever more detailed operations on the data in order to produce more sophisticated analysis. This means that the auditor may be able to follow the data into the machine but could never hope to cross-reference and sort all the information to arrive back at the final results.

3. The introduction of real-time and distributed systems in larger firms meant that data was being received from all over the country while increasingly less information was being printed out by systems. The result was a total loss of audit trail in certain application areas.

   Auditors soon came to realize the futility of auditing around the machine in this manner and sought a better way of performing their work. In the audits of non-computerized systems they had successfully used the systems-based approach for some years but seemed to have discounted it when they were first faced by the need to audit computers.

The emphasis with the systems audit was on checking that a suitable system existed and that it was consistently operating properly. With the introduction of computers the system became far more formalized and once installed was less likely to malfunction than manual systems had been. A return to the systems-based audit seemed to provide an answer to many of the auditors' problems, who again therefore began to evaluate the controls within systems and to develop methods of compliance testing to check these in operation.

To evaluate the system controls they soon developed *test packs* of data to be run against the client's system (see Fig. 14.2). The auditor needed to produce a detailed audit file on every application area audited, showing how the system worked and the controls included in it. Fictitious data items then had to be prepared with values that would test whether these controls were operating properly or not. This might be seen more easily from a simple example.

A payroll system might include controls to:

1. check that timesheets are input for all staff,
2. validate the hours worked and query anyone working over 50 hours in one week,
3. calculate the gross pay and overtime at the appropriate rates.

The auditors' test data would be designed to include a number of standard items which should be processed with no problem. In addition some items would be included where more than 50 hours were worked and certain payroll numbers would be totally omitted from the batch, as a check on continuity.

The auditors would know in advance what the results should be and what exception reports to expect. The actual output would be checked against what was expected and any differences investigated.

Setting up a test pack that will test all the possible outcomes of every control is a slow and costly business. However, once prepared the pack can be used again with only relatively minor amendments from year to year.

When auditors attended and ran their test pack through the system they gained some insight into how the controls were operating but they were still very much in the hands of the data processing staff they were there to audit. They needed them to load and run both the test pack and the programs and the staff knew that they were not testing a live run. A number of audit firms therefore tried inserting their test pack data in with live data and running it

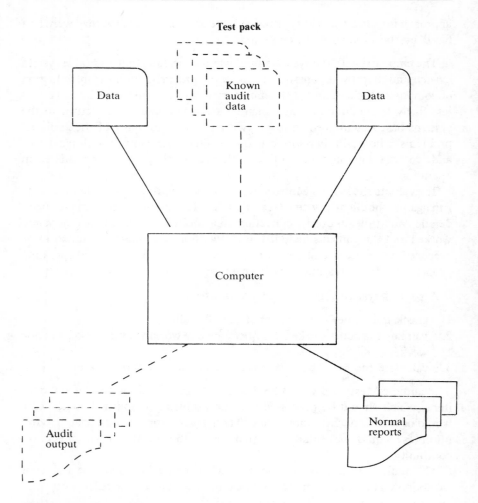

Figure 14.2 Test packs

through the normal channels. They obviously had to design further data items
to correct these false transactions later, however, and there were cases where
this was not done properly and the result was corruption of the client's files as
a result of the auditors' work. This highlighted another audit problem. How
could they test live data and yet avoid such corruption of the client's files? As a
result such data is now normally run using the client's programs but working
with audit copies of the files, rather than the originals.

Developments such as test packs moved the focus of auditing away from testing individual transactions towards auditing the programs and looking at the way they worked. With this approach auditors were better able to evaluate the extent of reliance they could place upon a system and the information it produced. However, they still had to perform some detailed tests and this involved selecting items, setting up sampling schemes to select them, extracting the required information from the files for testing and evaluating the results. This had been common practice with manual systems for many years but presented special difficulties where computerized systems were concerned. There was, however, a way of reducing the work involved. The auditor could use the client's own computer as a tool to help with its own audit. A range of tools was developed to allow this and they are often referred to under the general heading of computer-assisted audit techniques (CAAT).

A variety of such tools allows auditors to select those that are most useful for the type of testing they wish to carry out and includes the following.

Specialist audit software

This has become the most widespread and trusted method, where available. It involves the auditors using specialist programs written for audit purposes and used at the client's premises during the audit. We shall look first at the type of general testing software that is used and then go on to look at the way many firms are developing microcomputer-based audit tools.

GENERAL TESTING SOFTWARE

This has been developed by the larger audit firms and tested internationally. It can be very sophisticated and allows the auditor to choose from a very wide range of tools.

There are a number of file utility programs on the market and some auditors do make use of these to allow them to access files and read and manipulate particular data. However, such programs are general in nature and only help the auditor to a limited extent. International audit firms therefore developed their own specialist software to allow them to carry out a far wider range of detailed tests on clients' files. These systems generally work as follows.

The package (Fig. 14.3) is made up of a large set of subroutines (small programs each of which performs a particular task) which together can perform most types of work that auditors need to perform, e.g. calculate random samples and merge particular data. These routines can be called upon and combined in many different ways to create an individual audit programme to suit each client.

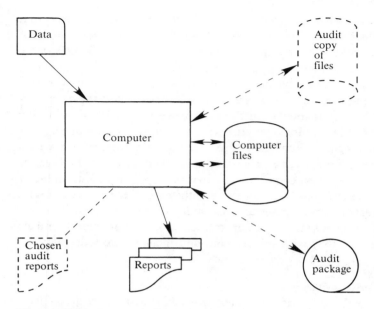

Figure 14.3 Computer audit package

We have seen that computer programs can only work on files that are prepared in a format that they recognize. However, auditors must work on many different client systems and across a range of machines so their own software will be unable to work on most of these files.

The answer to this problem is to include within the system a subroutine that can translate the client's files into the audit program's own recognized format. For this to happen, the client's file structure must first be described to the auditors' own system. Audit staff interview clients and then input this data on a special form. This in itself is one of the first checks with this type of system.

One of the largest computer frauds known to date took place on the computers of the Equity Funding Corporation of America. This large insurance company programmed its system to create non-existent policies and so boost its income. To prevent any of these policies being printed out for audit purposes a simple code field was added to each record, containing a number showing if it were genuine or not. In setting up the file descriptions for their program the auditors had to be told of the existence of this field. If they had not been, the audit program would have found an unrecognized field and notified them accordingly.

The output from this conversion subroutine is a full copy of the client's file(s) in a format which the auditors' own subroutines can operate upon. They can then devise their own tests, extract the data they want and work on it in the way they wish, and all this is done without affecting the client's files.

The auditors could, for example, select and list all debtors with balances between particular parameters, select samples from each group, produce individual letters asking them to confirm their balances and finally use the package to help interpret the validity of the results obtained.

The flexibility and approach of such software is illustrated by the fact that certain audit firms have been able to use their packages to help provide additional client services. There have been cases where clients' own systems were not programmed to produce certain information that was needed for a particular purpose, e.g. to prepare a tender for a large contract. The only solutions within the client firm were either to prepare the details manually, which was not possible, or to create a special program which would have taken far too long to create and test. The auditors were able to copy the files into the audit format and use their powerful search and merge routines to rearrange the data and produce the necessary information in just a few days. This did not break any of the firm's security rules because it did not involve working on the live files and did not require the development and testing of a new system, so their work was totally unaffected apart from the need to find computer time to run the audit packages.

MICRO-BASED AUDIT TOOLS

Audit firms are increasingly using microcomputers as tools for use by audit staff. These are still in a relatively early stage of development and although the time will eventually come when they will be able to pull data down from a client's large system and audit it, they are nowhere near that yet. Their main use at present is in the critical review stage of auditing.

We saw that auditors must test the computer system to ascertain whether they can rely on the results. If they are satisfied then, when the results are produced, they will look through them and identify any areas that differ from budgets or from previous reports. They will then satisfy themselves that there are reasonable explanations for these differences. This is the critical review and from the systems audit and the critical review together they can form a good opinion on the validity of the results.

Within the review function most firms seem to be using the Lotus 1-2-3 spreadsheet package or a computer language to prepare review schedules that allow the firm to hold several years' final figures on a particular client. When the current year's figures are entered the machine produces ratios and trends to highlight areas that may need further investigation. The firm will also use these tools to prepare detailed trial balance, final accounts and supporting schedules to back up the figures in the accounts. They are particularly helpful in dealing with the large number of closing adjustments normally encountered at the year end because as soon as an adjustment is made in the trial balance it is automatically reflected both in the accounts and in the various working schedules that refer to it. Updating and cross-referencing these manually is a very slow and monotonous task.

PROGRAM ANALYSERS AND LOG ANALYSERS

These are specialist software tools used to read through the computer log records or through details of the library records. They allow the auditor or management to identify what work was done and when changes were made to programs, etc. They are not extensively used by external auditors, partly because they cannot be used generally across different machines. They would probably be of more use to internal auditors, but even here many scrutinize logs manually.

TESTING INTEGRITY OF THE PROGRAM IN USE

The audit staff will know what the client's programs are supposed to do and will know that they have been tested and approved prior to acceptance. However, they must wonder at times whether the program actually running has been amended since it was commissioned. The files will show details of all authorized amendments but they will be particularly concerned with detecting unauthorized ones.

Some auditors have software to compare the current program in use with a master copy that has been kept at a secure location. These program comparison tools will read both the secure and the current version and compare them line by line at high speed. There are also core image comparison programs which can check the safe copy against the loaded version of a file held in the machine's memory.

This sort of check would seem an obvious development and the reader might be surprised to find that these are not very widely used. Once again they are not portable across machines and they are also very difficult to use. The computer works on the object version of the program file, held in machine language. If the auditors find that changes have been made at this level it is very complex work to identify what they mean and assess their importance.

EMBEDDED CODE OR AUDIT MONITOR

Some auditors, particularly internal auditors, make use of special software known as an audit monitor. This may be placed into the operating system or the applications software and will monitor data entered into the system. It can be set up to search for any items that appear to be unusual and that may require further checking. The monitor will then copy these out on to a special audit file for later checking.

The main weakness here is that the auditor will have to define in advance what will constitute an unusual item and this would make it very difficult for such a tool to detect a fraud of the Trojan horse type. These monitors also take up machine time and can therefore slow down processing speeds, which may not be acceptable to the systems manager. One way around this is to use a monitor that can be switched in and out of use at random.

The audit monitor is a useful tool where no audit trail exists and it has a useful psychological effect on users as they know items are checked even while auditors are not present.

Summary

1. Auditors have to rely on the internal control system of a firm in arriving at their audit opinion. However, they are not responsible for installing such systems, nor do they have the authority to alter them; these responsibilities rest clearly with management. The auditors are therefore users of the system and this gives them both a responsibility and a right to have their needs considered at the systems development stage.
2. Today's audits are systems based rather than transactions based. Auditors carry out compliance tests to check that control systems are operating and, if they feel justified in relying upon these, they will perform only limited substantive tests to check the accuracy of the information involved.
3. Early auditors attempted to avoid the new problems posed by auditing around the computer as if it did not exist.
4. At the next stage of development they realized the need to check the controls in the computer systems and place reliance upon these. Test packs and other methods were developed at this stage.
5. The next stage of development involved the use of the client's computer as a tool to help audit itself. A range of techniques and programs was developed, including:

- computer audit software,
- microcomputer worksheet packages,
- program comparison techniques,
- log analysers,
- audit monitors.

Part 6

Information technology and the accountant

15

Business applications of information technology

Introduction
Information technology is affecting all parts of our lives from medicine through to leisure, while in most sectors of the economy developments in computers and communications are increasing the output per employee. Information technology is, however, far more than a collection of tools to allow increased output and in many of these sectors it will greatly change the way we perform our work.

This has already been seen happening in many sectors. For example, the world's money market operates 24 hours a day as dealing moves around the world from London to New York to Tokyo. Dealers across the world no longer meet at specific markets, as trading is carried out from high-technology electronic dealing rooms across the world. In the field of medicine hip joint replacements have been very common for some time and a great deal of research has gone into the problem of creating replacement joints for insertion. One new method utilizes the techniques of CAD/CAM. Special X-ray pictures are taken of the patient's joint and from these a three-dimensional model of the hip joint is created within the computer. A number of possible alternatives can then be tried out against this model, rather than in the operating theatre, saving much time and discomfort for the patient. Finally, a joint can be manufactured specifically to fit that patient, and when it comes to the operation the medical team will know in advance what problems they face and that they have a joint designed with these in mind.

It can be seen therefore that the applications of information technology are very wide. In this chapter we shall confine ourselves to those aspects that affect the financial world. In our field the technology has resulted from the convergence of three areas of development:

1.   business computing,
2.   communications,
3.   office technology.

The accountant's role is right at the centre of these developments as he or she earns a living from the provision of business information. If accountants are to continue to hold their prominent place in the business community, they will need to be aware of these developments and able to realize how business can benefit from their application. Students on both business and computing courses in the colleges are learning to use these methods and there will be plenty of others willing to offer advice if accountants fail to take up the challenge which they are so well placed to take on. As we have already seen, accountants have a history of dealing with mechanical and electrical data processing systems. Their work takes them into all areas of business and in many cases they gain experience across a large number of firms. It is hardly surprising that several of our larger accounting firms also operate respected consultancy businesses and are large users of the technology and are at the forefront of advising firms on its adoption.

Throughout this book we have considered various aspects of computing which would come under the general heading of information technology. In this chapter we will briefly outline some developing areas of communications and office systems of which the reader should have a basic knowledge. This area is fast changing and even at the time of going to press there are further reports and developments the authors would like to have mentioned. Accounting students will therefore need to read current journals, observe clients' systems and visit trade exhibitions if they wish to keep up to date with developments.

Communications

Anyone preparing information needs to trace relevant data from various sources, discuss this with colleagues, obtain their views on the results and, if necessary, amend the first drafts accordingly. It can be seen therefore that this type of work involves a great deal of interaction with fellow staff and users. The stand-alone computer brought great benefits to data processing but had one great weakness when it came to creating management information; the inability to share information with other users greatly restricted its usefulness.

Developments in the world of communications have been equally important as those in computing in helping to bring about the information technology developments we see today. Mainframe business computers were multi-user from the early days and it was not long before microcomputers and mini-computers started to develop in a similar way. The purchaser of small systems today can buy multi-user mini and micro systems or may network individual machines together. There were early delays and problems in the development of networks for small machines but things seem set to improve as industry standards are emerging.

To network computers the users have to be able to transfer data and programs between them at high speeds and for this to work the machines at each end must be able to recognize the form in which the data is stored. The ASCII code mentioned earlier is the form in which most computers now transmit such data, and even where computers hold their data internally in some other format they will normally translate it into this format for onward transmission, leaving the receiving machine to translate it back if necessary.

Given a suitable code for transmission the next problem is to establish the physical links between the computers. There are two types of network communication system to consider here:

1. *local area networks* (LANs) consisting of private links between computers and peripherals over relatively short distances;
2. *wide area networks* created by linking machines over much wider distances, possibly in other countries.

LOCAL AREA NETWORKS

If a firm connects a number of microcomputers together at its own premises then, given the necessary software to control the process, data can be passed between the microcomputers and they can share certain peripherals such as printers and plotters.

Being designed to store data rather than speech, local area networks are simpler to operate than wide area networks, as the messages are transferred in digital rather than analogue form. In the future network circuits of this kind will be built directly into the fabric of new offices, houses, etc., and, as currently happens with electricity circuits, equipment will be plugged directly into these to gain access to the firm's information system.

This will allow far more flexibility in the choice and location of equipment once suitable standards have been developed. Development work is improving networking facilities but the problems experienced with early systems have made some users cautious about their adoption. A major problem up to now has been the lack of an industry standard system, but with the movement of IBM into this area we are likely to see an expansion of such facilities in the next few years as integrated office systems become more common.

WIDE AREA NETWORKS

Where equipment needs to be linked over wide areas, it is not feasible for firms to run their own lines and so the links are normally made over the British Telecom public system or, as it develops, the Mercury system. These are often referred to as the Public Switched Telephone Network (PSTN), as the telephone system is really just a large number of individual sets sharing a number of trunk lines between them. There are far fewer lines than there are handsets but each set spends most of its time unused. Switching equipment at the exchange connects and disconnects various equipment to the network and finds a route through the system for the user's messages or data.

There are problems with the main system so far as computer communications are concerned. The present system has run for many years using mechanical switching at exchanges but these are now all being converted to electronic switches which are faster and more efficient. The main setback is the fact that our public system is designed to transmit analogue signals; however, it is currently being converted to a digital service which will give improved operation and lower costs. Faster transmission media such as microwave, satellites and optic fibre cables are also being used to upgrade the system.

As computers are digital devices their messages consist of strings of 0s and 1s which can be easily represented by using two different voltage signals. These digital signals must be converted into analogue signals for onward transmission along the PSTN. A piece of equipment called a *modem* must be interfaced between the computer and the telephone socket to do this.

DEVELOPMENTS IN TELEPHONE SERVICES

The most used and least noticed piece of office equipment must be the telephone. Many firms do not realize its importance and the cost of the delays involved in having insufficient lines or using old equipment that does not offer the services currently available to business users. Over the next few years the telephone seems likely to stay at the heart of new systems development and, as we shall see shortly, it will have an important role in the development of integrated office systems.

Through the 1981 Telecommunications Act the British Government sought to break the monopoly that had previously been granted to British Telecom and to introduce competition into the market. Mercury were granted rights to compete with them on the provision of the telecommunications network, and equipment suppliers could now sell approved products directly to the public. Up to that time anyone requiring a telephone system with less than 100 extensions had to buy it from BT, but customers can now go direct to the manufacturers.

We noted above that the system is being converted from analogue to digital equipment. Until this is completed new equipment manufacturers are having to provide dual standard equipment which can be converted when the need arises.

The reader may have noticed the effect of some of the changes at his or her place of work or on visits to offices. The number of telephonists employed on larger systems has fallen and the equipment they use appears far simpler. Gone are the old plugboards and even the switching units that were so common until recently. Today a small electronic console and handset is all that visitors see, and this is supplemented by a control box normally placed out of sight beneath the desk. This equipment allows one person to operate what is a very complex internal switching exchange offering a wide variety of features. This equipment has brought great changes to internal systems and is called a PABX (private automatic branch exchange).

Despite its importance and usefulness to business, the telephones can be very inefficient. Users can often spend half an hour or more trying and retrying an engaged number before getting through only to find that the person sought is out at another premises or in the car. Most users will fume and fret while a business microcomputer takes perhaps 30 seconds to load a file they are working on, yet they will accept this waste of time on the telephone as a fact of life! The new telephone systems offer a variety of services which may not at first glance appear revolutionary but which can save a great amount of time and effort (Fig. 15.1).

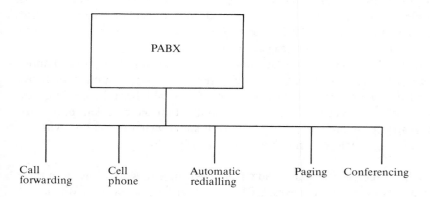

Figure 15.1 Telephone services can put most people in touch with their offices

Call forwarding or diverting

The proprietor of a small business in particular relies on the telephone to pick up a great deal of business. If he or she has to leave the premises on a job, there may be nobody available to take a message and business can be lost. One answer to this is to purchase one of the range of telephone answering machines currently available. These will record all phone messages and some make it possible to ring in from a distant phone and hear messages. However, many people do not like leaving messages on this type of system and it is certainly not very helpful if the caller needs to be questioned for detailed information.

Many telephone systems now offer a call divert option which will automatically transfer any calls from the office phone to any other stipulated extension or telephone which may be situated in another building or even in a car. A colleague of the authors who sells this equipment has his calls rerouted to the car from his office phone when he leaves the building. Should he leave the car, he will further divert the calls from the car to his BT pocket pager. Some rerouting systems will search up to ten different numbers in rotation until an answer is received.

Telephone pagers

These are small electronic bleepers carried on one's person which are activated by a selective radio signal. To page someone who is not currently available on the telephone, the office rings the pager number. A recorded message informs them that the call has been accepted and they replace the phone. Within seconds the person's pager will start to bleep—a warning to contact the office—and the person can phone in and accept the message. It is possible to leave a message in a person's electronic mailbox (see below) and have the system page him or her. In such a case the recipient can contact the mailbox and collect the message.

The writers know of some auxiliary coastguards who carry two-channel pagers with a different tone for each channel. If the pager sounds they know immediately whether they have to call the office or whether it is an emergency call from the coastguard marine rescue coordination centre. Silent pagers are now available, as are special pagers with a small visual display on which a short message such as a number to call can be displayed.

Facilities such as the above allow business people to work away from their base for short periods. However, BT has a further scheme for those who might work from home for longer periods. Under this scheme, callers can dial the office and will be charged at the call rate to that office. The calls will, however, be routed to the user at his home or any other diverted number which may be some distance away.

Automatic redialling
If a number is engaged, this facility allows the user to replace the handset and carry on working while the system will continuously recall the number until it obtains a free line at which time it notifies the user.

Call logging
The total cost of calls, particularly in a large system, can soon mount up. Many systems therefore include call-logging facilities which monitor the cost and duration of calls. These will print out details of individual calls, analyse the number and cost of calls from any extension, and identify those that are under-used and possibly not required.

To allow a further level of control, private extensions can be barred from making all but local calls and the system will block them off as soon as they dial the first digit of a long distance code (normally zero).

Memory facilities
Many systems can hold a set of phone numbers in memory allowing the user to call up long complicated numbers by entering only two figures.

Call conferencing
This allows a number of users on different phones to be linked together and each contribute to a telephone conference. Private data or speech lines can be rented by firms to link their own equipment and with larger systems they may even use their own microwave links.

Facsimile transmission
Equipment is available to transmit copies of documents along ordinary phone lines. Only a small proportion of larger firms have this equipment, but it can be done through some post offices.

Electronic mail
These services are provided through Telecom Gold, Cable and Wireless, etc., and offer a wide variety of services over the telephone. This is outlined as a separate service below.

Both BT and ICL have produced desk computer systems which contain a small desk-top computer, a telephone handset and communications equipment. They see this as an early development towards integrated office systems (see page 278).

The reader will note that several of the facilities above have been marked as specialized services; they will be dealt with in later sections, which show how the telephone system is at the heart of many of the office systems developments currently taking place.

ELECTRONIC MAIL

Once a firm has computers that are able to transfer data to each other it is a small step to using these to send messages, rather than typing them out and posting them. It is far more immediate and saves the printing and posting time. Electronic mail is a formal system offering a range of services based on such messaging.

If users were only able to communicate with other users currently working at a terminal, this service would not be as helpful as the telephone. An electronic mail system, however, resembles a set of electronic pigeon holes, as users rarely communicate directly but leave their messages in private mail boxes, on a central computer, for later retrieval. The recipients will have their own passwords and will be able to access their own mail boxes at any time.

Several firms offer commercial electronic mailing services based on the PSTN which can link users around the world. Such services are offered by BT. Cable and Wireless, and Prestel and—increasingly—firms with their own LANs are running their own internal mailing systems as well.

The procedure for using a public electronic mailing service works as follows. We will consider some of the work that a single user might do in checking the mail box.

1. The first task is to log on to the mail system by dialling up the host computer and identifying the user. This identification will consist of a two-part codeword, the first part being the user's allocated system code and the second a personal password created by the user to control access to the box.
2. Once the user is on the system a screen message will state whether there are any messages and if any are coded urgent. The user may scan these and for any of them may decide to:
    - hold it on the file,
    - pass it on to another person (and keep a copy if required),
    - print out a hard copy.
3. Having dealt with incoming mail there may be a few letters to send out:
    - A note to a supplier who is on the system can be written, corrected and then sent to the appropriate mailbox. If the letter is urgent it can be

marked as such and as requiring acknowledgement. The system will notify the recipient of this and if he or she is in touch with the system a reply may even be received within the hour.

- The next task is to announce to all the departmental staff, and to selected managers in other departments, the promotion of one of the supervisors to the role of manager. As the user has an appointment with the new manager at 14.00 h, to break the good news, the memo will be drafted with a system date and time on it for 14.15. The other staff will then be notified automatically through their mail boxes just as the interview is finishing. The circulation will be to all staff on one of the files, which will be specified. The system will then copy the message to each mail box on the file without any further action on the user's part.

A public electronic mail system is not cheap as users are charged joining fees and line charges while connected to the system. However, it offers facilities not available with other media. It is faster than conventional mail and avoids the problem of repeated telephone calls and, given access to a terminal, users can contact the system from anywhere in the country. Also, the service allows the development of flexible working methods. Users can check and update their mail from home and many do so at any time that suits them, e.g. late at night or between flights, when they would not be able to gain access to the office to check hard mail.

TELETEXT AND VIEWDATA SYSTEMS
These are systems designed to provide information to homes and business premises using the standard colour television as a display medium.

Teletext
The Ceefax and Oracle systems transmitted by the BBC and ITN networks are British examples of this medium. Teletext signals are transmitted along with television signals and can be picked up by viewers with a teletext converter fitted to their set.

Such systems are used to provide general information and news updates and do not therefore provide much in the way of business information.

Information is arranged on individual screens or pages which can hold both text and graphics, and make good use of colour. The presentation is therefore attractive and the teletext form of presentation is also used for viewdata screens.

Because of the broadcast medium, teletext is a one-way system, i.e. the user has no communication with the computer. The system cycles through all the screens in turn and the user after keying in the chosen screen number must wait up to 30 seconds until it is next broadcast. The decoder will then pull down the picture data and display it on the screen as long as required.

There are no transmission charges (apart from the television licence) and all screens may be viewed at no cost.

Viewdata

Viewdata is a form of communication which resembles teletext in appearance, but the system is interactive. Prestel is the British example of this system; it uses telephone lines to provide a two-way link between users and the computer.

Prestel uses a screen of 24 lines, each of which can hold up to 40 characters. The use of colour and graphics allows a very user-friendly presentation but limits the amount of information each screen can carry. This is often criticized but for some applications it can be an advantage as it prevents users trying to put too much information on one screen.

Prestel holds thousands of screens of information arranged in a tree structure. A main menu allows choices between several main headings, and submenus allow the user to close in on specific information by working down through the system. This method of search is very slow (and costly in telephone charges) so Prestel is working on developing a word search system to speed up data retrieval.

When it started in 1979 Prestel was the first system of its kind in the world and BT forecast high sales and 100 000 users by 1980. However, six years later they had sold only half this number. They originally tried to sell it as a commercial system marketing general information to the public but experience has shown that most of us do not require such general information. Recently they have changed to marketing more specific services to specialist 'closed user groups'. This has led to a significant increase in their income and the general information is now seen as an additional benefit.

Users are not able to alter information screens, which have to be prepared and input by specialist firms called information providers who have the necessary equipment. There are other screens known as response screens that allow users to send messages back to the computer. In this way a wide range of special services can be provided. The user is charged for the time the telephone line is occupied and may be charged for access to particular screens.

Users need either a Prestel adaptor for their television or a hardware add-on for their computers to access the system.

The interactive nature of viewdata allows it to be used to offer a number of services, some of which are listed below. To be commercially successful the system requires a large user base and Prestel does not have this. The French government has supported their system Minitel by providing units free to households as electronic telephone directories. As a result they have a large user base which makes schemes such as those outlined below economic to provide.

Telesoftware The system can transfer information that has been converted into the correct format, and is used by groups such as the home computer users' group Micronet to transfer programs to users.

Electronic mail With individual protected mail boxes set up in the computer a viewdata system can be used to provide electronic mail services.

Electronic selling A number of firms, the best known of which are travel agents, use Prestel to advertise goods and allow products to be ordered using response frames. Many travel firms now issue screens updating agents' information on holidays available. Using the system the agent can book any of the holidays on offer immediately.

In the West Midlands a local group, Club 403, offers links to retailers, theatre bookings and other services

Electronic banking The Bank of Scotland has linked with the Nottingham Building Society to provide home banking services. Clients can obtain details of their balance and make deposits and payments through a Prestel closed user group.

While there are problems with the take-up rate of Prestel, due partly to the method of marketing, viewdata does offer another great advantage. There is a great deal of incompatibility between different computers so that it is not always easy to transfer data from one to another without special software. However, viewdata is a common standard across a range of machines, and information on a viewdata system can be accessed from any of them if they have the necessary equipment to give them viewdata capability. Private viewdata services provided within a firm or by a local group are becoming more popular and seem likely to provide a bigger market than that of public viewdata systems. The authors are working on the development of such a system at the Polytechnic of Wales and see a wide variety of services that could be offered on such a system. For example, in the future it could prove a useful and user-friendly link for technical updates to accountants' clients and it is also a useful medium for advertisements.

Office systems

Journalists have looked forward to the 'electronic office' or the 'integrated office' for many years. Despite the great progress made with most office equipment, as microchips have been incorporated, until recently these have been mainly piecemeal developments with little attempt being made to integrate them. With the development of good local networks it is now possible to link up the various office services and make them available to all users from their own desk tops. A number of firms preparing to move into new offices are planning their information needs in advance and intend to install the necessary equipment and networks prior to moving in, as is done with all other services.

The office sector is still generally a low-investment area of business and while production, storekeeping and other areas have shown great gains from investments in modern methods general office work has seen nothing like the investment per employee that has been allocated to those areas. The average office employee is provided with a desk, filing cabinet and possibly shared access to photocopiers, etc.; in some cases add a personal computer and that's all. As a result the way office work is performed is still relatively inefficient, with work on a job often being done in small bursts of activity, interrupted by periods of searching for or waiting for files. Then the work will be sent off for draft typing and returned for checking often a week or more after it was done. After this delay the writer may need to spend some time revising the work before he can edit it.

Integrated office systems provide office workers with their own desktop terminals or workstations networked into a whole range of office services which can be accessed without leaving the workstation. Some of these are illustrated in Fig. 15.2.

The following scenario shows how the preparation of a sales report might proceed using such a system. On arrival at the office one morning the sales supervisor was called in by the sales manager and asked to produce a 'once-off' sales forecast and report for a management meeting that afternoon.

He returned to his workstation and asked the PABX operator to arrange a conference call with the five area sales managers or their representatives.

In this short discussion he made clear what figures he required and where they could be extracted from the local systems. These were to be sent to his electronic mail box by ten o'clock.

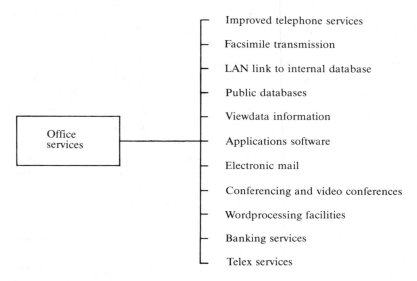

Office
services

- Improved telephone services
- Facsimile transmission
- LAN link to internal database
- Public databases
- Viewdata information
- Applications software
- Electronic mail
- Conferencing and video conferences
- Wordprocessing facilities
- Banking services
- Telex services

Figure 15.2 Integrated office services

In the meantime he loaded the spreadsheet program into his workstation and drafted the form of report, setting up formulae to present ratios, etc.

He wanted sales details for the whole industry for the same period so he put the report aside into a small window on screen and called up the trade association's database. A fast search based on certain keywords allowed him to obtain what he wanted but not laid out as he wished. These figures were downloaded to his machine and stored in a wordprocessing file.

He then checked his mail box and found that all but one of the area figures had been received. As the area numbers were stored in memory on his workstation it was quicker to use it to autodial than to go through the switchboard. Unfortunately the number was engaged so he replaced the handset and left the automatic recall to keep testing the line until it was clear.

In the meantime he went back to the wordprocessing program and started to draft out the text of his report, changing the industry figures to the format he wanted. When it came to inserting the figures from his spreadsheet model he left a space. From the small screen window he could see the general layout and figures if he required.

The phone rang with the reply from the remaining sales area where due to illness the work was being performed by a junior member of staff who did not really understand what was involved. A few minutes' discussion showed that he did not know how to obtain the required figures from the reports in front of him and there was no one there to help him. The best alternative seemed to be to ask him to transmit facsimile copies to the supervisor at once. While these were coming over the line the supervisor finished the draft on the wordprocessor and incorporated the other departments' figures into his report.

When the reports from the final area were in, he extracted the figures required and incorporated these into the spreadsheet. He then tested the model to ensure that it was correct and tried some forecast figures through it. Then he used the graphics facilities to produce several types of graph from the data.

Next he rang the sales manager for final approval but was told she was engaged. He used the callback facility available to staff on his grade. This he knew would switch on a warning light on the manager's workstation and put into store a voice message saying that the report needed her final approval.

He was finalizing the job when the sales manager rang back. Over the telephone he explained what he had done and showed on screen the format of the report and the graphs. They agreed the general format and decided to incorporate bar charts. He was asked to save the model so that it could be used to try out various alternatives at the meeting, and to come over to the manager's office to discuss the report.

Before leaving he incorporated the table and graphs from the spreadsheet into his wordprocessor and saved the file.

At the manager's office he asked her secretary to check the report against the spelling checker in the wordprocessor and print it out through the laser printer as it required high-quality print and graphics.

While the supervisor was discussing the model with the manager, the secretary brought in two copies of the final report. As there were no further changes to be made, it was agreed that it should be duplicated for the meeting. This involved transferring the file to the laser printer and stipulating the number of copies.

The technology mentioned in the above scenario is currently available and the software is commonly used on computers. However, it is only in recent years that suppliers have started to market them as integrated systems. Firms such as ICL are marketing linked office systems and both they and BT now market a small workstation which consists of monitor, keyboard and telephone. It includes wordprocessor, spreadsheet, data management and graphics software, and can be linked to other computer systems. At present these are relatively crude devices but would seem to be pioneers of more sophisticated systems yet to come.

Expert systems

Science fiction films regularly portray the computer as a friendly source of advice for the hero. Computers from Hal through to R2D2 have been shown listening to users' problems and coming up with expert advice given in helpful everyday language which the user can easily comprehend. Accountants working with computers and trying to find out some piece of non-standard information have found, to their cost, that unfortunately computers do not function in this way. A group of students working with computers told us that they got on better with them when they started to think of them as high-speed morons. Comments such as these illustrate the facts that computers lack intelligence and that their method of working can be difficult for human users to adapt to.

Science fiction often foreshadows what people feel will eventually become scientific fact. At present, manufacturers world-wide are competing to develop fifth-generation machines which will be very large powerful machines capable of handling work that is impossible with today's machines. While we are on the subject of science fiction it is interesting to note that the world's largest computer was used to animate sequences for the film 'The Last Starfighter'. Even this five-ton monster took five minutes to produce just one frame of a sequence and it is not yet possible therefore to produce a whole feature film in this manner.

If today's largest machines face such problems in recreating one aspect of human imagination, what sort of machines will be required to simulate human intelligence? This is what the fifth-generation project is about—the development of machines with the power to handle artificial intelligence. Of course the machines will only provide the hardware, and special software will be required. A great deal of research work has already been done into this, and special languages such as LISP have been developed to program them. The research teams have to be multidisciplinary because in addition to computer science this project crosses the boundaries of psychology, linguistics, etc. In fact the study of the meaning of language has proved very important. If they are to be really useful these machines will have to be used by business people in their everyday work. These people will not be computer scientists and will need to be able to frame problems in simple language. Look again at that last sentence. You probably had no problem with the term 'simple language'. You hardly bothered to define it but took its meaning in the context of the sentence. Try teaching that to a computer! This is the sort of problem that will have to be solved before we reach higher levels of artificial intelligence.

There are, however, applications of artificial intelligence which are being developed for use already. The main one is *expert systems*. These are an attempt to take the knowledge of an expert or group of experts and place it on a computer. People working in the same field can then consult the system and obtain the sort of analysis and advice that the expert would provide. A specialist called a knowledge engineer works with the expert to build up a set of decision rules that represent the expert's knowledge. The system must be flexible and set up in a form of language that users can understand, because such systems are not static but will develop over time as an expert's own knowledge would do.

Examples of expert systems are currently running in the area of investment advice. Such systems seem likely to prove useful in those applications where there is much data which is constantly changing and where opinions have to be offered on this. It seems likely, therefore, that in future years accountants will see such systems developed to assist them in areas such as taxation, planning personal finance and the interpretation of accounts.

The systems of this type currently in use are very costly to produce. However, their users in general seem satisfied that the investment is worthwhile and claim that they can produce savings that more than cover their costs and in many cases yield a very good return. This is, however, an early spin-off from technology which is still being developed, and with the new generation of machines and further software development artificial intelligence could well become very important and may greatly influence our lives.

Summary

1. Information technology is affecting most sectors of the economy. For our purposes we must concentrate on the aspects that are currently affecting the financial world. However, important changes in production and other specialist areas will eventually have an effect on our area.
2. Information technology means far more than improvements in areas such as photocopiers and telephones. It is the result of the convergence of developments in computing, communications and office technology and is so fundamental that it is making information more important in the economy and affecting the way we live and work. This is not going to be a once-and-for-all development but rather an ongoing revolution which is

likely to increase in speed. Accountants and other professionals will therefore need to work to keep up with the pace of change; to fall behind in the race will prove costly both to nations and to individuals.

3. The ability to link computers is one of the basic developments that have led to the facilities we see today. Local area networks are used to link computers and other equipment within firms. We have a standard form of organizing data for transmission in the ASCII code. Until now there has been no standard system for networking, but the adoption of the IBM standard seems likely to achieve this.

   Wide area networks are used to connect equipment over longer distances, using public lines. At present the public system handles analogue signals rather than the digital signals used by computers, so modems are required to convert the signal as it enters and leaves the public network.

4. The telephone system has a central role in the development of office systems. It will continue to handle voice messages, and a number of new services have been developed here. It is also playing an ever-increasing role in the transmission of data, and developments such as fibre optic lines are improving its capacity to handle such traffic.

5. Electronic mailing provides a number of services which complement existing services. It is faster than traditional mail and avoids the need to repeat unanswered telephone calls. The use of facsimile services allows copies of documents to be transmitted where the post is too slow.

6. Viewdata provides an interesting medium for transmitting information to a range of machines. Public viewdata services can be used to provide electronic banking and shopping services plus community information. However they require a large user base to become economic. This has not been achieved in the UK where closed user groups are providing the main custom. However, in France, a different form of promotion has achieved the necessary user base.

   Simple viewdata systems can be set up by firms or local groups and developed to serve particular interests.

7. These various new services and products have been developed into integrated office systems. The average investment per worker is lower in the office than in other areas of business, and developments such as these seem likely to improve output and change methods of working.

8. Great efforts are being made to develop fifth-generation machines which will offer services not presently possible. Artificial intelligence is being developed for implementation on these machines and should allow

ordinary users to perform very complex work. One aspect already being developed is that of expert systems, which allow the knowledge of an expert or group of experts to be put on the computer. Other staff can then use the system to obtain the sort of assistance they would gain from the expert. Some of these are in use and others are being developed, but they are at the first stages of development. The greatest impact will come with the next generation of hardware.

16

Information technology in action

Introduction

We have seen how information technology is creating a range of new services for the financial world and it has been stated that it will affect the way we perform our work. In this chapter we shall consider its effects upon the banking profession, one area that all accountants have some dealings with.

It is no accident that the banks are among the largest users of information technology in most developed countries, because their whole business is one of transferring information around the world. In fact, due to their operations, coin and notes finance only a small proportion of world trade and have become merely the 'small change' of the monetary system. Bank credit which finances so much of the world's trade is really a form of information transfer as charges between banks are set off against one another at the bankers' clearing centres. Relatively little cash or gold changes hands, even between the banks themselves. It is information that is transferred around the world.

The banks operate world-wide, processing billions of transactions in a field where delay costs money, and the whole fabric of their business rests on confidence in their ability to manage this information. Without information technology they would find it very costly to handle their current volumes of work in the required time.

The larger banks are increasingly coming to be seen as major computer systems to which other organizations can link in order to pass data. There are advantages in this both for the client and for the bank; direct computer links with clients allow banks to handle large volumes of transactions at high speed, and as virtually all the paperwork is eliminated this keeps down the administrative costs to both parties.

Client services

Banks deal with an extremely wide range of customers from young savers through to major international financial groups. A large proportion of the working population is paid by direct transfer to their bank accounts. Britain lags behind Europe in the proportion of its working population so paid, but most employers prefer to pay this way and various bodies (including, naturally, the banks) are trying to increase the proportion. To small clients such as this they offer a range of personal financial services. At the other end of the range their clients are multinational companies handling many thousands of transactions daily, working in several major currencies and requiring fast cash transfers around the world. Such clients will also require highly technical advice and information gathered by the banks through their world-wide networks of branches and associated companies.

To serve their very wide client base they have to offer a very wide range of client services from personal loans to portfolio management. In this chapter we do not have sufficient space to look at all of these and must concentrate on those that illustrate particular applications of information technology. At the end of the chapter we will briefly touch on some other uses which banks are making of information technology.

ELECTRONIC FUNDS TRANSFER AT POINT OF SALE SYSTEMS (EFTPOS)

A large proportion of consumer spending takes place at garages, supermarkets and shops where payment may be by cash, cheque or credit card, with the latter two methods of payment increasing in volume. The sums collected by the trader must be totalled, recorded and reconciled and then taken to the bank and paid in. These procedures are costly and the handling of large volumes of cash increases the risk of theft. From the bank's point of view they must handle a huge volume of documentation in the form of cheques, paying-in documents and credit card billings.

EFTPOS systems are designed to do away with many of these costs by bringing the bank's data capture forward to the actual point of sale. The customer will be encouraged to pay using any bank or other credit card recognized by the system. To pay, the card is inserted into a special terminal at the checkout or garage and the customer is required to key in a private iden-tification number. If the card and number agree, details of the transaction will be transmitted directly to the bank computers where the customer's account will be charged and the supplier's account credited. The retailer will issue the customer with a sales slip in the normal way but does not have to handle cash or visit the bank. There is the added advantage that retailers do not have to wait for payment as their accounts are updated immediately.

A series of trials have taken place at various locations and it is claimed that we could have a national system by 1988. Some of the test machines at petrol stations were actually fixed to the petrol pump and a customer could complete the transaction without visiting the cashier's office. Machines of this type could have a number of self-service applications across a wide range of firms in the future and could allow us to purchase goods at any time of the day or night. They have the attraction that although, like any other machine, they may be vulnerable to vandalism, they contain no money and are less likely therefore to attract such attention.

This is an interesting application of both communications and computers to provide a network that serves both banks and retailers. There have been problems in developing the system because, in addition to the arguments one might expect over who shall bear the costs of such a system, many retailers now issue their own in-store credit cards in direct competition with the banks and do not want to see the banks steal a lead over them by excluding such cards. The proposed British system will therefore recognize a variety of different cards from banks and other organizations.

AUTOMATIC TELLER MACHINES (ATM)
These are the cash dispensing machines which are frequently seen at banks and other locations such as shopping centres and building societies. Their main purpose is to allow customers to draw cash at any time and to provide banking services where it would not be viable to open another branch, e.g. on a college campus.

The machines currently in use allow users to draw any sum up to a limited amount, view the current position on their account and order a new cheque book. To obtain money from the unit the customer needs a special ATM card and is notified of a personal identification number which is not shown on the face of the card. The card must be inserted into the machine and the personal number typed in. The machine will validate the code number and if correct will allow access to the bank's computer both to check the account balance and, if there are sufficient funds, to withdraw cash.

With such systems security is a paramount concern because the machines must hold large amounts of cash which they dispense to customers. The machines are said to cost £20 000 and may cost half as much again to install as they in fact resemble a mini-strong room and must be cemented into place. This illustrates the additional costs involved when the banks have to handle hard money rather than information. There have been some problems with acceptance of this form of technology. Stories in the press have stressed that customers who claim to have been charged with sums they did not withdraw found themselves unable to prove the fact, and apparently some customers have returned their cards. One customer who came across a generous machine managed to fill a suitcase with the money the machine paid out to him. He was rather annoyed when he returned the money to the bank and told them what had happened because they then charged him interest on the money.

As the machines are so expensive they are not provided at all banks and outside normal banking hours a customer may have to travel some distance to find one. The position is being improved, however, as a number of banks and building societies are networking their machines together for the common benefit of all their customers who may then use their cards in any of them.

HOME BANKING SERVICES

We have already noted early developments of this form of service to domestic and small business users. The problem, however, lies in the communications link between the computer and the customer. While the telephone could be used, customers would be unwilling to pay trunk call charges to access their bank. Prestel has been identified as one medium allowing local rate calls to be used, but the small customer base of Prestel means that most people do not have access to it. However, the current developments in cabling several of our cities may well lead to a service such as this on a local basis in the future. At the time of writing, the French viewdata company Minitel has announced its intention to enter the British viewdata market and it remains to be seen whether it will achieve a greater market penetration than Prestel.

BANKERS AUTOMATED CLEARING SYSTEM (BACS)

This scheme was developed jointly by the main banks to allow customer data to be taken directly on to bank machines, avoiding the work involved in keying it in manually. At first it was used by large firms and local authorities to pay wages and salaries and to make payments to their suppliers. The banks themselves also use it to handle the large number of standing orders that they pay every month.

Originally customers could arrange for their computers to output details of payees, account numbers and branch codes on to a tape in a format specified by BACS. This had to be delivered to the BACS centre in London which would then process it and pass the details to the appropriate banks. Using this system a large number of payments can be transferred directly into the appropriate accounts across a number of banks and one payment, covering the whole amount, is paid out of the client's own account. The system saves a great deal of detailed work and is far cheaper than normal processing; while a cheque costs the bank about £2 to process, a BACS transaction costs only a few pence.

The system has been well used but the need to send up to 1000 tapes a day to the London centre created problems and led to delays, particularly for branches and clients outside London. As a result the BACSTEL scheme was developed to allow clients to send data directly into the BACS system using the public telephone network or rented lines. This has speeded up the transfer of data and about 2000 payments can now be entered in two minutes. It has also encouraged more businesses to make use of the service, which is now looking at the viability of allowing micro users to send details into the system on floppy diskettes.

CLEARING HOUSE AUTOMATED PAYMENT SYSTEM (CHAPS)

For many years banks and branches in London have operated a fast system which allows them to offset payments between them, called the 'town clearing'. Under this system they could be assured that local transfers of funds would be cleared on the same day and this allowed customers to treat amounts so transferred to them as available cash. However, transactions from other parts of the country could take several days to clear with resultant costs and inconvenience to customers.

Under the CHAPS scheme large payments (over £10 000) can be treated in the same way. It is an electronic messaging system within which all transactions are transmitted in code to help reduce the risk of fraud. The appeal of the system is that in return for the cost of the transfer, any sum so transferred will be entered into the recipient's account that same day and can therefore be treated as available cash, thus reducing borrowing charges. The bank making the transfer must ensure beforehand that its customer has sufficient credit because, once performed, the transaction is irrevocable under the rules of the scheme.

SOCIETY FOR WORLDWIDE INTERBANK FAST TRANSFERS (SWIFT)

This has been running for almost ten years and is a computerized messaging system which links banks around the world. In 1986 it was updated from a centralized system to a decentralized computer network because of the increasing amount of work passing through the system. They are also aiming to improve the speed and service in order to prevent the individual banks setting up their own computerized messaging systems in opposition.

At the time of writing it is open only to the banks but there have been repeated requests to allow large multinational companies, which run their own treasury functions, to use it. These firms operate rather like banks in their own right and transfer large sums around the world. Up to now the banks have refused this access as it would inevitably result in the firms performing their own cash transfers on this system, thus depriving the banks of a source of income.

CASH MANAGEMENT SERVICES

Banks offer a number of sophisticated services to larger clients to help them manage their funds world-wide. Such clients will have many subsidiaries around the world, each with their own bank accounts held in local currencies. In such cases the treasury department or holding company frequently acts as banker to the group, covering overdrafts in one country by transfers from another company's accounts.

Using these cash management facilities they can quickly bring together information about balances across the world and transfer funds from one part of the world to another to cover shortages or to invest temporary surpluses. They also offer customers the facility to build this information into complex cash forecasting models which are held on the bank's computers.

Using a terminal to the bank such clients can also obtain special details and reports on the international currency markets. Those organizations with large overseas interests stand to lose a great deal if the exchange rates move against them. Their finance staff are therefore willing to pay for accurate information and good forecasting to help offset these risks. In addition to regular market reports some banks allow customers to access complex currency models and use these to evaluate alternative policies and forecast likely outcomes.

CHEQUE HANDLING

The major system that has not yet been fully computerized in British banks is that of cheque handling. This involves a great deal of work and, it is claimed, costs £2 per cheque to process. All cheques are marked with magnetic ink characters to allow them to be sorted at high speed. Local cheques, i.e. those affecting only one branch, may be processed there and input to the main computer using the branch terminal. However, most cheques are sent off for processing and although current equipment can handle almost 2500 of these every minute this is still a large task which must be performed to a strict timetable.

Some continental banks have fully computerized this system and details of cheques are entered through the terminals of the branch where they are presented for payment and then retained there. This saves a great deal of movement of paper, and once the information is captured it can be used to provide any information produced under the present system.

Internal management

DEALING ROOMS

Banks are major dealers in the foreign exchange and bond markets and employ teams of specialist dealers to buy and sell on their behalf in these markets.

When multi-million-pound transactions are involved a small fall or gain in market rates can earn or lose large sums for the bank so dealers require up-to-the-second information on rates which are constantly changing and on the degree of exposure of their bank in terms of each major currency.

The currency markets now operate 24 hours a day across international boundaries and specialist information services such as Reuters continuously transmit details of market rates to their subscribers. Dealers in electronic dealing rooms around the world can enter the market at any time to make deals from their desks.

The deregulation of the city, commonly known as the 'big bang', has brought increased competition as new firms move into this area. As a result orders for new electronic dealing rooms have increased greatly. One merchant bank recently paid £750 000 for a new 70-position dealer room to deal in securities, and the Midland Bank has a new room with 130 positions at its headquarters. Operators will have four screens at their desks, providing access to 23 different information sources. While working, dealers will watch the Reuters' rates on one screen while keeping a view of their own bank's rates and their degree of exposure on others. In some dealing rooms another screen which is touch sensitive links the dealer to BT's City Business Service. By touching a particular part of this screen a fast call can be put through to a particular dealer in some other part of the world. When deals are agreed, details are entered by the dealer at the workstation and are then immediately transferred to the firm's main computers which then amend the in-house information and take over the work of recording it. The dealer is then free to concentrate on the market movements and negotiate the next deal—this is an area where the old maxim 'time is money' certainly applies.

The whole method of working in this part of the bank revolves around information technology and the banks look to their systems to give their dealers the edge over the opposition when making decisions. In some of the new dealing rooms minicomputers and personal computers are used to provide additional backup and help dealers keep up with events. With all the complex factors involved and the second-by-second changes, this would appear to be an area where expert systems might prove invaluable in the future.

MANAGEMENT SERVICES

Behind all these services the banks are running a business and their managers, like those in other areas, use computers to assist them with their work. Their earliest uses of computers were to perform their own accounting work and they are still looking at how to improve their systems. There have been experiments with a hierarchical network where branches would hold their own customer data on local computers, networked into mainframes, but these have not yet been adopted.

At main offices wordprocessors and microcomputers are used to assist management and some branch managers have been equipped with micro-computers that allow them to access branch information from their desks.

Decision support software is used by staff to prepare a range of models in a number of areas such as finance and foreign exchange.

Fascimile equipment is used to transmit copies of documents which are queried by the BACS centre.

To help combat some of the losses on credit cards traders can contact a hotline where operators with computer terminals can check the validity of British and American cards in seconds.

The banks have large training organizations to prepare staff for their role in operating these systems, and in this section of their work they also use informa-tion technology, making much use of video for both internal training and customer relations; viewdata is used as a training medium on some courses.

The benefits of IT
The banks turned to information technology for a number of reasons and generally appear pleased with the results. Over the years their staff numbers have grown but at a rate well below the growth in business handled. They appear to have removed many of the basic clerical tasks that were involved with the handling of paper-based transactions, but some of this still exists in connection wih cheques.

Banks argue that they are able to offer services they could never have provided without information technology. Developments like BACS have cer-tainly kept their costs down—without them bank charges would have to be much higher than they are. Technology has allowed them to improve their traditional services as well. For many years customers complained about the unhelpful trading hours of banks, yet the banks themselves faced difficult problems even in providing a limited service on Saturday mornings. Automatic teller machines now provide banking services around the clock and allow customers to view the state of their accounts.

Banks certainly do provide a wide range of services, many of which would not be available without developments in technology. Teller machines have improved customer services and it is argued that EFTPOS and increased payment of wages through banks will not only reduce bank costs but will reduce the amount of cash in transit and therefore should reduce the incidence of certain cash-related crimes.

The banks' use of IT has allowed them to remain more competitive than they might otherwise have been compared with other financial institutions, and we are already seeing building societies and other firms moving into this area and adopting similar technology in order to compete.

Summary

1. This chapter considers the banking profession as an example of how information technology is affecting one sector of the financial world.

    Banking was chosen for two reasons:
    - The banks are among the largest users in all countries.
    - This is one aspect of business that affects every accountant.

2. Banks are major users of the technology because their business is information based. Very little money is moved around the world; banks set off their claims against one another daily with the net indebtedness being settled mainly by transfers between their accounts in the Central Bank.

    The details of the individual transactions, however, have to be communicated between the bank branches and the clearing houses, and speed and accuracy are vital. Banks are therefore in the business of transferring information rather than money.

3. One trend today is to increase the facilities for clients to access bank computers and transfer their data directly on to them. This benefits the banks and their customers by allowing cheaper, faster and more efficient data capture. The cost to the bank of processing a cheque is about £2, while the same payment processed through BACS costs just a few pence.

4. Through increased use of technology the banks are able to offer a range of client services not previously possible:
    - EFTPOS will be a new service allowing clients to pay bills with credit cards, etc. The banks will pick up transaction details at the point of sale and the trade and customer accounts involved will be updated in real time. This may well affect the provision of services in the economy as it can allow self-service outlets to operate without the need for cashier staff.
    - Automatic teller machines are the machines installed outside banks. The range of services offered on the machines is expanding and allows banking services to be offered at all hours or at locations where it would not be economic to site a branch. The machines are costly and need a great deal of protection as they handle paper money rather than information.
    - Home banking services have started slowly in this country though there has been an increase in the range of services offered within such systems. The main barrier to expansion appears to be the provision of a

suitable communications network. At present viewdata and cable links do not have sufficient penetration in this country to provide the critical mass of customers necessary for such services to expand.

- The BACS system allows organizations to make large numbers of payments by direct transfer from their own computers through to payees' accounts in a wide range of banks. The system was originally based on tape files that had to be transported into the BACS centre but it now allows direct transfer of information using telecommunications links.
- CHAPS allows a fast, guaranteed same-day clearing service for large payments. They can treat sums so transferred as available funds and reduce interest charges, etc.
- SWIFT is the bankers' own international computerized messaging system which allows them to transfer funds and messages across the world.
- Sophisticated cash management services provide large corporations with high-speed specialist information to assist in managing their treasury function.

6. The banks also use information technology to help manage their own work. Their dealer staff have to be highly competitive in order to operate efficiently in the money markets. The dealing is now done in high-technology dealing rooms where staff are supported by a wide range of communications equipment.

They also use the technology in other areas of management, ranging from training and customer relations through to their own accounting systems.

17

The accountant and the future

Introduction

We have seen how information technology is affecting the way business operates and how the developments of integrated office systems will affect individual working patterns. As current developments are taken up and as new developments come on stream this speed of change will certainly increase. Other factors, such as moves by government to increase competition and falling markets, will all add to this trend. Faced with such changes one must wonder about the effect on accountants and accounting in the future.

The need for accounting in the future is fairly certain. However, the questions of how it will be done and who will do it are far more complex. The amount of information available to business is greatly increasing and accountants of the future will spend far less time on the collection and return of data. They will need to understand where data can be obtained and in what form it will prove most useful to the business. Accountants in the future will also have far more time available to interpret the information they produce. This will allow them to provide more meaningful information to assist management in their decision-making role.

Although the work of accountants has been in the forefront of computerization from the very beginning, accountants' professional bodies have been slow to react to the importance of information technology to their members. However, in recent years they have taken steps to remedy this situation. The accounting professional bodies are now deeply involved in researching the area, have made resources available for it, and are also engaged in developing policies for the future.

The last four years have seen several developments:

1. The Chartered Association of Certified Accountants (CACA), with the Department of Trade and Industry, carried out an accounting sector study entitled *Information Technology and the Accountants*. A follow-up is to be performed to test the prophecies made and this will also look at the position in the Far East with a view to collecting competitors' opinions in the same areas.

2. The Institute of Chartered Accountants in England and Wales (ICAEW) published a report by international accountants Coopers and Lybrand (themselves large users of information technology) entitled *The Chartered Accountant in the Information Technology Age*.
3. The Chartered Institute of Management Accountants (CIMA) published *Importance of Information Technology on the Management Accountant*.

Each of these studies was carried out to ascertain what is currently happening and what effect this is likely to have on the demand for accountants.

Other developments to date include:

1. the setting up by the ICAEW of an information technology working group to review and coordinate its policies in this area;
2. the issue by the ICAEW of guidelines for assessing accountancy software;
3. the formation of a committee of accounting software houses to coordinate the testing of accountancy software and its evaluation, which will be undertaken by the National Computer Centres (NCC) with costs being borne by the software companies;
4. ICAEW work on the creation of a special public network database for accountants on legislation and accountancy standards.

These are specific responses to the changes currently taking place in all sectors of the economy, but what will need to be done in the longer term?

Updating of qualified staff

All the main bodies place emphasis on the need for regular updating after qualification and run courses to this end. However, results from the various reports show that these appear to have relatively little effect in this area. Users are more likely to be self-taught or to have attended short commercial training courses on specific software.

Professional image

We see therefore a picture of a profession that is in general coping with the level of change to date, to a great extent by self-study, perseverance and self-motivation (possibly the legacy of a profession trained by correspondence courses). However, in most of the businesss world accountants do not have a good image; they are often seen as narrow in outlook and far too tied to the technicalities of accounting. The survey in one report mentioned that 'a large proportion of accountants did not seem to understand the requirements of their own training'. A general manager talking with one of the authors commented 'they were too busy making money'.

Many people consider accountants as only interested in auditing and traditional accounting. Hence clients do not as a rule think of asking their accountants for advice on computers. From the findings published in the reports, this is obviously not a fair view of all accountants. However, the profession has much work to do in informing the business community and the Government of the role that accountants can provide in computerization advice.

Likely future demand for accountants

Respondents to the various surveys showed an awareness of the changing role of accountants and the need to adapt their training schemes to meet this. They also noted in some cases that they themselves lacked many of the skills needed in this area. However, despite all this, the general feeling was that IT will offer challenges as well as problems. None of the reports forecasts serious job losses for accountants, although they have already noticed a reduction in the numbers of clerical and administrative staff employed. If we adapt to these new challenges and train to meet them in competition with other groups, it is probable that the demand for accountants will continue to exist. However, if accountants fail to keep pace with these changes others will step in and provide what the market needs.

Involvement of accountants in information technology

All of the reports found that accountants are generally taking on the challenge and becoming involved with IT. However, the speed of take-up varies across firms and across the country and much may depend on the degree of enthusiasm of individual accountants or their superiors.

Accountants have been involved with computers from the first days in business and as we have seen in this text they have worked with a whole range of data processing methods. This expertise together with the fact that their work covers all aspects of the organization should fit them to provide useful advice in this area.

The various reports show the areas in which accountants are involved and foremost among these are the following:

1. Installation of accounting systems, as we would expect, is a major area and, again as expected, accountants are seen to be involved in advising on control aspects in systems. However, there does not seem to be much evidence of their contributing to the wider role of planning for computer systems.
2. Decision support software, i.e. spreadsheets and modelling packages, represents a large and fast-growing area of their work.

3. The Institute of Cost and Management Accountants' report found that a surprising 25 per cent of its respondents had actually written and used their own programs though this is not likely to be a growing trend.

As yet most accountants do not seem to be using a wide variety of IT equipment. Many work indirectly with mainframes or more directly with microcomputers, but when it comes to communications equipment they are most likely to use telephones or telex. It is interesting to note that one report comments on old-fashioned telephone equipment causing delays. However, the sort of services we have mentioned are coming along soon and Coopers and Lybrand, the writer of one of the studies, is reported in the press to be planning a full system ready for a move to new premises.

Professional training

The reports sought members' opinions on whether newly qualified accountants were being trained for the sort of skills needed. The response from the ICAEW report was very worrying, a large proportion of members being unable to express an opinion and apparently unaware of the training needs of their members. In most reports people were not happy with the educational content and argued for more IT coverage directed towards preparing students to use IT to solve business problems and less towards computer science.

The Chartered Association of Certified Accountants went further and listed the specific skills they felt students need to acquire in the future to handle IT. These should enable the student to recognize suitable applications of IT and work with others towards their implementation. The report also emphasized the need in the future for accountants with more analytical ability.

In general, accountants who have qualified did not feel that they had the knowledge and skills they needed. Those who work in industry and commerce were happier that the necessary skills were available in their organizations.

Accountants felt that there was a need for students to start learning about IT in schools and colleges before they even started professional training. They also felt that this earlier training should be less directed to computer programming and more towards acquiring a general understanding of IT and a willingness to try out new ideas. They would probably be happy to see the developments in a number of business studies departments where this is now being done and where programming has given way to the use of spreadsheets to teach problem formulation and solution.

Conclusion

Information technology is affecting accountants' working environment each year and adding new challenges and problems to their role. The dominant position in industry held by accountants as the managers of information is under threat from data processing departments and their analytical role is being challenged by business school graduates proficient in analytical skills.

In many cases accountants in the profession are being bypassed by their clients when they seek IT advice.

The accountancy professional bodies recognize the problems but appear slow to act. The reports commissioned by the accountancy bodies refer to the lack of depth and quality in appraisal of IT in the professional examinations. However, the solution does not lie in adding more to what in some cases is already an overloaded set of syllabuses or in assuming that high examination failure rates will convince people that those who pass have a high level of expertise in IT. The accountancy profession's progress will depend on the IT training given to students. This training must incorporate the all-embracing influence of IT on the role of the accountant. The profile of the accountant in the future will be one of:

1. a broad-based information specialist with the knowledge to manipulate databases,
2. a generalist who can use specialist technology.

The future is and always will be a mystery. However, the accountant must be equipped with the latest knowledge available to exploit the potential that IT is bringing to the business world.

Glossary of computing terms

Access   We have used this term in connection with access to a storage medium. It refers to the action of locating data stored on the medium. For further information, *see* Serial access, Random access and ISAM.

Accounting package   A software package designed to process all or part of a firm's accounting data. These are normally sold as a series of subsystem modules which can be integrated to produce a full accounting system.

Accumulator   A register inside a central processor where mathematical calculations are performed. All data has to be transferred here for arithmetical or logical work to be performed on it.

Alphanumeric   Refers to characters which may be entered into or printed by computer. Alphanumeric characters include letters, numbers and certain other characters, e.g. * , + / . Numeric characters would only include the numbers 0 to 9.

Applications software   Software designed to allow the computer to perform a particular task or problem. Accounting software is an example of applications software, being designed to allow a general computer to act as an accounting tool. *See also* systems software.

ASCII   (American Standard Code for Information Interchange)   A widely used code which allows eight bits to be used to represent any character on the keyboard. It is widely used within computers and in the transmission of data.

Assembler   A systems program written to translate programs from assembly language into machine language.

Assembly language   A programming language which is very low level. However it replaces the operation codes (sets of 0s and 1s) with a set of mnemonics which are easier to memorize.

Backup It is dangerous to rely on data, programs, etc., stored on magnetic media, as heat, dust, magnetism, etc., can easily destroy them. It is normal therefore to take copies of important files and store them away from the main records. With accounting applications large volumes of important data are produced and specific procedures on backing up data have to be followed.

Bar code reader An input peripheral that uses a laser device to read information coded in the form of printed bars. It is now much used in supermarkets for stocktaking and to read in the details of goods at the point of sale.

BASIC (Beginners All-purpose Symbolic Instruction Code) A high-level programming language devised to help learners use microcomputers. It has become very popular and is now well used commercially with micros.

Batch controls Controls imposed on batches of data to ensure that errors are avoided or detected during processing. They involve manually listing figures from the input data and then, later, comparing the totals so produced against totals produced by the computer during processing. *See* Control total, Hash total and Document counts.

Batch processing A form of data processing where data is not processed as it is received. It is stored up and a whole batch of data is then processed when the appropriate software is next run. Under such systems the programs are stored off line and data cannot therefore be obtained from the files on demand. As a result far more reliance is placed on detailed printouts in such systems and the information provided is rarely fully up to date.

Bit All characters entered into a computer are stored as a series of 0s or 1s. A bit is an individual 0 or 1. A whole group of such bits (termed a Byte) is required to represent one character. An 8-bit micro is so called because it works on a byte consisting of 8 bits. Other micros use 16 and 32 bits while mainframes use even larger bytes.

Block When transferring records to or from a tape file the computer handles a block of records rather than a single one. The size of the block used in any application greatly affects the number of records that may be held on the file.

Bucket   As with the block on a tape file the machine transfers a whole group of records to or from a disk file when saving or loading.

Byte   A group of bits which the computer sees as one character.

CAD/CAM   (Computer Assisted Design and Manufacturing) The use of computer graphics to help design and define a product and the use of computer-controlled equipment to manufacture it.

Central processing unit (CPU)   The main operating part of a computer which consists of the processor and the internal memory unit. With today's microcomputer the microprocessor and the memory chips are normally separate from one another.

Character   Each letter, number and symbol on the computer keyboard is a character and can be recognized by the machine. One byte is used to hold each character, normally using the ASCII code representation.

Chip   As electronic circuits have become smaller and smaller so separate components such as transistors, diodes, etc., are no longer attached to special boards. Electronic circuits are now etched into small pieces of silicon (chips) on which the individual components are too small to be seen with the naked eye.

COBOL   (COmmon Business Oriented Language)   A high-level language specially designed for business applications and which has very powerful file-handling facilities. The majority of mainframe business systems are written in this language and it is now also available on microcomputers and minicomputers.

COM   (Computer Output on Microfilm)   A form of computer output that replaces paper in some large systems, e.g. in banks. It is far easier to store printout on film than on paper.

Compiler   A systems program written to translate from a high-level language to the machine language used by a particular machine. Each computer has its own compiler program for each high-level language offered. Programmers write their applications programs in the high-level language and the compiler converts this into a machine code version which is the one that will be used on the computer thereafter.

Computer security The computer hardware and data stored on the system need to be protected from illegal access. A whole range of physical security devices has been developed and many programs include software protection devices. The increase in computer communications links has led to further problems as intruders gain access through communications lines.

Control total This is a form of control frequently used to detect errors in processing accounting data. Certain fields on the data documents are prelisted and totalled before being processed. After processing these totals are compared with the totals generated by the computer, and any difference between the sets of figures signals that errors have occurred.

CP/M (Control Program for Microcomputers) An operating system first developed for use on a range of eight-bit micros based on the Zilog Z80 chip. This allowed software houses to develop programs that could be run on a wide range of microcomputers.

CPU *See* Central processing unit.

Cursor A symbol on the computer screen (often a flashing box line or arrow) which indicates the current print position. With the development of Window Icon Mouse Pointer software the cursor is moved around the screen and used as a pointer to choose between various tasks.

Cylinder When storing data on disks it is normally stored vertically across the disk surfaces rather than on one disk face. A set of such tracks taken vertically through the disk constitutes a cylinder. Storing data in this manner reduces the amount of head movement required and increases access speed.

Daisy wheel printer A type of printer where the characters are stored on the spokes of a removable wheel. These preformed characters are printed by being struck against an inked ribbon. Alternative print fonts are available by mounting different print wheels.

Data Raw facts which tell us nothing about the business; they have to be processed to provide useful information.

Database A system where data is common to all user departments and is cross-referenced so that it can be organized in a number of ways to suit a variety of users.

Database management system A complex set of programs used to organize the database, and to add and update information.

Data capture The act of picking up data and entering it into the computer. Traditional methods involved keying in large amounts of data manually. Modern systems are increasingly capturing data early and as a by-product of some other process, e.g. point of sale devices in retailing.

Direct access The ability to access data on a storage medium without having to work serially through all records. This greatly increases the speed of access.

Distributed processing Computer systems made up of a number of processing units at different locations, linked together and able to pass data and information. They frequently involve the use of several types of machine ranging from micros to mainframe machines.

Document count A method of control whereby the number of data documents is counted before processing. This total is then compared with the computer total to ensure accuracy.

Dot matrix printer A type of printer where the print head consists of a line of small pins. The characters are formed by firing various combinations of the pins against an inked ribbon.

EFT (Electronic Funds Transfer) The use of electronic communications systems to transfer money and messages between banks and large companies across the world.

Electronic mail The use of computer networks to transfer letters, memos and other messages. It offers a number of advantages over conventional mailing. For example, it avoids the need to repeatedly ring back recipients as a message can be left in their mail box.

Electronic office The convergence of computing, office technology and communications to provide an integrated set of tools for use at an office workstation. It is claimed that such developments linked to increased investment in office equipment will bring great improvements in the efficiency of office work.

General ledger The main ledger in an accounting system. It is used to hold the main body of accounts that produce the accounts and main reports. To allow a greater degree of analysis, accounts are arranged in a hierarchical coding system that allows the computer to order them as required.

Graphics The use of computers to produce charts, diagrams, etc. To do this the screen is divided into a large number of dots called *pictels*. By lighting up various combinations of these, pictures can be produced. Graphics are often used with business software to provide graphs and charts, and have also allowed the development of services such as CAD/CAM.

Hacker Someone who uses communications lines to gain illegal access to information on a computer. At first it was mainly a nuisance, performed purely as an intellectual challenge. More recently it has become a tool of computer criminals.

Hard copy A printed copy of data or information normally taken to avoid total loss if the computer develops some fault.

Hard disk Also known as a Winchester disk, this is a high-volume storage device which allows greater security and speed than is possible with floppy disks.

Hardware The term used to describe the actual machinery of the computer, as opposed to the programs, etc., which make it operate.

Hash function A complex formula used to calculate the location of a piece of data on a random access disk.

Hash total A form of control total used to detect errors in processing data. When the control is over a value field such as invoice total it is termed a control total. Where it is imposed on a non-value field, e.g. pay number, it is termed a hash total.

Help screens Modern software increasingly includes instructions, notes and assistance within programs. These are normally stored on special help screens which are invisible to the user during normal operation. When facing a problem, the user can press the designated help key and will then be guided to the appropriate help screen.

Hierarchical network A computer network arranged on a hierarchical basis with overall control held by a central machine.

High level language A computer language that appears to be close to our own form of language. This allows the user to concentrate on dealing with the problem without many of the restrictions of working in the machine's own language.

Information Data that has been processed to provide some meaning to the users.

Input The process of taking data programs, etc., into the computer.

Integrated circuit *See* Chip.

Integrated software A set of programs able to work together in order to achieve some task. Accounting software modules can normally be integrated to produce larger systems.

Intelligent terminal A terminal which contains a microprocessor and is therefore able to perform some processing locally, before onward transmission of data.

Internal memory The storage capacity within the computer which directly feeds the processor. This is much faster than external storage and is therefore often called *immediate access store*.

Interpreter A form of translator program used to run programs written in certain high-level languages such as BASIC. This is not as complex as a compiler but it is far slower because it must translate code every time it is used.

Inter-record gap The gap left between blocks of records on a tape. This is needed to allow the tape to speed up and slow down.

ISAM (Indexed Sequential Access Method)   A form of file organization that holds records on a file in sequential order, allowing fast updating, yet through the use of indexes allows direct entry to records.

K (Kilobyte)   A term used to measure the capacity of a computer memory. One kilobyte represents 1024 bytes of data.

Keyboard   The most common input device found on computers. It closely resembles the typewriter keyboard but there are some differences.

Key field   The field used to match records across two or more files when processing data. The key field must appear on each file or the records can not be matched.

Key-to-disk device   A form of input device that helped to replace punched cards. A keyboard is used to enter data on to a hard disk device. A second operator can then retype the data and the equipment compares the two versions, highlighting any differences. It can then perform some basic processing on the data file before it is sent on to the computer where it can be read in at high speed.

Laser printer   A high-speed, high-quality printer that uses a laser device to create characters on a drum. Using toner these are transferred to paper and heat-fixed to give a permanent image.

Letter-quality printer   A printer that produces high-quality output suitable for business correspondence.

Line printer   A high-speed printer which prints a whole line of output at a time as opposed to the character printers normally used with small systems.

Local area networks   Networks where all the equipment linked is situated in the same building.

Low level language   A language that is similar to the computer's own language. This will mean that one programming instruction will need to be written for every operation performed by the computer.

Machine language The set of binary codes and rules recognized by the computer. All programs must be reduced to this form before the computer can run them. Translator programs convert from high-level languages to this form.

Magnetic disk A disk of magnetic material used to store data on a series of concentric tracks. Read/write heads can move directly to any part of the disk surface to store or retrieve data

Magnetic tape A very common storage medium. A magnetic coating on the tape stores data that is placed there as the tape passes over a write head. A read head can later detect the data as the tape passes underneath it.

Mainframe computer A very large computer normally capable of performing a number of tasks at very high speed but requiring a skilled staff and a special environment to house it.

Microcomputer A small (desktop) relatively cheap computer which requires no special environment and is often transportable. Normally of limited size and capacity. These can be used in the ordinary office environment and may be networked to minis or mainframes to offer a higher level of service.

Microfiche A small sheet of microfilm about the size of a normal domestic envelope. These are capable of storing a great deal of output from a computer, providing great savings of space compared with traditional printout. They are read using an optical reading device and a hard copy of any document can be produced photographically.

Microprocessor The heart of a microcomputer and many other electronic devices. This is a chip containing the main parts of a CPU except the internal memory.

Minicomputer A classification of computer between a mainframe and a microcomputer. It offers more power than a micro but is not a full mainframe. As the market has changed it has become progressively more difficult to classify systems under these three different headings.

Modem (MOdulator/DEModulator) A device used to allow computer equipment to transmit and receive signals using telephone lines. It changes the digital signal of the computer into analogue signals required by the telephone system and vice versa.

Mouse   A pointing device used with certain types of software to input data with less reliance upon the traditional keyboard.

MS-DOS   A standard operating system developed by Microsoft for use on 16-bit personal computers.

Multitasking   The ability of a computer system to perform more than one job at a time.

Nanosecond   One billionth of a second.

Network   A system of interconnected computers and/or peripherals.

Object program   Machine language version of a program produced by a compiler and then run on the computer.

OCR (Optical Character Recognition)   A form of input device which uses optical devices to recognize characters. This allows the computer to 'read' printed text.

On-line system   A system where the program and data files are linked directly to the computer, allowing them to be accessed at any time.

Operating system   A program that controls the running of the computer and allows the user to run application programs.

Operation code   A code in machine language used to represent a particular machine operation.

Optical disk   A storage device that records data by using a laser device that burns small holes in the surface of a disk. As a result this is a high-volume, permanent storage method. The device cannot be overwritten.

Pascal   A structured programming language designed to overcome some of the criticisms of BASIC.

Password   A security word or number issued only to authorized users to allow them access to programs and data.

POS device (Point-of-sale device)   An input device used to capture data at the point where a sale is made, e.g. a bar code reader in a supermarket.

Program   A set of instructions which tells a computer how to solve a particular problem.

RAM (Random Access Memory)   A form of memory which can be accessed by the user to hold data and programs.

Random access   The ability to access any record on file directly, without having to check others first.

Real-time processing   Updating master files at the time the data transaction is entered.

Record   A collection of related fields on a computer file.

ROM (Read Only Memory)   A form of memory that cannot be accidentally overwritten due to user error. It may be used to hold an important systems program. For example, the BASIC compiler on the IBM PC is so stored.

Salami fraud   A type of fraud in which very small amounts of money are repeatedly stolen. Although the individual amounts are very small the total amount taken may be quite substantial.

Sector   A subdivision of a track on a disk.

Sequential storage   The storage of records on files in a sequential order based on a key field.

Serial access   Locating an item by reading blocks of data, one after another, until the required item is found.

Software   The general term used to refer to programs.

Source program   A high-level language version of a program. This will be worked on by a compiler to change it into an object program.

Spreadsheet A highly popular type of software developed to allow users to create business models with the minimum of training.

Systems analysis The analysis of a system to ascertain what happens and what needs to be done to develop a new system.

Systems software Includes all the software which allows the system to perform the user requirements.

Terminal A peripheral device used to access a computer.

Track A magnetic ring on a disk surface, used to hold data.

Transmission The sending of data from one computer to another.

Trojan horse A type of fraud that involves adding a section of code to a program which will only operate if certain conditions occur.

Universal product code (UPC) A system of product codes designed to allow all products to be identified using bar codes for data capture with point of sale systems.

UNIX A multi-user operating system that is growing in popularity.

User friendliness The use of menus, help screens, etc., to make software easier to use.

Validation Using the computer to check input data for obvious errors, e.g. checking that values fall between expected limits.

VDU (Visual Display Unit) Term used to refer to a screen or monitor used for input and output to a computer.

Verify To check data preparation work by entering the data a second time and comparing the two sets of work.

Videotext The general term for viewdata and teletext communication systems which allow television screens to be used to display data.

What if analysis The use of spreadsheet models to ascertain what will result if certain variables are changed.

Wide area network   A network of computers and peripherals that are spread over a wide distance. Public communications links are therefore used to connect them.

Winchester disk   A fast solid disk storage device kept in a sealed housing.

Wordprocessing   The use of a computer program designed to allow users to enter and edit text.

Index